Praise for
Confessions of a Counterfeit Farm Girl

"Packed with droll humor . . . McCorkindale's memoir is a witty take on what happens when you try to 'take the girl out of New Jersey.'" —*Booklist*

"A rollicking, *Green Acres*–esque memoir." —*Working Mother*

"[McCorkindale] calls herself counterfeit but she is truly the real thing; witty, startling social commentary in a flawless voice." —Laura Collins, author of *Eating with Your Anorexic*

"Witty, devilish, honest, and laugh-out-loud funny. Susan tells it like it is." —Petroville

"The author is at her funniest when recounting her faux pas: assuming that 'riding' meant the subway, or not knowing what address to give the 911 operator (numberless estate name or P.O. box?). Her prose is chatty and upbeat." —*Kirkus Reviews*

"Deserves five John Deere tractors, an appropriate equivalent of five stars. The author is edgy and funny, and pulls no verbal punches." —*Middleburg Life* (VA)

"Nothing could be more amusing than reading about a shoe-loving, makeup-wearing, once-a-week-hair-salon-visiting, manicure-sporting New York City marketing director finding herself on 500 acres of prime cattle farm. Especially when the story is written by Susan McCorkindale, a woman with . . . wonderful self-deprecating humor and wit." —*The Trumpet Vine*

"*Confessions* is 350 pages of fall-down-funny anecdotes of Susan's adventures on the cattle farm she and her family now run. . . . Susan's sense of humor is as divine on paper as it is in person. Her style is unique and elevating and can be best described as Nora Ephron, only closer to home." —*Warrenton Lifestyle Magazine*

500 Acres and No Place to Hide

MORE CONFESSIONS
OF A COUNTERFEIT FARM GIRL

SUSAN M. CORKINDALE ·

NAL
NEW AMERICAN LIBRARY

New American Library
Published by New American Library,
a division of Penguin Group (USA) Inc.,
375 Hudson Street, New York, New York 10014, USA
Penguin Group (Canada), 90 Eglinton Avenue East, Suite 700, Toronto,
Ontario M4P 2Y3, Canada (a division of Pearson Penguin Canada Inc.)
Penguin Books Ltd., 80 Strand, London WC2R 0RL, England
Penguin Ireland, 25 St. Stephen's Green, Dublin 2,
Ireland (a division of Penguin Books Ltd.)
Penguin Group (Australia), 250 Camberwell Road, Camberwell,
Victoria 3124, Australia (a division of Pearson Australia Group Pty. Ltd.)
Penguin Books India Pvt. Ltd., 11 Community Centre,
Panchsheel Park, New Delhi - 110 017, India
Penguin Group (NZ), 67 Apollo Drive, Rosedale, Auckland 0632,
New Zealand (a division of Pearson New Zealand Ltd.)
Penguin Books (South Africa) (Pty.) Ltd., 24 Sturdee Avenue,
Rosebank, Johannesburg 2196, South Africa

Penguin Books Ltd., Registered Offices:
80 Strand, London WC2R 0RL, England

First published by New American Library, a division of Penguin Group (USA) Inc.

First Printing, August 2011
3   5   7   9   10   8   6   4   2

REGISTERED TRADEMARK—MARCA REGISTRADA

Library of Congress Cataloging-In-Publication Data:

McCorkindale, Susan.
500 acres and no place to hide: more confessions of a counterfeit farm girl/
Susan McCorkindale.
p. cm.
ISBN 978-0-451-23336-3
1. McCorkindale, Susan—Homes and haunts—Virginia. 2. Farm life—Virginia.
3. Urban-rural migration—Virginia—Case studies. 4. Urban women—Virginia—Biography.
5. Women—Virginia—Biography. 6. Virginia—Biography. I. Title.
II. Title: Five hundred acres and no place to hide.
CT275.M4155A3 2011
975.5'043092—dc22
[B]   2011009611

Set in Palatino LT STD   •   Designed by Elke Sigal

Printed in the United States of America

For Nancy and Doug

Contents

Prologue   *1*

Part Two

THE COUNTERFEIT FARM GIRL GETS REAL
(COUNTERFEIT FARM GIRL STYLE, OF COURSE)

Part Three

WILL FARM FOR LOVE

Part Four

EPILOGUE

Author's Note

This work is a memoir. For the sake of storytelling purposes and pace, aspects of the time line have been compressed. In addition, certain names and identifying characteristics have been altered out of respect for people's privacy. Of course, certain other names and identifying characteristics have not been altered. This doesn't mean I don't respect those people's privacy, just that I couldn't resist telling the world how wonderful they are. By the end of this book, I believe you'll love them as I do. But that doesn't mean you should friend them on Facebook. Following them on Twitter is fine.

*"Parenthood: that state of being better chaperoned
than you were before marriage."*

—Marcelene Cox,
twentieth-century humorist

"Nowhere to run to, baby, nowhere to hide."

—Martha Reeves and the Vandellas

500 Acres
and No Place to Hide

Prologue

TO: Friends and family

FR: Suzy@stuckinthesticks.com

Date: Wednesday, 10:35 a.m.

Subject: Nemo Knows Best

About the salmon farm. Hemingway[1] and I have decided that Nemo knows best: fish are friends, not food.[2] And so, much to the dismay of the livestock on our five-hundred-acre beef cattle farm, we're not swapping the tractor for salmon tanks just yet. We're staying right here in the middle of nowhere with the cows and the bulls and the goats and the hens.

God, how I hate the hens. You'd think that over the past few years we'd have figured out how to live together. But no. They

---

1. My nickname for my husband. Not that his real name is Ernest, but he's definitely the guy for whom my bell tolls.

2. As in *Finding Nemo*. Of course, the mantra actually belonged to Bruce the Shark, whose sincerity was, to my way of thinking, seriously suspect.

despise me and, frankly, I find them pretty distasteful, too. Unless they're breaded and deep-fried, fricasseed, broiled, barbecue grilled, or roasted with a dash of rosemary. Then I like 'em just fine.

But I'm getting ahead of myself. Before I launch into my foul relationship with our fowl, let me take a second to bring you up to speed.

Back in the summer of 2004, on a day so sweltering hot I'd have given anything (my favorite pair of Guccis, a kidney, maybe even one of my kids) to get back into our air-conditioned car, I let my handsome, former marine husband convince me to walk away from a six-figure job as marketing director of *Family Circle* magazine and move to the country. I admit I was burned out at the time and a stint—a *short* stint—in the sticks sounded like it might be refreshing, rejuvenating, and really good fodder for cocktail-party conversations when we came to our senses and returned to suburbia.

The thing is, we haven't returned to our senses[3] or suburbia yet, and it doesn't look like we'll be doing so anytime soon. Not that this bothers our sons, Casey and Cuyler.[4] If anything, they're fine with not going back to the 'burbs, and thrilled we're not trading our pitchforks for fishing poles. Casey because he's finally figured out that our back fifty is the perfect place for paintball, and Cuyler because he's got big plans for

---

3. As evidenced by the fact that we've actually toyed with the idea of moving to a salmon farm.

4. Pronounced "Kyler." Don't even ask why we didn't just use that easier and much more obvious spelling. Suffice it to say, women with advanced "pregnancy brain" would be best served not to select their baby's name off the wall at the Baseball Hall of Fame.

his five-hundred-acre playground "when Uncle Doug gives it to me for graduation."[5] The idea, according to my younger son, is to get an agricultural degree from Virginia Tech, make a living raising Black Angus cattle, and then supplement his income by hosting Civil War reenactments on the weekends.

You've got to love a little boy with a business plan.

It's a good thing someone's thinking about the future, because in all honesty? When I'm not staring out at the cows and pining for the days of expense-account lunches at Smith & Wollensky steakhouse, afternoon Starbucks breaks, and a designer footwear collection that rivaled a DSW, I'm thinking about the present. And trying not to have a panic attack.

Despite my mixed emotions about the farm, life in the boonies has netted me some neat new skills (come on, I'll show you how to band a bull!), a great new group of girlfriends, and a whole new career as a writer.

Of course, Hem says I don't write as much as rant about country stuff that drives me crazy, and about that he might be right.

He also says someday I'm going to regret my ranting and wish I could take it all back. And about that he might really be on the money.

I already feel bad about not painting a rosier picture of life here in the hinterland. I can't believe I didn't celebrate the snakes in the cellar, the mice in the utensil drawer, and the

---

5. Hem's brother owns the beautiful, people-free slice of heaven on which we reside, though clearly Cuy plans to restructure that relationship.

stinkbugs scurrying across my forehead while I was trying to sleep. I can't believe I didn't pledge to learn to make my own jam, can my own tomatoes, or wield a power jerky blaster. I can't believe I didn't replace my Spode dinnerware with the John Deere collection that Tractor Supply carries, or learn to drive a tractor, ride a horse, or bag a buck. I can't believe I didn't embrace NASCAR and Toby Keith, denounce the New York Giants, and stock up on Redskins jerseys.

And I certainly can't believe I bitched *on paper* about the bizarre attire that passes for women's fashion in these parts.

Oh, Lord, do you think it's too late to trade my stilettos for work boots and develop a taste for pulled pork? Is it too late to change my tune and say I absolutely, positively love life on the farm, or at least make one last push for us to move to the salmon farm?

As my dear friend Trish would say, "Sorry, Suz, that train has left the station." If it's got a bar car, I'd damn well better hop on.

Love,
Susan

Part One

SLEEPLESS IN STICKSVILLE

"There are good days and there are bad days,
and this is one of them."

— LAWRENCE WELK

Chapter One

CLUCKSTER'S LAST STAND

I have a confession to make: I've adopted an "if you can't beat 'em, join 'em—at least a little" attitude about farm life. I don't know if I'll ever love it, but I won't know if I don't try, right? Besides, it gives Hem a kick to see me pitching in to herd cattle, haul feed, or put in a fence post. And the fact that I'm doing it in heels only makes him laugh harder.

Today, for instance, I'm gardening. Replanting the window boxes counts as gardening, doesn't it? Hemingway packed them full of pansies and petunias in the spring, but since then the pansies have passed on, done in by both the warm weather and the last of our psycho chickens.

Apparently one night while we slept, the Great Banty Bloodbath took place in our side pasture. How we didn't hear the screaming and fluttering and flinging of eggs in the face of the attacker is beyond me, though I suppose it has something to do with the fact that Hemingway and I went to bed really late. See, my favorite farmer built a burn pit in the backyard, and on cooler evenings we stay up snuggling by the fire and talking about everything we need to do the next day. Of course, come morning we're too exhausted to do half of what we discussed, so maybe what we should really do is fill in the burn pit. But honestly, who has the energy?

In any case, when Casey went out to water and feed our crazy fowl, he discovered the carnage. Something— maybe it was a fox, maybe it was a raccoon, maybe someday I'll give a rat's ass[6] what it was—ripped our pretty rooster to shreds, and murdered six of our remaining ten hens. A seventh died later of her injuries.

So now we've got three cuckoo birds left and they absolutely, positively will not return to the coop. Who knew chickens could suffer post-traumatic stress disorder? Instead, they've commandeered one of the window boxes on the porch. It's there that they sleep, poop, and lay the occasional egg. Seriously. They lay, like, once a week. If I were running a bakery, I'd go belly-up. Oh, well. One more reason to thank God I can't cook.

The hens' favorite window box faces the site of the pullet pogrom. They sit in it, root their freaky four-toed feet around in it, stare at the empty coop, and cluck. And peck at themselves and one another. Until somebody gets pissed off. Really pissed off. In no time there're feathers

---

6. Ooh, maybe it was a rat!

flying, potting soil sailing over the side, and all the pansies and petunias are pushing up daisies.

Which is how I came to be replacing them today.

Usually, Hemingway does this stuff. But since I made the mistake of actually telling him about my plan to sorta, kinda get my farm game on, he said, and I quote, "Who are you and what have you done with my wife?" And then he ran off to Bush Hog[7] before I could back out.

Out. How I'd love to be out—for a pedicure or a latte, or just a quick look-see at Lou Lou.[8] (I swear I won't buy as much as a hair band!) But that's a daydream for another day. Right this sec I'm imprisoned on my porch until Cluckster and her pullet pals make their move.[9]

Cluckster is a tough old bird with a big mouth and a serious aggressive streak. I can't tell you how many times she's sauntered up the stairs to the front door, forced our portly and particularly aromatic dog Pete from the floor mat in front of it, and settled in. It would be one thing if she did this quietly. But no. Cluckster earned her name for her nonstop, crazy-making clucking. Every morning she awakens clucking at a level neither of our roosters[10] ever reached, every night she passes out clucking at the exact

---

7. Bush Hog is farm speak for "cut the grass," "mow the lawn," and my personal favorite, "spend all day deaf to the cries of your family."

8. One of Middleburg's best boutiques. I actually worked there way back when. I never brought home a paycheck, but my collection of Tribal pants and Free People tops is priceless.

9. Actually I'm imprisoned behind my front door, peeking out the window, and wondering, once again, how the hell I pulled pullet duty.

10. Hef and Kellogg, may they rest in peace. Make that pieces. Neither died a pretty death.

same deranged decibel, and one day, maybe soon, she'll pass away . . . a casualty of her uncontrollable clucking.

Or maybe Hemingway will simply try to shoot her. Again.

The first summer we had her, when she was just a puny pullet, her clucking reached the crescendo of one of those freaky PETA protesters during Fashion Week. It was a hundred degrees outside, and two hundred inside, thanks to a flash thunderstorm that lasted five minutes and left us without power for three days, and we were all pretty hairy from the heat. We took our lunch and picnicked on the porch. The scent of eau de Black Angus wafting in the warm breeze was pretty bad, but not so bad that it made us bonkers. But this, of course, is where McCorkindales and Clucksters part company.

As soon as we sat down, Cluckster showed up. She lunged at the boys' burgers and attempted to swipe the lemon slice from Hemingway's iced tea. He shooed her away and she made for the fern hanging above my head. Alas, chickens really can't fly. But they can fall, and when they do, they stick their landing. Which Cluckster did—in my scalp.

I went from zero to bun-free burger flying in less than a second. "Get it off! Get it off!" I screamed, tearing across the porch. Maybe I thought a good stiff breeze would dislodge the damn bird, but I was wrong. That hen hung on, digging her claws into my new, sophisticated " 'do." [11]

---

11. At this writing, I'm wearing my hair a whole lot shorter. It hits right below the jaw and is angled toward my chin. Very Gwyneth Paltrow. Hemingway hates it. He says women cut their hair only when they've given up on themselves. It must be true. Just look at how poor Gwynnie's gone to pot.

"I can't help you if you won't hold still!" Poor Hemingway. I was racing back and forth, swiping at my head, and howling like the epidural didn't last long enough.

"Oh, my God! Oh, my God! I'm bleeding!" Sure enough, there was blood trickling down my temple. And Cluckster? She had her claws in my cranium and was squawking at a level typically used to drive dictators[12] insane.

"Susan, you've got to stop moving!" Hemingway hollered.

"Yeah, Mom, come on!" cried Cuy. "Stop, drop, and roll!"

What the fuck, I'm on fire, too?

Something had to be done. So Casey did it. As I flew past for about the four hundredth time, he grabbed me by the waist and stopped me just long enough for Hemingway to clock Cluckster. She fell to the porch floor with a spectacularly satisfying *thwap!* and for one brief moment, we all breathed.

Okay, the McMen breathed. I bled.

Was she down for the count? Knocked senseless for even a second? Are you kidding? The Energizer Bunny's got nothing on this banty. Cluckster was back on her fetid feet Marshall Faulk fast, and this time she made a mad dash for our big dog, Grundy.

Now, if you know anything about chickens, you know that going on the attack is not the norm. Sure, we've all heard reports of Perdue roasters flinging themselves at the feet of unsuspecting supermarket shoppers, but really,

---

12. You know, like Noriega. They blasted him with AC/DC. But they wouldn't have had to if they'd had Cluckster.

such foul play among fowl is rare. But Cluckster charged, and Grundy charged off, and Hemingway turned to me and said, "Susan, I've gotta put that pullet down."

We interrupt this family lunch for a little gunfire. Now, there's a side I never served in suburbia.

A minute later, my honey returned with his rifle. He loaded it, took aim, and fired. It's tough to hit a moving target, and Cluckster was still in hot pursuit of our pup, so the first shot missed. As did the second. And the third.

By then I'd stopped bleeding, started breathing, and served the boys seconds. Frankly, it was like being in the stands at a sporting event; we kept an eye on Team Hemingway, cheered, and hit the concession stand—I mean kitchen—for more burgers and beer. Kidding, of course. The boys can't drink till cocktail hour. None of that "it's five o'clock somewhere" crap for my kids.

Of course, that rule doesn't apply to Hemingway, for whom I made a nice, tall Tennessee Snow Cone.[13] Sure, I could have brought him a Bud, but as those of you married to former marine sharpshooters know, when they're outmaneuvered by the bad guys or, God forbid, a bird, only the hard stuff will suffice.

Speaking of that damn beast, she's back, and she's disemboweling her favorite window box. Which happens to be one of the ones I just replanted. The balls on that bird!

"Cluckster! Knock it off! Scat!" I scream, charging out the front door. But oh, no. Not only does that painfully loud pullet stay put, she flicks potting soil in my face. And

---

13. Hemingway's name for a Slurpee-size glass of crushed ice smothered in Jack Daniel's.

then a pansy. A pansy! A pansy that I just planted! I'm stunned, so I do what anyone having it out with a hen[14] would do: I whip the pansy right back at her. And the root-ball? Bonks her right between the eyes.

In an instant, Cluckster's flopped to the floor, dead. My marine couldn't kill her with a .22, but I off her with an annual.[15]

You know, I'm starting to get why people love gardening.

---

14. Please tell me other people have it out with hens.

15. From the bottom of my heart, I swear I didn't mean to kill that hen. And according to one of our particularly experienced farmer friends, I probably didn't. It's more likely Cluckster was unwell (as evidenced by her aggression and ceaseless clucking), and being hit with the pansy put her over the top.

Chapter Two

STAYING ABREAST IN THE BOONIES

Recently I discovered several baby bottles as big as traffic cones, and huge, naughty-looking nipples lined up on my kitchen counter. Did it freak me out? Make me worry my honey had developed a fascination with Pamela Anderson, the St. Pauli Girl or, God forbid, the Frederick's of Hollywood catalog? Nope. It actually gave me hope that maybe Hemingway is finally on board with my having a few "improvements" made.

And then I wondered whether his expectations and mine weren't just a little different in the mammary maximization department.

In reality, this stuff's for the baby bulls he and Cuyler are bottle-feeding. There are four of them. Three are Holstein dairy calves my sweeties bought for a song at the local livestock exchange. Why were the oversize infants, who tip the scales at just under a hundred pounds at three days old, so cheap? Because they're boys, and you can't get milk from a male.[16] I think they cost us about twenty-eight dollars a pop; a female goes for more than two hundred.

The fourth was Cuy's gift from the Easter Bunny. You should've seen the size of that basket.

To digress for just a moment, the fact of the matter is that Easter on the farm is almost one hundred and eighty degrees different from Easter in the suburbs. For starters, we don't color eggs, 'cause they fall out of the hens in every hue under heaven. And we don't buy yellow Peeps because, frankly, we've got the real deal, and my kids can't stand anything with the consistency of marshmallows.

Except manure. And that they've been known to throw at each other.

We don't even load up on candy and celebrate the resurrection with a good sugar rush. Although I can see how sweets might have played a part in bringing Christ back from the dead; chocolate does it for me every day around three o'clock.

No, here in the hinterland, this holiest of days is just another opportunity to stock up on livestock.

Like I said, this past Easter, my younger son got Char-

---

16. Grief, on the other hand, you can get by the gallon.

lie, a Charolais bull.[17] The rangy, dirty blond beast joined Ky,[18] Eli,[19] and Fido,[20] the aforementioned trio of Holstein dairy calves, on Holy Saturday,[21] and when they're not sucking down more "milk"[22] than any human newborn's ever consumed, they're busy getting sick.

It's not enough that all of us have had the stomach flu; the baby bulls have had it, too.

To be accurate, they've actually had something called "the scours," which is farm speak for Old McDonald's revenge, which is further farm speak for Montezuma's revenge, which is really just regular old diarrhea.

Delightful.

You know it's bad when you're out shoe shopping and stocking up on footwear quite possibly fashioned from one of the bulls' family members, and your husband calls and asks that you pop into the Marshall Pharmacy for some Pepto-Bismol. And Kaopectate. And a rectal thermometer.

17. I got the world's smallest, hollowest chocolate bunny. Two bites and Mr. Rabbit was gone, but Charlie's here for the next year. By then he'll be about twenty-five hundred pounds of prime beef. Which makes Nate's Place the place for Easter dinner. So put it on your calendar and come on down. Bring the whole gang and maybe your set of Ginsu steak knives. But please, no Peeps, and no A.1. This guy's gonna be good right off the grill. (FYI: Nate's Place is our name for the farm, specifically our house, which looks like the birthplace of Nathaniel Hawthorne. At least, it does to us. But what do we know? Neither Hem nor I has ever been to Nate's real place.)

18. Whom Cuy named after himself.

19. In honor of our man Manning.

20. Whom Hem named because Cuy's pick, Polamalu, was just a little too long. Sorry, sweetheart.

21. Now, that's a miracle. Not even FedEx delivers to the way-back on the weekend.

22. They actually get something called milk replacer. It's basically baby formula for cows.

Hey, just don't ask me to play Dr. Doolittle, darlin'.

They're all better now, thanks to Hemingway,[23] and at this writing are probably closer to a hundred and thirty pounds each. In a few weeks they'll be off the bottle, freed from the barn, and encouraged to hang with the heifers. A heifer, for the uninitiated, is a cow that hasn't had a calf.

But that's just because she hasn't met the right Ky.[24]

---

23. Who I've decided should ditch farming for large-animal vet school, as he's demonstrated a true talent for saving the lives of livestock.

24. I'm sure Eli, Fido, and Charlie will make good mates. But I'm equally sure any bull named after my boy will be better!

Chapter Three

RUNAROUND SUE

*H*ere's the deal. I typically sleep a full eight hours every night. But these days, almost since the moment I made the decision to "fake it till I make it" in the farm-love department, I've really been stressed. Did I volunteer to "band" the baby bulls?[25] Scrub in during calving season? Physically examine the heifers to confirm we'd *have* a calving season? Oh, God, no. First of all, *yuck*. Second of all, my fear of failure is even worse than my fear of giving a pelvic exam to anything I might one day make for dinner. No, I asked to handle something I'm familiar with, something within my comfort zone, something much, much closer to home. Something, in fact, that actually involves homes.

---

25. Banding turns a bull to a steer by cutting off blood flow to his you-know-whats. They shrivel, die, and disappear. Similar to the reaction some men have to wedding bands . . .

I offered to play real estate agent and find renters for the three empty tenant houses on our property.

In hindsight, not only should I have offered to band the baby bulls; I should have donated my ponytail holders to the task.

Finding renters is much easier said than done, and, since I haven't yet done it, I can't sleep. I lie there, eyes closed tight, praying Bugs Bunny will bonk me in the head with a sledgehammer. All I want is sleep. But all I can do is think, overthink, and rethink my overthinking. This would be wonderful if I were Albert Einstein or Jonas Salk. But I'm me. And I assure you society is not getting anything remotely as remarkable as a theory of relativity or a cure for polio from this poor excuse for a farm girl.

I mean, maybe I can come up with a shot that'll stop the Crocs plague in its tacky tracks, but that's about it. Hmm. Now that I think about it, that wouldn't be a bad way to spend my sleepless nights. And it might net me a Nobel. Particularly if I pair it with a patch that stops women over age eight from wearing white stockings and velvet jumpers, and a pill that triggers cramps in any woman who can't quite kick bib overalls on her own.

But I digress.

You'd think that since I can't sleep at night I'd be comatose all day. But you'd be wrong. I have the frantic energy and attention span of a Concerta-deprived third grader.[26] One moment I'm a maid, cleaning each house top to bottom. The next, I'm a marketing director, making my pitch

---

26. Or a mom in her mid-forties.

on craigslist, my blog, and my Facebook profile. I tweet. I text. I e-mail my entire address book.

And several of my sweet friends from New Jersey respond. They'd love to come live on the farm, but the commute would kill them.

With panic fueling my every waking moment, I thought it might be interesting to log my lunacy. If nothing else, it's good for a laugh, and it could help Hemingway secure me a spot in a decent psych ward someday . . . soon.

Ready for a look at how today went down? Yeah, me neither.

4:45 a.m. . . .

Remove yummy-smelling meat loaf from oven. Throw tantrum upon sudden recollection of Hem's position on meal swaps: breakfast for dinner, yay; dinner for breakfast, nay. Ingrate!

5:00 a.m. . . .

Reread piece I penned yesterday. Ouch. Wonder if writing sober is really the best method for me.

5:47 a.m. . . .

Yikes! Three minutes late awakening Casey for the school bus. Hurry up and get dressed, big guy. There's no way I'm making the thirty-minute trek to the high school. Sure, I can make it in fifteen if we take the Mustang, but I don't like driving with the top down in the dark. And top-down is the only way my six-foot-four son can fit in the car. Otherwise, it's like trying to wedge Yao Ming into a Matchbox.

6:05 a.m. . . .
Watch in horror as firstborn breakfasts on cold pizza and Hawaiian Punch. And to think, he could've had meat loaf.

6:21 a.m. . . .
Eldest off to catch bus, elderly off to exercise. Gotta stay in shape to show houses. You know, on the off chance anyone ever asks to see them.

7:26 a.m. . . .
Shower. Dress. Drag anxious, antischool fourth grader from bed . . . but only with the promise of a Fender guitar. *Fourteen-hundred-dollar* Fender guitar he's been on me about for months. I know it's quite the carrot, but the kid misses too much school. And I miss having impulse control.

7:27 a.m. . . .
Wake Hemingway. Encourage OT! Second job! Dillinger-style crime spree! After all, someone has to pay for my foolishness.

8:45 a.m. . . .
Deposit Fender-mad little man at school. Leave basket of Hem's homegrown tomatoes for teachers. Pray Vitamin A–packed produce equals A-packed report card.

8:48 a.m. . . .
Ponder my growing propensity for bribery. Decide to feel guilty after both boys graduate. From med school.

9:00 a.m. . . .

Kick the goats out of the chicken coop and the bulls out of the goat pen. Rack tiny blond brain on subject of livestock "intermingling." Legal? Illegal? If they crossbreed, I call . . . ?

9:15 a.m. . . .

Go to garden. Cut flowers. Battle big, scary bugs intent on making a home in my hair. Scream *Psycho*-style while racing to shower, stripping naked, and running scalding water on my scalp.

9:45 a.m. . . .

Throw now-wilted flowers in vase.

9:48 a.m. . . .

Pull on fresh jeans and a T-shirt. Momentary pause in endorphin freak-out gives fear free reign. Chest tightens. Throat closes. Must. Find. Distraction. It's almost ten a.m. Do you know where the margarita mix is?

9:50 a.m. . . .

Check e-mail. Note usual morning onslaught of J.Crew and Victoria's Secret sales announcements, Staples coupons, and DailyCandy newsletters, but nothing from prospective renters. Curse craigslist, Facebook, Twitter. All the usual social media suspects.

9:53 a.m. . . .

Hit "refresh." Nothing from Craig or his cohorts, but look! A link to the wine country catalog! Save under "self-medication" and promptly suffer major panic attack.

9:59 a.m. . . .

Are you there, Ativan?[27] It's me, Susan.

10:32 a.m. . . .

Awaken to find myself, big surprise, on sofa and suffering from slight case of Ativan-induced dementia. Noise on porch propels me to door. It's the damn goats, and it looks like they're playing hockey with a groundhog. But wait. It's not a groundhog. It's a ham. A fourteen-pound Smithfield Ham. Talk about mystery meat, not to mention a really weird "Good Luck Faking the Farm Love!"gift.[28]

10:45 a.m. . . .

Log on to Ask Jeeves for ham baking and glazing tips. OMG! The butler's been fired. Who knew? Ask Ask instead.

10:47 a.m. . . .

Ohhh. Brown-sugar-and-pineapple-juice glaze sounds like heaven. And like it's bound for my butt.

11:00 a.m. . . .

Slide ham into oven, fatty side up. Vow from this point forward to always walk backward in a bathing suit.

11:02 a.m. . . .

Return to laptop, appetite suppressed for the foreseeable future. Check e-mail. Nothing. Reread descriptions I posted on craigslist. Hmmm. Houses *sound* pretty, but there's no

---

27. Ativan is an antianxiety medication used to treat panic attacks. Works almost as well as wine, and is a lot more socially acceptable. Particularly before ten a.m.

28. Only I could ask for hogs and get ham. It's okay. I know you meant well, Mom!

proof. Need pictures! Crap. Can't take any till somebody cleans the damn things. Somebody, huh?

11:03 a.m. . . .
My God, there's a big M on my chest!

11:15 a.m. . . .
Cleaning supplies, vacuum, and trash bags in tow, I race from one house to the next. I wash fingerprints off walls, scrub toilets, and wipe down ceiling fans nobody's touched since man first broke wind (because you know it was a man). I wash the floors, scour the sinks, and disinfect the refrigerators, the whole time thinking, *Universe, I'm ready. Bring on the renters!*

2:15 p.m. . . .
Check e-mail. The universe has yet to respond.

2:16 p.m. . . .
Break for chat with agent. Promise first fifty pages of new book by next month. Because no, I don't have enough on my plate. The fourteen-pound ham not included.

2:17 p.m. . . .
Jesus, Mary, and Jamie (Oliver, of course; he's cute *and* he can cook)! The ham!

2:20 p.m. . . .
Note to self: You cannot flip a *Hindenburg*-size slab of pork using two plastic soup spoons.

2:25 p.m. . . .
Do you think the five-second rule applies to food dropped on the floor of a farmhouse kitchen? Guess it depends how recently I scrubbed off the chicken, goat, and cow poop Hem and the boys track in on their boots.

2:27 p.m. . . .
Note to self: Always use oven mitts when washing scalding-hot ham.

2:28 p.m. . . .
Slide feces-free ham back into oven.

2:35 p.m. . . .
Practice deep breathing and calming techniques fabulous shrink showed me in desperate attempt to stave off second panic attack. And Ativan overdose.

2:56 p.m. . . .
Make mine Manolos. There's a big fat birthday check in the mail from my dad! Is it seven months late, or five months early? That, I couldn't tell you. But I can tell you those seven-hundred-and-forty-five-dollar leopard-print stilettos on the Neiman Marcus Web site are so going to be mine.

2:57 p.m. . . .
But wait. Blahniks or Botox?

3:00 p.m. . . .
Mirror, mirror, on the wall, who's the wrinkliest one of all? Not me. I've got a date with the derm.

3:05 p.m. . . .
And now I don't. Fabulous shoes on my feet, or no crow's-feet? I can't decide, and frankly, with nary a bite on my listings, I don't deserve either. And to think I used to call myself a marketing director.

3:10 p.m. . . .
Surprisingly, the prospect of utter failure does not impair my ability to drive. So it's off to retrieve future Fender-owning fourth grader.

4:00 p.m. . . .
Pull ginormous, I Can't Believe It's Not Burned! ham from oven. Set on counter to cool.

4:02 p.m. . . .
Suggest both sons share kitchen table to do homework.

4:03 p.m. . . .
Neosporin and Band-Aids for everybody! Please tell me No. 2 pencils no longer have real lead in them.

4:27 p.m. . . .
Take Casey for crew cut. Stupidly attempt conversation with sweet, foreign barber. Result? Son's marine-style cut makes stops at mullet and mohawk before arriving at boot camp.

5:00 p.m. . . .
Soothe infuriated, follicle-free teen with milk shake from McDonald's. Pull up to order board and request milk

shake. Pull up to payment window and pay for milk shake. Pull up to pickup window and pick up . . . speed.

5:05 p.m. . . .
Return to McDonald's. Retrieve forgotten McFlurry.

5:30 p.m. . . .
Head coach (aka Hemingway) and star player (aka Cuyler) off to football practice. Casey Guitar Hero–ing above my head. Ham hanging tough.

6:00 p.m. . . .
Still no prospective tenants. Why aren't the pictures I posted helping? Hmmm. Maybe it's because I forgot to take them. Oh, my God.

6:02 p.m. . . .
Pound head on desk. Wonder if it's too late to offer to band bulls.

6:45 p.m. . . .
Set table. Spy whopping huge check from Dad taunting me from side pocket of pocketbook.

6:47 p.m. . . .
Pour wine and wonder: Take ten years off my face, or face life without the latest Italian footwear?

7:15 p.m. . . .
Chow down on tasty (despite midbake bath) ham and a side of microwaved meat loaf. Make the mistake of mentioning

massive birthday gift to "God, I got up too early" husband and Fender-frenzied son, both of whom look at each other like, "Deposit!" Consider suicide as Casey rolls his eyes and mouths, *Dumb blonde*, in my direction.

9:23 p.m. . . .
Watch future rock star sleep. In ten years, he can foot the bill for my footwear and my face. The Ativan's on me. Unless, of course, I still haven't found renters. Then I think we're talking Betty Ford.

Chapter Four

WHEN IT RAINS, IT PAWS

All those novenas Dame Joan's[29] been making are paying off: I've found renters for two of the three houses. Whew! Hemingway's happy, too, or at least he was until I decided to celebrate my first farm success by getting a puppy. Specifically a six-week-old golden retriever puppy.

Everyone warned me it would be like having a newborn in the house, but did I listen? Do I ever? The dog is up with me at my preferred rising time of "really too early to confess to right now" and, instead of exercising, or writing, or sleeping like a normal person, I'm engaged in a tug-of-war with Tug, as we've so aptly named him.

The four-legged, blond ankle biter is bent on consuming chair cushions, table legs, wicker garbage pails, and

---

29. *Aka my mom.*

carpet corners, which, honestly, I'd be fine with if he'd just leave his jaws off the jumble of wires beneath my desk. He's got two hundred dollars' worth of doggy toys, but he prefers the power cord, the wire for the printer, and my cell phone charger. When he blows a fuse, I'm going to go ballistic. You know how I hate a blackout that's not char-donnay induced.

Tug is mine. And Cuyler's . . .[30] But guess who spends the lion's share of the day washing and rewashing the fre-netic fluff ball after every foray through our ponds and streams? That would be me wielding the Fresh 'n Clean tear-free puppy shampoo, Perfect Coat pet spray,[31] and more towels than the U.S. Olympic swim team uses in an entire season. I'm getting a little tired of the bath business, so I've been thinking of teaching him to shower. He al-ready drinks from the toilet bowl, so how hard can it be?

Of course, if I could just get him to use the toilet or even the grass, I'd happily spend the rest of my life hosing him down. Why? Because bathing him five or ten times a day would sure beat chasing the Master Defecator from room to room in rubber gloves and a state of near hysteria:

No! No! Not the living room rug!

What is that on your brand-new dog bed?

We do not defecate in seventy-five-dollar football cleats!

But didn't I just let you in?

At this point we're out of Bounty, club soda, and Clo-

---

30. My son and I share a fondness for the fluffy golden retriever pups flopped all over the pet beds in the L.L. Bean catalog. When Cuy was little, he thought we could order one right out of its pages. Don't laugh. I thought so, too.

31. Apple scented, for what it's worth; smells great in the bottle, so-so on the beast.

rox wipes. Not to mention butter knives. I used every last one picking poop out of the sea-grass rug.

What we're not out of is dog food. Sure, Grundy and Pete eat it. (Hell, Grundy and Pete will eat whatever I put in front of them.) But Tug is a pup of a different palate.

Right this second he's in the backyard feasting on a calf's head he found.[32] And my thoughtful farmer? He's photographing the whole thing to make sure I see the "meal replacement" my purebred prefers to the pricey stuff I purchase.

Guess I should be happy the Master Defecator doesn't bring a hunk in the house.

Of course, this may be Tug's way of telling me that the bones and raw food diet is indeed what he likes best. This "natural" approach is also known as BARF,[33] which is interesting, as that's typically my sons' response to almost everything I set before them. Who knew they had so much in common with a canine?

Breakfast. Lunch. Dinner. Doesn't matter. My boys gag and retch, roll their eyes and clutch their throats. And then, if it's a regular night and not one on which watching something on television rests on their actually swallowing something I've made, they sidle up to the garbage pail and spit.[34]

Tug, of course, is having no such response to his entrée. He's chowing down and enjoying it just fine.

---

32. Found or exhumed? You make the call.

33. *I kid you not. BARF, aka the* bones and raw food diet, *was popularized by Australian veterinarian Ian Billinghurst. And now you know what they really do "down under."*

34. *Newsflash, kids: I'm blond, not blind. And you're not squirrels.*

Which makes me wonder: If the meals I fix make my honeys hurl, maybe they should simply have dinner with the dog. I'm unsure he'll share his calf's head, but I spied a plump hind portion he might be convinced to part with.[35]

But back to the glaring fact that my first official farm task is unfinished.

I still have one tenant house available.

It's the most romantic little cottage, tucked out by the old grain silo, just before the woods. The views from the quaint front porch, with its sweet swing and steps that beg for flowerpots, cross-legged copper frogs, and signs that say things like, I LOVE IT WHEN YOU TALK DIRT TO ME, and HENS, GO HOME,[36] are spectacular. The prettiest on the property.

It's got two snug-as-a-bug bedrooms, one bath, a bite-size eat-in kitchen, a sunny entry foyer, and a petite but bright living room. I absolutely love the place. And that's the problem. I don't really want to rent it. I want it for me. To work in. Think uninterrupted thoughts in. And sometimes—dare I say it? Hide in. Virginia Woolf was right: A woman needs a room of her own. And if I could finagle a whole house? I think she'd be pretty damn proud.

Yeah. Like that's gonna happen.

We need the income, and honestly? I'm just too type A

---

35. In exchange for my headphones and the cord to my iHome, I'm sure.

36. If I lived there, I'd have a sign that said that. After what happened with Cluckster, can you blame me?

to quit before something's a hundred percent *t*'s-crossed, *i*'s-dotted done.

On top of that, there's the fact that I put the cart before the horse and bought myself a congratulatory gift. A gift that's suddenly finished with its calf's head and running for my sea-grass rug.

Anybody got a butter knife?

Chapter Five

DRESSED TO KILL

I've worn shoes that pinch, bras that bruise, and sweaters that suffocate. I've worn khakis that camel-toe, suits that scratch, and ball gowns that guaranteed I'd spend all night sipping Beano.[37] But never in my forty-something years of suffering for beauty has an article of clothing actually attempted to take my life.

Until last week.

That's right. Around eleven o'clock Wednesday morning, my cousin Lisa's one hundred percent silk, one hundred percent sexy Rag & Bone dress tried to kill me.

Now, I can see a tube top trying to take me out, particularly since I'm over the age of twelve and probably

---

37. You keep it in your purse, pour it in a rocks glass when no one's looking, and everyone thinks you're drinking a White Russian. You won't get buzzed, but it sure beats bloating in your skinny silk chiffon.

shouldn't even be in the same time zone with that junior fashion staple, but a sleeveless, V-neck sheath? Shocking.

At the time of the attempt I was staying at Lisa's and enjoying a brief break from wrangling cattle, kids, and Tug, whose new trick is coming home so covered in manure and flies that he looks like a light brown cow.[38] As befits her *Sex and the City*, take-no-prisoners, single, successful, professional-woman persona, Lisa lives in a glorious, glass-walled, three-story town house in Edgewater, New Jersey. Of course, her home overlooks the Hudson, and the views of the New York City skyline from each floor of her totally "I read *Vogue*" abode are spectacular. But the best thing about the place, other than the fact that there are four wall-to-wall, double-shelved, multimirrored closets, and the fact that those très big repositories are *bursting* with all manner of fashion fabulousness, is that Lisa and I? Wear the Exact Same Size.

Okay, that's a lie. The really, truly, absolutely beautiful best thing about Lisa's is that Nate's Place? Is Six Hours South.

This means there are no ornery billy goats trying to barrel their way through the front door, no dogs dropping germ-infested, still slightly fur-covered cow, deer, or fox bones at my feet,[39] and no mice living large among my soup ladles, spatulas, and other assorted utensils (which I almost never use to cook with, but that doesn't give them the right to commandeer them, does it?).

---

38. Or so Hem claims.

39. Why, thanks, guys. Who knew a maggot-ridden femur could so beautifully complement my Louboutins?

I know you think I'm exaggerating about our lively livestock and three dog-obedience-school dropouts, but I'm not. The cows frequently make a break for the farm next to ours, necessitating full-scale search-and-recover missions followed by hours of manicure-busting fence board repairs. The hens, still traumatized by the Great Banty Bloodbath, won't lay eggs in the coop and instead prefer one particular window box on my front porch, which they flock to like a fertility clinic for fowl. And the goats? They do their damnedest to get into the house at least every other day. In fact, the morning I left for Lisa's, Duke, one of our two Boer wether billies, tried to accompany Pete, Tug, and Grundy when they came in from their morning constitutionals.

For a full fifteen minutes, while I gathered my iPod and a couple of bottles of water, threw in another load of laundry, and brought toilet paper up from the basement,[40] the stubborn beast beat his head against the front door. Why did he want in? Hell if I know. Maybe he'd gotten wind of my reputation as the world's worst housewife and figured I wouldn't notice if he ditched the goat crib for my crib. But this, my dears, is why they call them dumb animals. While it's true I'm no Hazel, and ages ago a local cleaning service deemed my domicile too tough to tackle,[41] that doesn't mean I'm good with livestock in the living room. Or kitchen. Or anywhere other than the great outdoors.

---

40. Lest the McMen run out and resort to using tissues—which are great on noses but piss-poor on plumbing—again.

41. I think it was the half-eaten, congealed, dead-stinkbug-filled containers of Velveeta microwavable Shells & Cheese beneath the beds that got them.

Anyway, I certainly didn't let him in, and to say it really got Duke's goat when I stopped him is an understatement.

What's not an understatement is that shopping my cousin's designer clothes–filled closets makes me happier than a pig in shit.[42]

Lisa leaves for work, and I employ myself by rummaging through her things, trying stuff on, and calling her with every find. "Do you have plans for the naughty black-and-white BCBG Max Azria necklace dress or can I borrow it? And how 'bout the bodice-hugging floral from Blumarine? Can I take that, too? Great, thanks. Now tell me about the Michael Kors merino sweaterdress. Black boots with that, or chocolate?"

Heaven.

But back to nearly being bumped off by that racy Rag & Bone.

See, I've developed a habit of bringing nothing when I visit my cousin. Except for my toothbrush and some underwear,[43] I don't even pack. I simply strolled in, gave Lis a hug, and headed for the closets. I spied the hot 'n' homicidal Rag & Bone beauty sometime after my arrival

---

42. Just so you know, the whole business about pigs loving shit is a myth. It's mud they have a thing for. They can't sweat, so they lie in it to cool off. Unfortunately, their favorite place to seek relief is also their favorite place to relieve themselves, so their reputation as shit fans is their own damn fault. I know this because around the time we got Tug, I was campaigning hard for hogs, specifically Hampshires. They have black bodies with white "belts" around their shoulders. Pretty snazzy for swine, no? I did all the research, prepped the hog pen, and picked names. And then I shared my plan with my man. His exact response? "Suz, that pup is pig enough." Who knew he wouldn't be on board with my raising boars?

43. And my MasterCard. Lis lets me borrow everything. The least I can do is buy dinner!

late Sunday and thought, Hmmm, that would be perfect for Wednesday night. I'd better try that on.

But I didn't. I simply stepped out of the shower and attempted to slip into it while I was still damp. Okay, maybe I was a little more than damp. Maybe I was closer to dripping. Okay, let's be safe and say I was soaking. There, I said it. I was soaking.

And, of course, it got stuck.

I had my head and right arm in, when suddenly the fabric shellacked itself across my shoulders. I couldn't shake it loose or pull it down and yet I tried, like a lunatic, to put my left arm in. It snagged around my wrist and there I stood: naked, wet, and wondering whether Lisa would have to leave work to cut me out, or if I'd have to really humiliate myself and call 911.

Hello, Officer. What's that? The nature of my emergency? That I'm au naturel? Yes, see, I was duking it out with a dress and it got stuck and now my privates are public, which is where the whole au naturel thing comes in, of course, and, well, do you think you could just send, say, a few of your female associates and a pair of scissors to assist me?

Worse yet, the V-neck was wrapped twice around my neck. I couldn't breathe, couldn't move, and couldn't imagine what people would say if I showed up with all my girly goodies hanging out.[44]

It took about fifteen frantic minutes of yanking, pulling, and praying I'd suffocate before I froze to death, but finally I wrestled the dress off and hung it up. Then I dried

---

44. My guess is they'd probably call the police and the papers and, while I believe there's no such thing as bad publicity, even for me this would be pushing it.

myself practically to the point of chafing and slipped that baby right on. It fit, it looked good, and I wore it that night.

Then I stepped out of the restaurant and into a downpour. Trust me when I tell you, that sucker's no fun to sleep in.

Suzy's Pig-Buying Primer

. . . .

Remember the Mother Goose nursery rhyme, "To market, to market, to buy a fat pig. Home again, home again, jiggety-jig"? It was always one of my favorites, though I think Mama G really copped out on the closing. I mean, "jiggety-jig"? How's about "Home again, home again, to roast it with figs"? Of course, I don't intend to roast or fry or bake or in any way cook and consume my hogs (because, believe me, sooner or later Hem will tire of my begging and I'll get those haute Hampshires). No, my plan is to treat them like pets. Two-hundred-and-fifty-pound pets that can do double duty as flypaper, but pets nonetheless.

If you've got it in your head that you've got to have hogs, here are some tidbits to help you get started:

Determine whether you really have space for swine. I know how tempting it can be to say, "I simply must have that adorable Duroc!" and just assume the boar can bunk in with your kids. But real swine need a real pigpen, something with a roof and walls to protect them in bad weather, and a decent amount of ground to root around in, get muddy, and, as I've already mentioned, take a poop and a chill in. If you place the pen near the vegetable garden, you can toss them discards. And if you build it a bit bigger than usual, the little piggies you gave birth to can have pajama parties with the ones you bought.

Learn the lingo. The pursuit of the porcine has a language all its own. And unfortunately, it's not pig latin, so eventually I'll have to learn it. For now, here are the basics. A boar is an intact male, and a barrow is a male tweaked to sing soprano in the Vienna Boars Choir. A gilt is a female that's yet to have piglets, and a sow is a mama hog that's had at least one litter. Armed with this impressive volume of knowledge, it's time to . . .

Pick your breed of pig. Will it be Berkshire, Black Poland, Yorkshire, or Chester White, and why? I love the Black Poland because its white feet remind me of the cowboy boots I wore as a gun twirler on my high school color guard (boots that were, I'm relatively certain, a direct descendant of Nancy Sinatra's). Of course, there are more practical reasons to select a particular breed of pig. For instance, if you'd like lots of litters, spotteds are reputed to make good moms. And if you're the low-key type, the Landrace has a docile temperament (and really cute, droopy ears). The best way to choose is to get online and do some research, and pay a visit to a pig farm or livestock barn. Getting a copy of *Storey's Guide to Raising Pigs* is also a good way to go.

Sow, what's in a name? There are no hard-and-fast rules to picking pig names. Babe's nice, and Wilbur works. But both are a bit overused. To help you get creative and think outside the hog pen, try this trick. Pretend you're an A-list celebrity about to have a baby or adopt a child from some country the rest of us didn't even know existed, like the People's Republic of Crest. (National motto: Gingivitis Can Bite Us.) Then open a book or a newspaper, close your eyes, and—quickly, now, speed is of the essence—point to a word on the page. See? Taxi is a perfectly good name for a pig. And Lunar is lovely, too.

Please pass on these pigs. I'm not talking about the ones sporting manicures or pinky rings, or reeking of cologne, or unable to talk about anything but their golf game, what they earn, how much property they own, or how frequently women tell them they should be a porn star (*wink, wink*). I'm sure you already know enough to 1) not let these pigs engage you in conversation, and 2) hit them with your car. I'm talking about the pigs you're considering purchasing. A head that looks too big for the animal's body could mean the hog's "over the hill," swollen feet might mean arthritis, and a lackluster hair coat can indicate stress. (Yes, pigs suffer stress; they're afraid one of the aforementioned assholes will buy them.) In any case, if you see any of these signs, please skip that swine.

Chapter Six

WHO SAYS YOU CAN'T GO HOME?

Woke up, slipped on my sneaks, and hit the streets of Ridgefield, New Jersey, for a speed walk early this morning. When I'm home, I Jazzercise and kickbox. When I'm away, I speed-walk. When I've stolen something, like the Calvin Klein sleeveless shift I shoved in my bag when I left Lisa's, I run. Of course, I intend to return it. It's too wrinkled to wear.

I departed my cousin's two days ago to stay with my mom. In the house I grew up in. Where, it turns out, my room is about the same size as Harry Potter's spot under the stairs. How I hid a six-month supply of Lipton instant iced tea, several cartons of Chips Ahoy!, and a case of Aqua Net in there, I'll never know.

For musical motivation and to keep my mind off the searing pain of the shin splints I gave myself yesterday tearing around town, I cued up some home-themed songs and set off. First up, "Who Says You Can't Go Home?" Not Jon Bon Jovi and Jen Nettles. Jen's great, of course. And Jon? *Ooooooh, Jon.*

Jon Bon Jovi is my second-favorite Jersey boy[45] and in my opinion, the only reason to watch *Ally McBeal* after Robert Downey Jr. left for a stint in yet another celebrity rehab center. Much to my relief, and that of millions of other women who lust after dark, brooding, tousle-haired, high-cheekboned bad boys with more talent in one arched, smirking eyebrow than the rest of Hollywood has in its collective body, RDJ is just fine now. Which is a damn good thing; Iron Man certainly can't save the world if he's strung out. He could, however, have Jon cover for him. And if you've ever seen that boy rock, you know I'm right.

Waving to the grinning, Day-Glo-vested crossing guard and maneuvering 'round the black-jeaned, charcoal-eyelinered, Hello Kitty–T-shirt-wearing tweens double-doused in Clinique Happy Heart and humping backpacks as big as worm bins,[46] I whipped past W. Arthur Skewes Middle School, where my dad, aka Mr. C.,[47] taught seventh-grade English since the discovery of the dangling participle. How a kid who took first grade twice because he spoke only Italian grew up to become a tremendously

---

45. My heart belongs to the Boss.

46. A large plastic storage container for red wigglers (aka worms). Frequently upgraded to worm condo and kept under the kitchen sink. You feed the worms food scraps and use their poop to enhance your produce. Oh, for God's sake, some of this farm stuff's starting to stick.

47. Short for Mr. Costantino. He was Mr. C. and I was "Little C." And yes, that's my picture in the dictionary next to "daddy's girl."

popular English teacher is beyond me. But it does give me hope that a kid who to this day can't add and who did remedial math even in college—who does remedial math in college?—will one day be able to balance her checkbook.

Really, Suz. Zero plus zero is zero. Zero minus zero is zero. It's depressing, but it doesn't require a calculator.

I'm unsure when Lynyrd Skynyrd replaced Jon and Jen, but suddenly I found myself singing "Sweet Home Alabama." Out loud. This probably accounts for why the kids parted faster than Tony and Jessica [48] when they saw me coming, and why, for the first time ever, I was able to take Elm Avenue at a sprint. Elm's one of those streets high school cross-country track coaches include in practice routes to weed out the girls who can run from those who are just there to chase boys. Like Jack's beanstalk, it pretty much shoots straight up. And if you don't pop a quad or burst an ovary before you reach the top, you make the team. [49]

In any case, I did it. I took the whole thing at a sprint. And as I raced past a few of my high school pals' old houses, I felt so good that I thought I could do anything. Including stop in and say hi to whoever's living there now. But I didn't. Endorphins are good 'cause they make you happy. They're bad 'cause they make you think complete strangers are eager to meet you.

Once I regained some of my senses, I remembered

48. Romo and Simpson. But you knew that, 'cause you follow all that Hollywood garbage, too, right? Right?

49. And now you know more about my high school experience, not to mention my gynecological health, than my mom.

hearing that my friend Deb's parents might still live in town. If that was true, I really wanted to see them. As a kid, I spent entire *Partridge Family* seasons in the Glucksmans' TV room, using one of the pillows on the love seat to pretend kiss David Cassidy[50] and a silver candlestick to sing into whenever Deb, her sister Sheryl, and I "performed" along with our favorite TV family.[51] Did her mom and dad still live there? Maybe, but I wasn't sure. I jogged up, thinking I'd try the bell, but then I saw it. I mean them. I mean it. The statue of the Madonna and child on the front lawn. Clearly the Glucksmans had gone.

With a quick wave to the Blessed Mother and baby Jesus, I ran on, past the community center, which to this moment still looks as if no member of the community has ever set foot in it, and turned down Shaler Boulevard. The pizza parlor's still there, as is Anthony's Pharmacy. What's new is a Korean bagel shop and a nail salon. No, not in one space, silly.[52]

I stopped and peered through the window at the salon's polish selection. Nose pressed to the glass and leaving a sweat print bearing a disconcerting resemblance to a monkey's butt, I spied OPI's Suzi Sells Sushi by the Seashore, and Tickle My France-y, and one of my all-time favorites, Paint My Moji-toes Red. Oh, how I love Paint My Moji-toes Red! I wanted to paint *my* moji-toes red right

---

50. And his lips were so soft, too. Or maybe that was just the really expensive fabric I got my lip gloss all over. Sorry, Mrs. G.!

51. The only thing I hated was having to play Shirley. Deb got the coveted Susan Dey part. I mean, it *was* her house.

52. Actually, I kind of like that idea. I'd like a toasted, no-butter, cinnamon-raisin bagel and a spa pedicure, please!

then and there. But the thought of stinking the place up stopped me. I flexed my funky toes, felt the sweat squish between them, and knew in my heart I could inflict what was marinating in my Nikes on no one.

Particularly not the lovely Korean woman looking back at me who was, I swear to Saks, a dead ringer for Annette Bening in *The American President*.

Big, wide-set eyes. Short, dark hair swept back off flawless alabaster skin, and complemented by pearl posts a shade brighter than her complexion. Even her soft gray turtleneck, scrunched casually around her throat, screamed Sydney Ellen Wade.

My attire, on the other hand, screamed, "Stay back! She needs a shower!"[53]

For a moment I just stood there, wondering whether it was possible for a person to be pickled in perspiration, my hair frizzed and corkscrewed and quite literally curled like the tails of those sweet Hampshires I have my heart set on, and stared. And then, because I figured I was frightening her,[54] I smiled. I waved, too, and she waved back. She motioned for me to come in, but I just pointed to my sneakers and pinched my nose.

How would we survive without sign language?

As I took off to the sound of Daughtry[55] crooning "Home," I wondered if Miss Sydney Ellen Wade the Second knows who Annette Bening is. And if Annette Bening has

---

53. Preferably in a radiation decontamination tank.

54. And I was certainly doing a number on myself.

55. A guy who's living proof you don't need hair to be hot.

any idea she has a Korean doppelgänger. And if anybody besides me makes these weird connections. And, if so, what medication they take, 'cause clearly mine's not working.

I bobbed and weaved down the boulevard, sidestepping moms pushing strollers and kids trying to push one another into the street. Then I cut across the baseball field and headed for Wolf Creek, or, more accurately, the bridge that goes across Wolf Creek. And when I saw it, I stopped dead.

How the hell did *that* teeny thing hold all of us?

Thirty years ago, my friends and I hung out right here, talking and laughing, sneaking cigarettes, and stealing kisses. I can still see my first crush sitting on the railing, the hood of his bright white sweatshirt bunched like a cotton ball above his blue Ridgefield Royals windbreaker. He was trading fake punches with a teammate to get my attention, which he had in spades, so why he had to roughhouse and nearly fall backward onto the rocks, I'll never know. What I do know now is why my mom didn't want me or any one of my pals on this Popsicle-stick structure. It can hold two, maybe three people, tops. No, we wouldn't have been killed if it had collapsed. But somebody could have broken their neck. Or sliced themselves good on a rock. And did we need obvious scars on top of the broken hearts some of us already had? I think not.

Still in shock, I suddenly found myself in front of the high school, an institution from which I graduated only by the grace of God, and the pass/fail policy adopted by the math faculty. For me.

I was surprised not to see a blimp-size plume of smoke

obscuring the entrance of Ridgefield Memorial High, but heartened by the familiar expression on the students' faces. To a teen, they all looked like they'd rather be dipped in boiling oil than be there.

The more things change, the more they stay the same. Thank goodness. Speaking of RMHS, I'm speaking there later today. Sort of a "let this be a warning to you!" chat with the juniors and seniors. My message? Stay in school. Be doctors and lawyers. And leave the prime berths in Barnes & Noble to me.

Just kidding. I'm talking with the English honors students about writing and book publishing and, believe it or not, magazine marketing. If they ask me about my Top Ten Ways to Pass the Workday,[56] I'm going to plead the fifth. Grade. Though second might have been a better place for me to stop.

In an effort to prove I could truly hurt myself in my advancing age, and because I needed to get back to my mom's to get cleaned up, I decided to finish my workout by jogging up Edgewater Avenue. Like Elm, Edgewater is painfully steep and perfect for masochists whose hamstrings just don't have enough knots in them yet. Once again, I ran the whole way nonstop.

And then, for some reason, I kept running.

Past St. James Nursery School, where getting snack duty was the equivalent of scoring a spot on *American Idol*. Past my dear friend Roma's old house, where I spent many a Sunday ducking Mass and Sister Patricia's cate-

---

56. Page seven of *Confessions of a Counterfeit Farm Girl*. For best results, place tongue in cheek before reading. After all, that's how I wrote it.

chism class. Past Slocum Skewes School, where fourth-
grade recess meant "Red Rover" and butterflies in my
stomach till a certain cute, curly haired boy called me over.

It was as if death were nipping at my roots and I
couldn't rest till I connected with something Redken.

I didn't actually do that yet, but I plan to when I visit
Panico[57] in about an hour. All this racing around has ru-
ined my blowout, and you know I can't talk to anybody
when my hair looks like a hay bale. Hell, I can hardly
speak when it's straight.

Okay, time to shower, dress,[58] and charge the iPod. I
also need to put together tomorrow's playlist for the ride
home, which will of course include "Ninety-nine Boxes of
Louboutins on the Wall" and "See Ya, Jersey," a little ditty
I wrote to the tune of "On the Road Again." Care to channel your inner Willie Nelson and join me in a chorus? And
a one, and a two . . .

> *On the road again, down to VA to hang with the hens.*
> *The life I love is where the shopping never ends,*
> *but now it's time to get back to the McMen.*
> *And the goats and deer, and the cows and bulls that get*
> *   out on the byways.*
> *They're not my favorite sight, but I'm getting better at*
> *   corralling them my way . . .*
> *on the byway. . . .*
> *On the road again, down to VA to hang with the hens.*

---

57. The Garden State's best salon.

58. *Shhhhh.* My mom steamed the Calvin Klein sheath.

It's been fun seeing all of you, my friends,
but now I've got to get to the farm again.

Maybe, before I hit the highway, I'll make a quick detour and return my cousin's Calvin. After all, it's the right thing to do. She loves that dress. And with any luck, she won't notice her Nina Riccis missing until I'm in Maryland.

Chapter Seven

THE COWPOKE WORE PRADA

$\mathcal{I}$ always joke that, unlike me, Hemingway hates to leave the farm. That he'd rather be here dealing with animals than "out there" dealing with people who behave like animals. But the truth is that I don't *let* him leave the farm. In fact, I'll do anything to keep him here, or at least keep him checking in every few hours or so.

I promise him something hot at lunch,[59] and cold, sweet iced tea and a couple of chocolate-chip cookies if he'll take a break around three. Come six, I've got his Budweiser poured into his favorite tall, frosty mug and his pretzels in a bowl, and by seven his mac and cheese and fish sticks are in front of him.[60] It's okay if he runs errands,

---

59. Sometimes it's even food!

60. Hey, he has no palate and I can't cook; we're a match made in the frozen-food section.

like going to the local co-op or Tractor Supply in Marshall. And it's certainly fine if he jumps on Route 50 and heads to Winchester for . . . whatever. But if he picks up 81 it's guaranteed I'll be on the phone with 911, or the plumber, or the principal of the high school. But the real reason I never let my honey leave the farm is because as soon as he does, one or another of our barnyard beasts escapes, and I'm forced to play cowpoke in my Pradas.

Of course, this time it was a little different. The eighteen-hundred-pound cutie that pulled the pasture break is not our property. She belongs to our neighbors at BlueRidge Farm. Yes, we have neighbors; you just can't walk to their house unless you pack a lunch. In any case, just a few hours after Hemingway headed north for a weekend with friends from his fantasy baseball league, Henrietta[61] got out and our phone rang.

"Sue? Hate to tell you, but you've got a cow strolling Rokeby Road."

Hmm. My honey's in Harrisburg. Think he'll come home to help? Me neither.

I grabbed Cuyler and my camera,[62] and we jumped in the car. At the end of our private road I turned right, expecting to run headlong into my future filet mignon,[63] but nope. No cow. So I turned around and headed away from our property, toward BlueRidge Farm and Route 50, and there she was.

---

61. My name for her. I'm unsure what my neighbors call her, but dinner comes to mind.

62. If I've got to corral cattle I've got to take pictures of it, too. Plus I need them for proof; Hem thinks I make this stuff up. But I don't. At least, not all of it.

63. I do so love filet mignon. And hanger steak's heaven, too.

"She's not ours, Mom. She's Mike and Leslie's," said Cuy. Damn. Now I needed to be neighborly.

First stop, Mike and Leslie's house. We ring the doorbell. Nothing. We pound on the door. Nothing. We rap on the windows. Nothing. Nothing, that is, except the sound of someone vacuuming. So we open the door and shout, "Hello! You have a loose cow!" The vacuuming stops, but no one responds. Ah, the beauty of the mute maid service. We shout again. "You have a cow on Rokeby Road!" The vacuuming resumes. We're on our own. Shit out of luck. Up the creek without a cattle prod.

We jump back in the car and return to the scene of the cow. There we're greeted by a very brave Good Samaritan who's stopped and is trying to move the big moo all alone. Quickly, we hop out and assume our positions. Cuy opens the gate. I stand in the middle of the street blocking the big beast from making a break for Rectortown Road. And the Good Samaritan attempts to oh, so sweetly urge hungry Henrietta to stop eating thistles, cross the road, and return to the pasture. Things are going well until the cow spies Cuy and makes a beeline back to her snack. This doesn't unnerve my son, but the rapid approach of the twenty or so head of cattle he's been holding off sure does.

"Mom! Mom! They're closing in fast. Get that damn cow now!"

Did he just curse at me? He cursed at me! God, I love this kid.

I burn rubber in my heels and in seconds am just inches away from Henrietta, arms out and fingers pointed like a traffic cop toward the field. Jen,[64] aka the Good Samaritan, is doing her cajoling thing and wielding a twig. And Cuy? Well, the poor thing was hollering, "Hurry!" when God finally said amen, Cuy stepped to the side, and Henrietta ran home.

We locked the gate and checked it twice, and then Cuy and I hit the Old Salem Restaurant in Marshall for a celebratory dinner.[65] Cuy's a natural at this country stuff, and I guess I'm going native, too. Hemingway, on the other hand, is never going anywhere again.

---

64. We introduced ourselves midwrangle.

65. We both had chicken. We were afraid if we ordered any kind of meat they'd make us catch it first.

Chapter Eight

BRUMFIELD FOLLIES

"*I* have nothing to write about!"

"Sure you do," I urge, smiling and slipping immediately into mega cheerleader mode in front of twenty-two fifth graders I'd met just moments before. I should have been terrified. I'm no teacher. But no; I was so ready for this. Prepared. I'd done my homework. Quizzed my mom, the elementary school principal; my dad, the retired seventh-grade English teacher; and my little brother, the big New Jersey college creative-writing professor. They told me how to handle kids who draw a blank when faced with a blank piece of paper.

"Get them talking about things they're passionate about," suggested my mom. "Bring a stash of writing prompts, just in case," counseled my dad. "For God's sake, talk up your state schools, Suz," teased my brother.

55

Ah, yes. There's nothing like the loving support of one's siblings.

"Of *course* you have things to write about," I cajole. Still smiling, I add bouncing on the balls of my feet and bounding around the classroom to my tornado-style approach to teaching. And the kids? They're watching me like somebody locked them in a room with the Energizer Bunny on a Red Bull drip. "It's all in how you look at your life. At the details, you know?" I nod, fast, like a blond bobble head, and the kids at the table to my right nod back. They're with me! That or they're so freaked out they're too afraid not to agree.

"Think of it this way: This morning you got up and came to school. But you didn't just roll out of bed and onto the bus, did you? No. You woke up. And maybe you hid back under the covers for a minute because the room was so cold. Or maybe you popped out of bed, raced to your closet, and, holy mother of Hannah Montana!" I pause and look directly at a pretty, ponytailed brunette in a long-sleeved pink tee with rhinestone flowers on the front. "Your favorite jeans are missing!"

She giggles. Lots of the girls do. Oh, yeah: the clothes connection.

"So then what did you do? Did you sneak to the hamper and hope they'd be on top, you know, so they wouldn't be too stinky?"

More laughter. Seems the boys have some experience with this as well.

"Were they on top? Or did you have to root around in all that yucky laundry to find them?" Twenty-two scrunched-up noses stare back at me. "And when you found them, maybe they were a little soggy 'cause they'd been squished beneath a towel your dad used to wipe up your dog's drool."

"That is so gross!"

"My baby brother's barf is worse."

"You're wearing jeans with baby barf?"

Oh, yes. This was going even better than I hoped.

"And then what?" I stop and look slowly around the room. They know what's coming. Several of them even have their hands over their mouths. Dog drool. Baby barf. For a split second I hope the school nurse has nausea medication.

"You slipped those soggy suckers right on, didn't you?"

"Eeeeew!"

"Uh-huh. While your mom was busy with breakfast or your baby brother or whatever. And then you put on a nice, fresh shirt to hide the smell and hopefully, literally, throw her off your scent." I pause for effect. "Did you get away with it? Are you sitting here in jeans that spent the night marinating in dirty sweat socks and damp dish towels?" They look totally appalled. It's priceless. I sniff the air. *Sniff, sniff. Sniff, sniff.* They squirm. "Ladies and gentlemen!" I cry. "Do I detect the presence of some champion hamper divers?"

"Mine are clean!"

"I'm wearing shorts. See?"

"Only my stupid sister does that stuff."

"Or . . . or maybe you got caught, and your mom pitched a fit and took your iPod. And then you had to ride the bus next to some blabbermouth you couldn't tune out because you tried to sneak out of the house in stinky jeans."

My new friends at Brumfield Elementary School[66] dissolve into laughter, and it hits me: This is a great gig. The kids are cute and enthusiastic, and despite the fact that they clearly think I'm crazy,[67] they're also completely captivated. Or at least, they were. I need to quell the clean-versus-dirty debates raging around the room before things get dicey. And that means I need to make my point. Pronto.

"So, guys. Guys!" I shout. "What's the moral of the story?"

"Clean clothes are overrated."

"So's showering!"

"Just do what I do. Wet your head, and your mom'll think you're clean!"

Great. I haven't cursed once and the principal's still going to get complaints.

"No, sillies. The point is this: Every single day, almost every single moment of the day, something happens in your life that's worth writing about." The chatter's stopped, and they're looking at me, and their faces say they might actually be weighing what I'm saying. "But the trick is, you have to pay attention. You have to be aware. Don't just float along and let your life happen to you. Be conscious of the moment. Make note of it. This way, the next

---

66. Just one of the twenty-two terrific schools in Fauquier County. And as long as you can pronounce Fauquier (faw-*keer*), we'll let you attend them!

67. Which, to my way of thinking, is simply testament to their impressive intelligence.

time you walk into your classroom and there's some *waaaayy* too happy blond woman cheering you on to write about whatever you'd like, you'll have a whole slew of stuff to pick from."

Silence, and then a small voice.

"So, um, are you going to write about us?" It's my little pal in the pink tee.

"You bet," I reply, "soon as it's just me and my notebook."

She tilts her head and gives me a shy smile. "But what are you going to say?"

"That's easy," I begin. "I'm going to say—"

"That the Ravens suck!"

"No way. Redskins! That's what I'm writing about!"

"I think I'll write about Aerosmith. Or Nickelback. I'm still deciding."

"Nickelback's so lame!"

"Maybe I'll write about my nana's new horse."

"I have my *own* horse. And my dad says I can show it next spring."

"My story's about my dog. This morning? He brought me my backpack!"

"Your dog's *so* cool. Can I write about him, too?"

And suddenly it was raining writing prompts. Pencils hit papers and the kids wrote and chatted and laughed and shared and asked a hundred questions, and I hopped from table to table reading their work and offering suggestions and encouragement, and by the time we had to wrap up, a case of Red Bull couldn't revive this Energizer Bunny.

Okay, that's a lie. I was totally high from the whole experience. I loved it. I loved *them*. I wanted to come back the next day and do it again.

I jumped in the car and called my mom. "You were right! Once they got started, they were unstoppable!" Then my dad. "I didn't need a single prompt!" And finally my brother.

"Hey, ye of little faith," I said with a smile when he answered the phone. "What're you doing?"

He groaned. "I'm suffering through one of my students' short stories."

"Not short enough, huh?" I laughed.

"It's called 'Love in the Time of Facebook.'"

Ouch. I felt the start of a sympathy headache. "True love?"

"True crap."

Forget headache. Migraine was probably more like it. "You need to work with fifth graders."

"So that was today, huh?" I heard his pen click and his chair squeak. I could picture him, my enviably thin brother, sitting at his enormous,[68] immaculate desk in front of his equally enormous computer monitor. He was smiling and warming up to tease me. I could tell. "Anybody survive my sister, the human Energizer Bunny?"

"Yup. All of 'em. And not one of my budding authors wrote about Facebook."

"They're probably more into MySpace."

"No lie, little brother. They wrote some funny stuff. In

---

68. And I mean big enough for the New York Giants to host the Washington Redskins for dinner. You know, to thank them for being good for two wins a season.

fact, I think my favorite was a tale of two hobos with a Food Network addiction." I could hear him laughing.

"*I* think your favorite was the piece about you."

What the . . . ? "How'd you know they wrote about me?"

"There's one in every crowd."

"You're just jealous. But okay, her piece *was* pretty great."

"Suz, doesn't anybody down there know you're certified to teach kickboxing, not kids?"

"Shut up. I'm a writer. I'm local. I guess they thought it would be fun to invite me." I pause. "And besides, that could change."

"The whole certification thing?" He was genuinely surprised.

"Yeah. It's crazy. All of a sudden, I'm doing all this coaching. Helping with the writing club at Cuy's school, giving a workshop for a group of teens, and I guess about two weeks ago, one of Brumfield's gifted and talented teachers asked me to come here. Pretty funny, considering I couldn't even get into the G and T program when I was in school."

"I believe it had something to do with your considerable math skills."

"So I couldn't add. I had no problem putting two words together!"

"I'm not sure 'screw you' and 'bite me' were what the G and T folks were looking for."

We both laughed. "I guess the point is, I'm enjoying it."

"Well, that would make Mom really proud. And Dad,

too." He paused and I stayed mum. Not an easy move for the Energizer Bunny. "Suz? You there?"

"Mmm-hmm," I mumbled, as passive-aggressively as possible.

"What? You're waiting for me to say I'd be proud, too? You *know* I would."

What to do, what to do? Give in, or make him work for it? "*You* told me to talk up state schools." I pout.

"Great. The bunny's gone and I'm stuck with Sensitive Suzy."

"Say it, and I'll put the bunny back on."

"You know you have to pass a mental competency test to teach, right?"

"And you know I can still take you, right?"

"All kidding aside? You'd be great, Suz. You're a natural." He paused. "Just do me a favor, okay?"

"Anything."

"Don't miss your medication."

Ah, yes. There's nothing like the loving support of one's siblings.

Chapter Nine

🌿

THE LAND THE TAKEOUT TAXI FORGOT

When we lived in New Jersey we had a wonderful little service called the Takeout Taxi. With one call I could order a burger with fries from Smith Brothers for Hemingway, penne marinara for me[69] from La Piazza, and sweet-and-sour chicken for the kids from Ivangie Tea House, and the Takeout Taxi would pick up at all three places and deliver the whole thing lock, stock, and two smoking egg rolls.

Oh, how I loved the Takeout Taxi.

My passion for the TOT, which is what we regulars called it, bordered on addiction. I knew its order takers well enough to ask after their families, and its delivery van was in our driveway so frequently my own family

---

69. Because back then I was *the* carb queen.

came to associate the smell of carbon monoxide with meal-time.[70]

I had the TOT number in my cell and on speed dial in the kitchen. And that's saying something. Our phone system had just three programmable spots, and the other two were dedicated to my favorite wine store and salon. I would have given up a slot for something responsible, like the kids' pediatrician, but he did a really bad job on my eyebrows.

But back to the Takeout Taxi.

Oh, how I miss the Takeout Taxi!

Here in the hinterland we have no such animal. We have *other* animals that we raise, slaughter, and serve, but nothing like the Takeout Taxi. Hell, we don't even have a pizzeria that'll make the trek to the backcountry.[71]

No, here at Nate's Place I'm expected to cook. And you can expect to need a couple of Tums to chase whatever I make. Sure, I can open a box of macaroni and cheese and serve it with fish sticks, or pour a couple of jars of white clam sauce over linguine. I can even make a pretty good meat loaf (and heat up a ham when one shows up on my doorstep but not, as I'm sure you noticed, the brown-sugar-and-pineapple-juice glaze. Two ingredients, a bowl, and a spoon? Stop. I'm completely confused). But that's only three dinners. What about the other four nights of the week?

---

70. And now you know why you never want to get stuck in traffic with my sons.

71. As of this writing, we're still out of the delivery area for both local pizza places. Rumor has it that's about to change, but I'll believe it when I catch the cows sharing a cheese pie and a couple of chicken Parm subs.

Oh, how I hunger for the Takeout Taxi.

I guess I could crack open a cookbook. I have a collection of beautiful, hardcover tomes on my kitchen counter that's done almost nothing but collect dust since the day I put it there. I say *almost* because sometimes I use the smaller ones to kill flies. And the larger ones I press into service as hot plates. Does it count that I use them to support dishes they didn't help me make? I didn't think so.

They're good cookbooks, too. I've got Betty Crocker and *The Barefoot Contessa*, two of Rachael Ray's thirty-minute-meal deals, and one about cooking with kids, which always makes me wonder how Case and Cuy would taste (my guess: gritty). I even have *The Joy of Cooking* and something called *All-time Family Favorites You Can Make in Minutes!* My only problem with it is that I'm the "you" they're referring to.

Maybe I should open one of those books and try something. Not because I expect to discover a meal my family will a) like, or b) not make too much fun of me for attempting.[72] But because maybe I'll be able to show Hem and my dear friend Jenn, one of these amazing women who bakes, makes her own curtains, and can diagnose and fix the mysterious pinging sound her car's making without messing a single hair on her gorgeous curly head, once and for all that I can't cook and therefore I can't can.

That's right. The two of them want me to learn to can tomatoes. Why? Because Hem can't learn to produce less

---

72. I still bear the scars from a disastrous bid to master the Manwich in '92.

produce.[73] Every year he grows enough to keep every single Italian restaurant and pizzeria, from Hoboken to Sicily, in sauce for six months.

I believe the conversation—well, part of the conversation, the most important part of the conversation for our purposes at this particular moment—went something like this.

"Why can't you just plant enough for the four of us?" I asked as Hem heaved two huge baskets of just-picked beefsteak tomatoes onto the kitchen table.

"I can't believe you're complaining. Look at these! Learn to can and— Catch those, will ya?" Two of the firm, perfectly proportioned, baseball-size orbs tumbled toward me. I caught them, and gave a split-second thought to freezing both. You know, to show the plastic surgeon someday when I've saved enough pennies in my "Mommy's Boob Job" jar.

"Thanks," Hem continued. "Like I was saying. Learn to can and we'll never run out of homegrown tomatoes for tomato sauce."

"But you don't like tomato sauce," I said, placing both back in the basket. "You don't eat tomato sauce. You always tell me it bothers your stomach."

"Sweet thing," Jenn cooed, coming in behind Hem and plopping yet another filled-to-the-brim basket of tomatoes on the table. "You can use them for more than tomato

---

73. And ever since Jenn failed to teach me to knit, through no fault of her own, I assure you, she's been committed to teaching me to can. When I nix that—and as you'll see, I do—she's going to help me make skin-care products "from stuff in the crisper drawer!" Who knew mold worked as a moisturizer?

sauce. You can use them to make . . ." She paused and thought for a moment. "Salsa! You like salsa, right?"

"Yes, but *he* doesn't like salsa," I said, nodding my head in Hem's direction. "And the *kids* don't like salsa. And if *I'm* eating salsa, it means there are Tostitos involved, and if there are Tostitos involved, you can bet there are margaritas involved, and since I only drink margaritas with salt, you can bet, the next day, between the salsa and the chips and the tequila and the salt, I'll be retaining, like, Lake Superior."

Jenn laughed. "Okay. So salsa's not really an option."

I shook my head.

"Well, you can always can them and then give them to your friends."

I flashed on those precious little pink-and-white-gingham-bordered labels that say things like MADE WITH LOVE IN MARY'S KITCHEN and practically started to cry. "I've got a better idea. How's about I give the tomatoes to my friends and they can do the canning themselves?"

In the end, that's what I did; I gave the tomatoes to Jenn and she canned them. Only it turns out you don't use cans for this little endeavor. You use Ball jars, which I heard as bell jars and thought, Oh, my God, isn't that what Sylvia Plath used? It drove the poor woman to suicide! And you accuse me of exaggerating when I say cooking makes me want to kill myself.

Right this second I'd really like to stick my head in the oven, but I'd have to share it with the Easy Chicken and Vegetables Pie I just put in. Easy, my ass. The only thing easy about it was reading the directions and selecting a tasty-looking specimen from Hem's flock of meat birds.[74] Where'd I get the recipe? From a cookbook I completely forgot I had, as I was using it as a decorative accessory in the dining room. I'll have to find something else to act as a doorstop, but I'm not worried.

My collection of Takeout Taxi menus just might work.

---

74. Yes, I do that now. Mr. Perdue, it's been a pleasure.

Chapter Ten

COCK-A-DOODLE SUE

I knew this social networking stuff would come back to bite me. Here I sit, doing my best to "friend" and be "friended," join cool if totally fabricated fan clubs like Capezio Can Keep Its Dancing: We'd Rather Be Drinking, and change my profile picture often enough so that my friends don't get bored but not so often that I look like I'm fleeing the FBI, and what do I get?

Outed by Facebook.

I'd expect such behavior from LinkedIn or Twitter or maybe MySpace. But Facebook? I thought you liked my "Live and Let Drink" philosophy. And you certainly seemed to get a kick out of my "Born to Shop, Forced to Farm" funnies. Hell, you joined my new group, "Wine. It's What's for Dinner" in droves.

Oh, I feel so betrayed!

If you have any familiarity with Facebook—and, unless you're still spinning forty-fives, talking on a princess phone, or curling your hair using jumbo-size cans of frozen orange juice, I'm betting you do—you know it's all about the status update. You log in, write a few pithy, provocative words, hit "share," and faster than you can say, "Ooh! A sale!" all your friends are treated to the most intimate and, if you're me, occasionally mortifying details of your day.

Thanks to the status update, there's no longer any need to say, "Wish you were here." Your friends *are* there. They're there replying, "STOP!" the second your status changes to "At the salon, thinking 'bout bangs." They're egging you on with "do it!" moments after you make the mistake of posting from Nordstrom that you're "trying to choose between the Choos . . . and the Choos, and wondering if I dare buy . . . both." And they're the first to declare you "smooth" when you confess to "rocking the big meeting with my hotshot marketing director stuff that I still *so* have, right up until the moment I reached into my purse for a pen. And pulled out a tampon."

And thanks to the status update, there's no longer any delay in announcing the results of your most recent research studies. It's a damn good thing, too. Your friends need to know, and they need to know now, that the new math is as simple as Snow + Escaped Cattle + Monday = Margaritas (frozen, with salt, especially if there's no school and you don't care if your wedding rings or your fat jeans fit till the fall equinox), and that after several weeks of testing and three trips to the ER for X-rays, you've proved your hypothesis that aerobics and merlot don't mix. Though the high heels certainly didn't help.

In any case, it seems my status updates of late have gotten lots of attention. Not for their wit or descriptions of life here on the funny farm, or even because the Master Defecator continues to be my muse: "Awakened to the sound of Tug tinkling by the bed. Just what I always wanted: an indoor pool," and, "This morning's gift? Dog barf on the rug. My throat's sore from screaming, but my feet have never felt so soft."

Nope. My short blurbs about whatever I'm thinking, doing, discovering, or dying from have been singled out for something I had no idea anyone would notice.

The time they're posted.

What? Four in the morning's not normal?

In the last three days alone I've gotten at least a dozen comments and notes on my "wall" asking why I get up so early, what do I do "in the dark," and the big question, what time do I pass out at night? The answer: nine o'clock if there's no wine involved; eight o'clock if I've had a glass with dinner. Yes, it's been a long, long time since I've made it much past the seven-o'clock *Seinfeld* rerun. And no, Hemingway doesn't find it funny.

I have to tell you, the "what do I do 'in the dark'" question really cracked me up. For starters, I turn on a light. The last time I brewed coffee in the pitch-black, I made it with milk replacer. As I believe I've mentioned, it's like baby formula for cows.[75] Great if you like a cuppa joe that

---

75. And it's all over my kitchen counters. Thanks, Cuy.

gets your gag reflex going. Since I don't, I opt for a little illumination.

My predisposition toward rising with the roosters set in sometime in middle school. I don't know who I pissed off during puberty to be saddled with the same internal alarm clock as livestock, but Saint Peter and I are having a big old "come to Jesus" meeting when I get to the pearly gates. And I do hope Jesus will join us. It's high time some- body called Him on the carpet for the Taliban, Al-Qaeda, and the ankle-socks-with-clogs craze of 1976.

Thirty-something years later, my morning routine re- mains much the same as when I had big hair and a mouth- ful of braces. I get up, brush my teeth, and slip on my exercise stuff. I make coffee—minus the milk replacer— guzzle it down, and force myself to go to my computer.[76] There, I work out my angst. What angst, you ask? The ceaseless, unyielding, twenty-four/seven, three-hundred- and-sixty-five-days-a-year fear that I'll never be funny again. That the last humorous bit, piece, or post I wrote will be the Last I Ever Write.

And then, when I've been at my desk about an hour and given myself at least one good giggle (I subscribe to the Mel Brooks school of comedic writing, which says, "If you laugh, they're gonna laugh"), I reward myself with my own private Jazzercise class. Led by me. For me. Just to kick my own ass. And to celebrate the fact that I don't suck.

---

76. Back in the days of bunny-fur jackets and crushed-velvet hip huggers, I grabbed a ream of paper, a new ribbon, and a whole lot of Wite-Out, and went to an IBM Selectric typewriter. The writing implement of choice of all Cro-Magnon coeds, the Selectric was better than scratching words on a cave wall with a sharp stick, but not by much.

Yet.

Tomorrow? Anything's possible. It could be a whole different story. But at least I know how it'll start. And when. And what my Facebook status might say. I'm thinking, "Done working out with the roosters. Tomorrow it's back to real weights."

Feel free to post your reply.

Now I Lay Me Down to Sleep,
A Pair of Stilettos at My Feet.
If I Should Die Before I Wake,
Bury Me in Them,
For Goodness' Sake!

. . . .

TO: Friends and family

FR: Suzy@stuckinthesticks.com

Date: Saturday, 4:36 p.m.

Subject: No goody bags at this girl's funeral

Life on the farm is lovely, calming, a veritable feast for the senses. It's low-stress, peaceful, like living in a postcard. At least, that's the party line.

Fact is, some days, when there're no goats to chase off the porch, fence boards to bitch about fixing, or houses to show to prospective renters,[77] it's downright brain-deadening.

So what do I do to stay occupied, off the street, and out of trouble?

---

77. I'm happy to report I've found renters for all three tenant houses. Hem was so proud of me, he bought me a new set of butter knives.

Sometimes I write letters to the local chamber of commerce asking, again, why there's still no Starbucks in town. Other times I flip through a Pantone color book left over from my marketing director days and choose new color combinations for the twenty-eight buildings on the farm. Currently I'm campaigning for periwinkle with lime green trim, because I really think there's a whole Key West Goes Country thing coming and I want to be out in front of it. And still other times I dream up elaborate plans for a Takeout Taxi–style service I call Suzy's Pickups by Pickup. It's sort of a rip-off of the TOT but with one important difference: not only will Suzy's Pickups by Pickup stop at your favorite Italian restaurant, we'll also hit the wine store. Because what good is penne marinara without a nice pinot noir?

But even daydreaming doesn't last all day. So what do I do for shits and giggles and barnfuls of fun? What do I do to pass— dare I say kill—the time?

Frankly? I plan my funeral.

And at this point, I've left directions down to the minutest detail for a party you won't want to miss.

I want music. Loud, fun, feel-good music like Linda Ronstadt's "Heat Wave" and Gretchen Wilson's "Redneck Woman." And throw in some Black Eyed Peas, too, please. I want a martini bar *and* a margarita bar, and more chardonnay than you can shake a corkscrew at. The good stuff, please. Stick the Turning Leaf in a tree. Toss the Monkey Bay back in the water. And tell the Smoking Loon to put that shit out. Only J. Lohr and La Crema, *capisce?*

And, of course, there has to be food. Get Forlano's Market in The Plains to cater hanger steak,[78] frites, and a succulent green salad. Then top the whole thing off with Hershey's. Hershey's bars. Hershey's kisses. Some with almonds. Some without. But please, skip the white chocolate. It's beyond blasphemous to us purists.

Whether I die today, forty-something years old, two kids, two cats, three dogs, two goats, three hundred head of cattle, a couple of chickens, and twenty-plus years of marriage to my best friend and the only man I'd ever try to love farming for, or thirty years from now, the rules are the same:

No crying.

And no goody bags.

You heard about that, right? Some poor unsuspecting woman went to a funeral where the guests were given a lovely satin satchel that contained a dollop of the remains of the dearly departed. I guess the host felt it would be nice if the bereaved could bring a little of that very special someone home with them.

And I guess I feel … *ick.*

Is it just me, or does this smack of a kid's birthday party gone berserk? Maybe I could understand if the deceased's favorite expression was, "You want a piece of me?" but I have a nagging sense that this was not the case.

---

78. Supplied by Martin's Angus Beef, of course.

And I'm absolutely, positively not trying to speak ill of the dead. On the contrary: I'm trying to defend them against the alarmingly poor judgment of a few of the living.

Like I said, I happen to think celebrating someone's life is a wonderful way to go, if you'll pardon the play on words. But let's not go too far.

I want you to drink my favorite drinks. Dance to my favorite songs. Tell stories about my farm foibles, and laugh about my shallow passions for shoes and the Jersey shore. I want you to tell my favorite jokes and joke about how I loved my sons to the point of incapacitating them.[79] I even want you to say, "Suz, you *Glamour* 'don't.' You had to wait on that highlight. Now you're going to spend the rest of eternity with roots."[80]

But please don't parcel me out like a premium. Unless I died in battle, there's no reason to resort to body bags. Even pretty, shiny ones.

If anything, you might just want to buy doggy bags. There's bound to be too much food at my funeral, not to mention alcohol. So please, divvy up the steak and the frites, the martinis and the margaritas. Send me off with a bag of Hershey's

---

79. The little guy still can't make his bed because I insist on sniffing his sweet pillow and smoothing the covers "mommy style" so he'll be comfy at night, and my older son still can't do his own laundry because I can't risk his fouling up the fabric softener and hurting his sensitive skin. And no, I don't care that I'm ruining them for their future wives. My mother-in-law certainly didn't care about me. (*Oh, hi, Hem! What's that? You'd like your roast beef* warmed up *before I put it on* untoasted *rye with* just a hint *of mayo and a* very thin slice *of tomato? You got it. And is today's preference* crushed ice *or* cubed *for your Coke? Crushed? Of course. No, no, don't strain yourself. You know the Giants can't win if you're not watching!*)

80. And a three-month-old manicure, I'm sure.

kisses, a bottle of chardonnay, a corkscrew, and, of course, a glass. Oh, and somebody please make sure my favorite stilettos are on my feet.

Because, Lis, if they're missing? I am so coming back for your Calvin.

Love,
Susan

Chapter Eleven

JEREMIAH WAS A PEEPING TOM

It's funny, but one of the things I like most about farm living is also one of the things I like least. I'm talking about the lack of people. I much prefer having people, particularly my girlfriends, close by.

Especially at cocktail hour.

And when I have writer's block.

And when I just feel like claiming I have writer's block so I can feel less guilty about goofing off.

And breaking out my blender.

But I also love bare windows. No drapes, shades, or shutters. Just spare, sparkling, sunshine-streaming-in, Windexed-to-within-an-inch-of-their-lives windows. Not exactly an option when you live so close to your neighbor that you can see the tag on their T-shirt and only one of you has to have a television. If I could choose people or stark-naked windows, I'd choose people. But as that's not an option on our five-hundred-acre slice of near solitary confinement[81] and I'm one of those folks who pride themselves on making lemonade when life gives them lemons, I decided from the start to view Nate's Place as a once-in-a-lifetime chance to live curtain-free forever.

Or at least until somebody complained about having to wear sunglasses inside.

Of course, they could have worn one of the two dozen New York Giants, John Deere, and Tractor Supply baseball caps I keep handy, or popped open a beach umbrella. But no. They had to bitch. And I had to buy blinds.

In fact, within six months of living here I was forced to forgo my curtain-free fantasy and valance, sheer, and drape the entire downstairs.

"Now we can see the TV!" cried Case the day the blackout panels went up in the den.

"Now I can see my computer screen!" cried Cuy the day dark blue denim curtains went up in his room.

"Now the cattle can't see me in my birthday suit!" cried Hem[82] the day he realized the whole first floor was dark enough to harbor fugitives and treat them to a matinee. Nothing new, of course, and no online ticketing; I draw the line at putting the farm on Fandango.

Before long, the McMen coerced me into covering the windows upstairs, too. And this I really couldn't compre-

---

81. Three rental houses set pretty darn far from ours do not a neighborhood make.

82. Winner of the "Most Modest Farmer, Football Coach, and Father of the Year" award and the man voted Most Likely to Shower in a Bathing Suit Lest He Make His Body Wash Blush. Because that's just the kind of nudie he is.

hend. Sure, we've all heard talk of clouds calling 911 on behalf of some poor woman who's way overdue for a bikini wax, but the fact is? They do that only to purists who won't even put up a shower curtain.

Now please don't get the impression I'm an exhibitionist or some kind of closet nudist. On the contrary. I love clothes and unfortunately have (and have *always* had) the credit card bills to prove it.[83] I also love decorating and accessorizing, picking paint colors and fabric patterns, and yes, back in suburbia I was all about window treatments.

But in suburbia I had neighbors, for Pete's sake, and if they were watching me like I was watching them, it was only a matter of time before somebody hollered, "Suz, give the bleach a break!" and Hem's T-shirts would look like shit.

And I'd be back to hiding my roots with a yellow highlighter.

In any case, I very quickly caved and created the veritable man cave my men desired. I put curtains on every window in the house, with one exception: the upstairs bathroom. The sun floods it all day long, and the only plant I haven't killed yet owes its life to living on the sill.[84] But more important, we hardly use it. Sure, it's our middle-of-the-night "go-to" loo, but when it comes to showering? That we do in the downstairs bathroom, where the water comes in from the well and not the *Exxon*

---

83. By my junior year of college I'd done so much shopping and so little working that several of my friends took to calling me Dances with Debt Collectors. I think they were just jealous. I mean, some of those guys could really cut a rug.

84. And the fact that I always forget it's there.

Valdez, which, I'm relatively certain, supplies our second-floor facility.[85]

My point is, we're never in there naked.

So even if the cattle sprout wings, what can they see? Toothbrushing? Deodorant application? A barely awake blond woman fussing with a plant?

Bingo. It just wasn't flying cattle that caught me.

One morning I got up as I always do, in the before-dawn dark, and tiptoed, as I always do, into the bathroom. Yes, the uncurtained one. It's four a.m., it's pitch-black outside, and, since I don't turn on any lights, it's damn dark inside, too. It doesn't bother me. I'm a mom. I can wash my face, remove the mascara I should've removed the night before, brush my teeth, put in my contacts, and, of course, pee by moonlight. And so I do.

To my left are the naked window and the sill where my benignly neglected, and therefore flourishing, jade plant usually sits. I say *usually* because a few days earlier I did a little light cleaning,[86] and I put it on the ledge of the tub. There's more room for it there, but it does better on the sill, and I want to kick myself for forgetting to put it back.

Since I'm butt-to-bowl at the moment, kicking myself will have to wait. But the tub's not two feet in front of me; I could just pop up, grab my happy, healthy jade, and return it to its favorite spot. It would take a split second, tops. And unless I cause some kind of unprecedented lunar eclipse, nobody's ever going to know I moved a plant and chucked a moon at the same time.

---

85. But just the shower. The water in the sink's fine. Go figure.

86. And I mean very little and very light. I spit on a piece of toilet paper and wiped some bug blood off the windowsill. At least, I think it was from a bug.

Quickly, I lean forward into what can only be described as a piss-poor (pardon the pun) squat and lift the one and only shred of proof that I'm capable of caring for a living thing that doesn't subsist on snack foods and video games. "Mommy's so sorry for not moving you sooner," I coo. Suddenly my sleep shorts slip down around my ankles and an image of Porky Pig in all his belly-shirted, pants-free fabulousness flashes across my mind. "You're all class, Suz," I whisper to myself and my plant, and the bulging-eyed bullfrog staring back at me through the glass.

Holyshitholyshitholyshit! I hiss, pressing my sun-deprived succulent into service as a fig leaf and shuffling backward as fast as anyone lassoed by a pair of pajama shorts possibly can. Which, of course, isn't fast in the least, but what I lack in the ability to flee I more than make up for in my ability to snag my foot, fall backward, ram into the towel rack on the door, and slide down to the floor.

Note to self:

1. *Replace cold, tough-on-bare-tush tile with carpet.*

2. *Replace metal towel rack with something less likely to cause spinal injuries. Like a pool noodle.*

The bad news is that the bruise on my back was definitely going to look like a tramp stamp done by a drunk.[87] The good news is that I didn't wake anyone up or spill a

---

87. Closer to my shoulder blades than my butt, which, as far as I'm concerned, is where those things really belong. I know I sound like an old fogy, but is anybody else as tired as I am of plumber's crack complemented by ass antlers? Buy a belt, dammit. Or maybe a pair of pants that actually fit.

drop of potting soil. And the round of applause from the frog was nice, too.

At least, I thought he was applauding. Turns out the poor thing was banging his head against the glass because he was stuck between the screen and the sash. My guess is that one of the rednecks I'm raising was playing sharp-shooter, and someone, quite possibly the other redneck I'm raising, shot back, and in ducking for cover redneck number one had just enough time to close the sash before he was hit by a hail of BBs. As the windows in our house have been known to close without any human assistance whatsoever, my other guess is that sometime after the skirmish Mr. Frog hopped in, the screen slammed down behind him, and he was trapped.

Until he spied me, pantsless and whispering sweet nothings to a plant.

Clearly Jeremiah wasn't just a bullfrog. He was a peeping Tom.

As I saw it, I had three options. One, I could try to free J.T.[88] myself, but, as this required opening the screen, which could be achieved only by first opening the window, which would most likely result in J.T.'s hopping into the bathroom and quite possibly touching me with his sucker-footed feet, which would almost definitely result in my fainting, hitting my head on the toilet, and adding a concussion to my spi-nal cord–cum–tramp-stamp injury, I said, *Nah.*

---

88. Short for Jeremiah Tom. Maybe it's weird to name animals I've just met and that aren't pets (remember Henrietta?), but that's what happens when you grow up with a duck named Duck and a female dog named Good Girl. Accurate? For the most part. Creative? Not so much.

Two, I could rouse my rednecks and make them dispose of poor, dear J.T. But as this would result in fighting and finger-pointing, and the fact that, ultimately, while they wrestled to the death on somebody's bedroom rug, the frog would get loose and we wouldn't find it until later in the day—when Tug threw it up—I said, *Nah*.

Or three, I could pull up my shorts, grab my plant, and go wake Hem.

Dammit, I thought. He's going to make me swear I've seen the error of my naked window ways. And worse, he's going to make me promise to put up a shade.

I didn't have a choice. I couldn't just sit on the floor, stuck between a toad and a window treatment.

It was time to get my farm game on.

I took a deep breath, got up, and tiptoed toward the window. "It's okay, little guy," I whispered, "I've got ya." Then I closed my eyes, lifted the sash, and stepped back as J.T. sprang onto the toilet seat.

"Cool! A frog!"

Holyshitholyshitholyshit! I whirled around. "Case! Where'd you come from?"

"My bed." He laughed sweetly.

"You scared the daylights out of me, dude," I replied. "I didn't even hear you." He looked so cute standing there, half-asleep in his green camo p.j. pants and brown Hendrix tee, which, frankly, could just as easily have been a Backstreet Boys tee. My eldest loves music. You name it, he listens to it. The Rolling Stones, *NSYNC, Pink Floyd, Slipknot, Maroon 5, the sound tracks to *Footloose*, *High School Musical*, even *Star Wars*.

"I heard you," he teased, looking from J.T. to me.

My God, I'm losing my mom powers. "Sorry, sweetheart." I fumbled with the screen. It went up, but it wouldn't stay up.

"You're hoping he'll hop out?"

I turned to reply and came eye-to-eye with the teeny, tiny, but big-enough-to-freak-me-out frog, cupped lovingly in my gentle giant's long, thin fingers. "What the—How'd you—"

He shrugged. "Animals like me, Mom."

And I love you, Case.

Ten minutes later, J.T. was safely outside, my hero was back in bed, and I was on the Country Curtains Web site. A week later, our pretty blue paisley button-up curtain came. It lets in a little more light than my men wanted, but we do have the plant to consider.

And a bullfrog to keep an eye out for.

Chapter Twelve

SUPERMODEL SUZY

"*Model for me!*"

It was my friend Tara, the lovely and talented woman who owns my absolute favorite boutiques in all the world: Lou Lou, and Lou Lou Too. Sunday service had just ended and I was making my way up to the piano to practice with the kids' choir. Unfortunately for these darling boys and girls, I'm their accompanist. They sing. I stumble. Somehow the pastor, the choir director, and the Big Guy—you know, God—are all good with it. It's the kids who probably want to clunk me with their clipboards.

But back to my plucked-from-obscurity Ford Modeling Moment.

"Susan," Tara said, touching my shoulder and stopping me in my "oh, please be speaking to me" tracks, "we're doing a fashion show as a fund-raiser for a local charity and I'd love it if you'd model for us."

Should I act like I didn't hear her? It would be kind of tough. I'd have to feign sudden, catastrophic deafness or some sort of seizure. And I really wasn't certain about collapsing in the sacristy. Playing the piano poorly is one thing. Playing the congregation for fools is another.

"Tara, did you miss your medication?" I cracked. Oh, God. Why didn't I just say yes? I so want to say, *Yes. Thank you. I'd be thrilled. Oh, goody. Me and Kate Moss. Maybe after the show we can smoke and skip meals together! What are we waiting for? Let's swing by the store and pick out my outfits!* But no. Needy wiseass that I am, I make her ask again. I am totally going to hell for my bottomless insecurity and bouts of massive ego.

"Susan, you are so funny," she said sweetly. "You'll do it, right?"

"Um, sure, if you really want me to," I finally reply like an adult. And then promptly permit my gumball-machine mouth[89] to get away from me. Again. "I mean, I can see the folks at animal crackers asking me to model, because frankly I've always thought I had it all over their regular bear, but if you want me to hit the runway for Lou Lou, I'd love to."

Nice save, O unsound one.

And thus began my Supermodel in My Mind career. Which was a blessing, really, as it put a stop to a bizarre plan I'd hatched to cohabitate with the hens. Don't ask

---

89. Symptoms include the inability to stop yourself from saying whatever you're thinking, and a terrible taste in your mouth, most likely from your feet.

what I was thinking. I was caught up in some misguided, Dian Fossey–ish, "Live with Livestock" thing. I guess I thought I'd get material to write about, but Hemingway said all I'd probably get was a spectacular case of scaly leg.[90]

In any case, I raced in from church, marked the calendar with the day of my big debut, and in that moment heralded the start of my own personal *America's Next Top Model* mania. There was so much to do and so little time. For starters, I had to grow six inches and shed twenty-six years. Hmm. Not going to happen. But what could I do? What did I have control over? And then it hit me: I'd develop a good old-fashioned eating disorder! Hell, I could binge and purge with the best of them. I drew the line at smoking, though. I joke, but it would really screw with my Jazzercise addiction. And no drugs. It's clear I've got crazy covered.

As I may have mentioned, I have always wanted to be a supermodel. Come on. Who doesn't? The lights! The cameras! The magazine covers! The closest I ever came were some hair shows I did for Sebastian when I was in college. Not exactly the Paris collections, but still, a room at the Plaza and oodles of free professional styling products are nothing to split your ends over.

For those of you who don't know, a hair show is like any other fashion show. There's a runway involved, and lots of six-foot-tall women who look like they live on black coffee, cigarettes, and a wide variety of appetite suppres-

---

90. Yeah, scaly leg. Just one of the many jaw-dropping avian diseases that'll leave you relishing your adult acne, age spots, mild rosacea, eczema, facial moles, and other much less leperlike medical conditions.

sants strutting their stuff on it. The main difference is the focus. In fashion, it's on clothes. In hair, it's on cut, color, and style.

The audition was a hoot: I was like a wombat in the land of the willowy. I was the shortest woman in the room, the least beautiful—and that's putting it mildly—and the only one carrying pictures in a portfolio not emblazoned with the Click, Ford, or Elite logo. In fact, the only reason I was there was because one of the Sebastian scouts saw me (or, more specifically, my hair) on a bus and suggested I come to the call. *Call* is short for *cattle call*. Appropriate, huh? By the time I'd reached the tender age of nineteen, it had already been preordained that I'd one day be stuck in the sticks. You've got to wonder whom I pissed off in a previous life.

In any case, the two Armani-suited, glasses-wearing, supremely well-coiffed Sebastian execs went down the line surveying the hopefuls. They selected six or so and dismissed the rest of us. I was walking out the door when the Pointer Sisters' "I'm So Excited" came blaring through the speakers and I did what I always do. I started to dance.[91] I was shimmying into my backpack when I heard someone shout, "Ladies! Loosen up, ladies! We need you to dance like . . . like . . . *that!*" I turned, saw them pointing at me, and ducked out the door.

"Wait! Wait!" shrieked the more stressed of the two Sebastianites as Anita, Ruth, and June kicked into the chorus. "Can you teach them that?" I wasn't sure; it seemed to

---

91. I still do this. Even to this day. Nothing embarrasses Case and Cuy more than when I bust a move in public.

me we'd need a case of champagne and muscle relaxers to get those mannequins moving. I shrugged. "Screw it," she continued, grabbing me by the elbow and dragging me back to the group. "We'll stick you in front and they can follow you. You're in."

Exhibitionism: Madonna just thinks she's cornered the market on it.

My desire to be a supermodel, or just plain gorgeous, goes back at least as far as sixth grade. And I really didn't think it was beyond the realm of possibility (which shows you how far back my mental instability goes, too). I remember kneeling by my bed at night and saying, "Dear God, I've been good. I did my homework. I cleaned up after dinner. And I didn't drown my brothers in the bathtub. Whaddaya say? Can you find it in your heart to give me Jacqueline Bisset's breasts? I promise to take good care of them."

Of course, it never happened, and to this day my collection of padded bras is second only to Victoria's Secret's. The Big Guy also never came through with Cheryl Tiegs's height, or Farrah Fawcett's face and hair. When I get to heaven, that stuff's the first thing on my agenda for a "come to Jesus" meeting even the Blessed Mother wouldn't miss.

But back to reality. Or at least the recent past.

A week before the fashion show, I found myself at a fitting at Lou Lou. "Tara said this screamed, 'Susan!'" exclaimed Toni, the shop's manager, as she shoved the most gorgeous beige, brown, cream, and white jumbo-check wool suit I've ever seen in my life in my face. "She picked it out especially for you. Don't you just love it? Oh! And she picked this, too." Toni took off for the back of the store while I stood there caressing the hip-length, double-breasted jacket and matching skirt. It was just the kind of thing I wore in my marketing-director days. I held it up to myself in the mirror; I didn't even have it on yet, and I wanted it. And I wanted a job to go with it. I felt so at home just hugging it. So comfortable. So ready to run to a meeting and instead get a manicure. But, of course, I don't have a job, my role as farm Realtor/maid service notwithstanding, and the chances of my needing a killer suit to perform either of those tasks were pretty slim.

About as slim as the Kay Unger cocktail dress Toni suddenly dangled before me. It was breathtaking. Rose colored, with a pleated sweetheart neckline that hung off the shoulders, it screamed, "Wine me, dine me, make me wear Harry Winston's discards!" In short, it brought me right back to the fact that I didn't really want a job. I wanted Hemingway's job to require that we socialize, press the flesh, hobnob with something other than cows and hens.

I got my chance the day of the fashion show. It was held at Sheila Johnson's[92] Salamander Farm, and my fellow models (as well as the hundred-plus guests) were comprised of the horsey set I so enjoy ribbing. If the eleven lovely ladies I shared the runway with thought about snapping my heels and hiding my accessories in retalia-

---

92. Sheila Johnson is the cofounder of Black Entertainment Television and the country's first female African-American billionaire. The fashion show was held in her spectacular stable/indoor riding ring. And all I kept thinking was, Wow, I wish I were her horse.

tion for my bratty riding-pants barbs, they didn't act on it. They were loads of fun, gracious, and absolutely gorgeous in their Lou Lou, B. Jolee, and Finicky Filly fashions.

To be honest, I felt pretty gorgeous, too. So what if I hadn't managed to get any taller or younger; sixteen-year-old skyscrapers are so overrated. I prefer my women petite and pushing fifty. And more important, so does Hemingway. He wasn't there, of course. He had a pasture to plow and a couple of bulls to de-ball. I'm hoping he'll come next year, though. Yeah, Tara asked me to model again. And this time I simply said, "Yes. Absolutely. Count me in. Thank you." And then I took off for my car before Needy Suzy could surface.

You know, for me, that's a pretty adult response. So maybe, after all these years, God's finally answering my prayers. Not exactly what I had in mind, but then, I never asked which version of *Roget's Thesaurus* He refers to. The moral of the story? Be specific. Pray for great hair, and you might find you can plait your armpits. Pray for boobs, and you might find yourself married to one. Pray to grow, and you just might turn out mature. Like me.

A Note from Suzy, Princess of the Pastures

. . . .

You've heard of the Horse Whisperer and the Dog Whisperer, right? Well, they've got nothing on the Chicken Whisperer.

Back in the days when I lived a slick, stressed, but well-dressed professional-gal-about-the–Big Apple life, I got e-mails that made my little clothes-horse/haute couture/bling-loving heart skip a beat. Notes like, "Sue, meet me at the Carolina Herrera sample sale at noon!" and "Sue, Paloma Picasso trunk show. Today! Tiffany! Twelve!"

These days I get e-mails like, "Sue, check out this guy's radio show at noon. He's called the Chicken Whisperer. Why? Because he talks to chickens. And *he* got a *two-book* deal!"

Like I don't consider throwing myself from the grain silo frequently enough.

I have to hand it to the Chicken Whisperer, though. His book titles, *Chicks are Easy* and *Peep Show*, are really funny. And I could use a laugh. I just Googled "local sample sales" and was directed to the farmers' market in Warrenton. I want Prada, but I get produce. Which is, of course, better than pullets. That, after all, is the Chicken Whisperer's job.

My job at this particular juncture is to stop day-dreaming about meal delivery services and prancing around in beautiful clothes (even if it's for a good cause). It's time to focus on being the wife, mom, and maid, cook, dog demuddier, and homework direc-tress. It's time to make a new pitch for pigs, figure out how else I might be able to help around here, and reacquaint myself with my computer.

In short, it's time to resume my position as Prin-cess of the Pastures and my role as Ranter in Resi-dence. After all, that's pretty much what the good people at my local paper pay me for. As far as I know, they're still running a column I contribute, so it might be nice if I wrote one.

I'd like to write about Cluckster and what that damn bird did to my window boxes. But then I might have to mention that I killed her. Unintentionally, of course, but still. And, as there are bound to be people who don't believe me, who could even conclude that root-balls (of geraniums, pansies, any kind of peren-nial) should be registered with the police, and who might possibly get so incensed they protest and carry picket signs that say, HAVE YOU HUGGED YOUR HEN TO-DAY? and, CLUCKSTER, WE HARDLY KNEW YOU, and, IT'S A CHICKEN. NOT A CHOICE, my best bet? Would be to skip the subject altogether.

At least until after I tune into the Chicken Whis-perer. Who knows? Today's topic could be "Letting

Go of Guilt after Accidentally Exterminating an Egg Layer." I'm relatively certain it won't be, but if it is? And I hear just one other listener confess to harming a hen?

Column, here I come.

Part Two

THE COUNTERFEIT FARM GIRL
GETS REAL
(COUNTERFEIT FARM GIRL STYLE, OF COURSE)

*"How many kids does it take to close the one and only gate
that keeps the cattle in the pasture? Two. One to say, 'What gate?'
and the second one to say, 'I didn't open it.'"*

—SUSAN McCORKINDALE

Chapter Thirteen

CALVES' HEADS AND BLACK SNAKES
AND GROUNDHOGS. OH, MY!

How do you know when spring's come to the sticks? Forget the tractors and the Bush Hogs and the hay making and the cows enjoying a population explosion over what seems like every inch of pasture. As far as I'm concerned, spring's come to the sticks when the dogs bring home groundhog carcasses and calf heads, and the cats smack snakes around on the kitchen floor.

Back when I lived a nice, safe, suburban existence, I gauged the arrival of the green season the same as everyone else. I watched the trees bud, the forsythia bloom, and the common sense of every child in town take a hike. And I include my own in that statement. Why, just because the calendar says it's spring, do they ditch their jeans and sweatshirts for shorts and T-shirts? Do they actually think surfer gear will suffice in the snow?

What was that song Whitney Houston sang? "I believe the children are our future. . . ." God help us all.

Here in the hinterland, it's a little different. Yes, the trees bud, the forsythia blooms, and my psycho seventeen-year-old puts on shorts,[93] but there are several telltale signs unique to the bucolic cow country that I'd never been treated to in the 'burbs. Including, but not limited to, the aforementioned cattle giving birth in my backyard.

For starters, there are the groundhogs Grundy kills, carts to the porch, and leaves for Pete, our ever-expanding pup, to consume. Then there are the calves' heads that Tug exhumes, brings home, and proudly bats around with his paws, as if to remind me he's a bones and raw food diet dog. This, as you might recall, is also called BARF. Which is what I'd like to do every time I see this stuff.

Grundy, Tug, and Pete have no such response to their entrées. They dig in and digest them just fine every time.

Now if I could only get them to do the same with the third unique-to-the-sticks sign of spring: the snakes.

Six-inch snakes. Six-foot snakes. Snakes in the tulip beds and in the grass around the goat pen. Snakes in the streams and the springhouse[94] and catching rays in the middle of the road. Snakes hanging from the gutters and giving me the evil eye. Snakes lounging along the porch rail and reclining, camouflaged, atop the wrought-iron picnic table. Not the most appetizing find at dinnertime, but damn good if you're on a diet, don't you think?

---

93. With *flip-flops.* "They're fine on ice, Mom, I swear!"

94. A lovely little stone structure built over a spring. Before the birth of the air conditioner, folks used to sit in it to escape the heat.

The worst are the slick, black, oversize kielbasas committed to creeping into the basement. I discovered two of them once while changing the litter box, a chore that's really Casey's, but since he was in bed with a cold[95] and the cats wouldn't hold it in, I had to do it. The snakes were coiled up in what looked like piles next to the stinking, huge gray container, and honestly? I thought they were poop that missed the pan.

Not only am I nearsighted, I'm proof of that popular adage "You can only be young once, but you can be immature forever."

It's probably a combination of my being a maturity-impaired individual (a phrase I totally stole from Dave Barry, a man I am someday going to marry, right after I divorce Robert Downey Jr.) and my growing resignation to having reptiles around that stopped me from screaming blue bloody murder when I discovered our cat Coca[96] playing with a good-size garter snake on the kitchen floor this morning. In fact, my exact reaction was, "Stay right there. I'm getting the camera!" And he waited. Oh, yeah. Just call me the Cat Whisperer.

Five seconds later, I'd snapped five pictures. Five minutes later, they were all up on Facebook. And five minutes after that? All my friends started freaking out.

Just the reaction I used to have.

These days I'm cool with the unique signs of spring in the sticks. The body parts of long-dead barnyard beasts

---

95. I'm sorry, sweetheart; what were you saying about shorts being warm enough in forty-seven-degree weather?

96. Big brother of—big surprise—Cola.

dug up and deposited on the porch by the pups. The goats grazing on my dainty but now dearly departed daffodils and butterfly bushes. And, of course, the snakes: the big ones, the little ones, the ones on the windowsills, in the cellar, under the sink, and in the backseat of the Mustang.[97] Even the ones the cats choose to use as chew toys. They're not my favorite sign of spring, but they sure beat the skater-dude stuff my son freezes his ass off in.

---

97. That'll teach me to leave the top down after dark.

FOR IMMEDIATE RELEASE

Contact: Dr. Suzy, Princess of the Pastures

Tel: 555-555-5555

Cell: 555-555-5556

E-mail: Suzy@stuckinthesticks.com

CHILDREN OF THE CHEETOS

Country's Foremost Fake

(And We Mean Totally Pretend) Parenting Expert

Has Good News and Bad News for New Moms

(UPPERVILLE, VA)—In a press conference earlier today, Dr. Suzy, president of Dr. Suzy's Fantasy Pharmaceuticals and bestselling author of *That'll Teach 'Em: Change the Locks on Your Latchkey Kid*, and *The Girlfriend's Guide to Motherhood by Intimidation* (or, *Why Threats Like "Wet Your Bed One More Time and I'm Tweeting It!" Should Be Part of Any Parenting Arsenal*), announced the results of her latest research study, this time on the eating habits of the human male.[98] Speaking at Molly's Irish Pub during the monthly breakfast meeting of her fellow moms and loyal followers, many of whom wore SCREW THE WHALES. SAVE THE WINE, GOTTA RUN. THE KIDS HAVE

---

98. Previous studies include "Kids in the Kitchen: A Look at the Mess that Tries Moms' Souls and the Meals that Try Their Stomachs"; "Haute Cow-ture: Strut It at Your Local Tractor Supply"; and the afore-referenced "Wine is Not Gatorade: Why Aerobics and Merlot Don't Mix."

GOTTEN INTO THE CUERVO, and MY CUP RUNNETH OVER
AND IT'S SCREWING UP ALL THE SALT T-shirts from Dr.
Suzy's signature line of overpriced, questionably cap-
tioned apparel, she said, and we quote,

"After years of careful observation and stepping in
stuff, I've got good news and bad news for new moms.

"The bad news is that your kids will never out-
grow the two a.m. feeding. The good news is that
eventually they'll ditch the breast for the bag. You'll
no longer need to get up. But you will need to keep
them stocked up.

"On what, you ask? Cheetos. Tostitos. Doritos. Fritos. And all manner of fat-filled, sodium-infused
snacks.

"Of course, I'd never assume it's exactly this way
in other people's homes, and based upon my research I'm relatively certain boys are guiltier of this
than girls. But it's been my experience, thanks to my
sons, the eldest of whom I've studied for the past
seventeen years, that not only does the two a.m.
feeding persist, but at some point the human male
adds ten p.m., midnight, and four a.m. kitchen raids
to the roster.

"Case in point: Every morning I go in to awaken
my oldest so he doesn't miss the school bus, and every morning I step on a bag of whatever he inhaled
the night before. Sometimes it's sour-cream-and-
onion potato chips, also known as the birthplace of
morning breath; other times it's Fritos. And every

now and again he ditches salty for sweet and I'm crunching a half-eaten sleeve of Chips Ahoy! beneath my feet.

"Of course, I don't like the junk he ingests, but I buy it, so I'm the one to blame. But I also can't blame him. He's six-foot-four, still growing, and hungry 'round the clock.

"He's also skinny as a Bachman pretzel stick. Oh, how I wish there were medication that could give me *that* metabolism.

"Up until recently I thought it was just my big guy who did the late-night noshing. But in the wee dark hours two days ago, I stepped in an unfinished bowl of chocolate pudding by my younger son's bed. As we have three dogs, two cats, and two goats with a knack for getting in the house, you can see why it's possible the people in Fairbanks heard me freak.

"You're right if you're thinking I could turn on a light and see where I'm going. But why blind my boys when I can deafen them with the 'What the hell was *that*?' scream I've got down to a science?

"Mornings in our house are pretty loud affairs, with laughter, back rubs, conversation, and, occasionally, the brazen consumption of whatever snack food I've played footsie with. Trust me when I tell you, there's nothing like starting the day with a handful of stale Cheez-Its and half a can of lukewarm Yoo-hoo. It's more than the breakfast of champions. It's the fastest-acting colon cleanse in the country.

"And yes, in case you're wondering, I hope to release the results of that study within the next six months, or at least as soon as I'm able to spend more time at my laptop, and less time in the ladies' room.

"So, new moms, take heart. You won't always have to get up for the two a.m. feeding. Eventually your kids will replace the breast with the bag. But just watch where you walk when you wake them. The folks in Alaska still haven't accepted my apology.

"Thank you."

Dr. Suzy maintains an office on her farm in Fauquier County, Virginia, where, when she's not busy filling Hefty trash bags with dead groundhogs and making sure the snakes in the kitchen don't eat the kids' snacks, she conducts cutting-edge research on such subjects as nails, males, and designer sample sales, jeans, heels, and buy-one, get-one deals. At present she's developing several new-mom-only medications, all of which are designed to be taken with wine, and one that induces short-term deafness when your kids start to whine. In addition, Dr. Suzy offers weekly bartending workshops at which she imparts the secret to making her famous Morning Margarita, and the trick to drinking it and staying coherent for your parent-teacher conference. (Hint: It involves a tote bag, a covered pitcher, and two cups. Swing some salt, and your kid's a lock for at least A/B Honor Roll all year.)

Chapter Fourteen

COMING AROUND TO COUNTRY

𝓘 warned Cuy not to get too attached to Marnie, our Rubenesque Rock Cornish hen. But did he listen? Not a chance. He said he had plans for that chicken. I said I did, too. He planned to show her. I planned to Parmesan her. As it turns out, neither of our plans panned out. Why? Because Marnie's true calling was cutlets.[99] From her one breast, I got enough for two meals. For the third marine division. From my two breasts I couldn't nurse a newborn. Trust me on this.

You would have liked Marnie, with her plump frame, pretty feathers, and piercing black eyes. But I liked her sliced thin, dipped in egg (generously supplied by one of her hen friends), coated in bread crumbs, and browned to

---

99. While I was visiting in New Jersey, my mom taught me to make chicken cutlets and chicken Parmesan. Two more meals and we'll be able to go a week without doubles!

perfection in lots and lots of big, bad, artery-clogging, butt-broadening oil, and served with a cucumber-and-tomato salad and a side of broccoli, all of which Hem grew, and which tasted great. Even the grubs.

Yes, we raised her, butchered her, and consumed her. What should you get from this incredible tale, besides stunned by the fact that I cooked and nobody keeled over, and the sense that Frank Perdue is probably pissed at me? Scared. Really, really scared.

Why? Because I'm becoming one of those folks who live off the land. Me! The woman who raised takeout to an art form and perfected it by not ordering from the same restaurant twice in six months. Me! The woman who awakened one Christmas morning and said, "Hmm, I've got fifteen people coming for dinner today. Should it be Thai? Italian? Chinese? Ooh! Only shrimp lo mein and moo shu pork can assuage that hunger pang. So it's . . . Chinese!" One phone call and three hundred and fifty dollars later, it was.

That's right. Everything I railed against is silently, insidiously seeping into the very fiber of my being. And I'm not the only one.

Case in point? Casey.

Tough as it is to believe, the family holdout has begun to succumb to the charms of the country. Not all of them, of course. Just little things, like the fact that his five-hundred-acre backyard means he never has to go to a paintball park ever again, and if he wants to shoot off Roman candles every night, nobody's gonna complain.

Time was when Casey would come in from school, work, wherever, and play his guitar. Or watch the History Channel. Or spend insane amounts of money on iTunes.[100] Sure, sometimes he'd go outside. But only under penalty of death—or worse, the possibility of my confiscating his iPod. In fact, Casey left the house so infrequently, we referred to him as Mr. Inside, and Cuyler as Mr. Outside.

These days Mr. Inside is outside before I even know he's home. He drops his backpack on the back porch, pulls on his helmet, and takes off on one of our four-wheelers. No, "Hey, Mom, ya here?" No, "Yo, Mom, what's for food?" Nothing. Sometimes, if I'm upstairs making beds or talking on the phone, I have no idea he's out racing around the property until he returns frozen, if it's winter, or covered in burrs, if it's spring or summer. And in the fall? Casey doesn't come in at all. Or at least not until Hem goes looking for him.

How awesome is that? I joke, but you have no idea how happy I am to see my son, the kid who collapsed into a snowdrift the first time he ever saw the farm, finally coming around.

Of course, that doesn't mean I'm not traumatized by how comfortable I'm becoming with country stuff.

The other day Hem and I hit Tractor Supply for chicken scratch and something called Laymore, which is, quite literally, chicken food designed to make the hens "lay more." From the moment the automatic doors slid open it was as

---

100. Buying songs we already own but, "It just can't be the same Boston, Mom!" Trust me when I tell you, I have "More Than a Feeling" Hem's going to flip when he gets the MasterCard bill.

if some other woman were shopping with my husband. I don't know who she was, but she couldn't get enough of the waterproof rose-colored gardening gloves and plastic orange ponchos with matching pull-on pants. She oohed and aahed at long-sleeved T-shirts dotted with livestock, and thought the snap-front, guy-style shirts in John Deere green were "So great!" She was a pushy bitch, too, dragging me through the shoe department and shaming me into trying on work boots.

"*You* want *those*?" Hem asked, watching me clomp up and down the aisle.

"God in heaven!" I said, looking down. "How'd they get there?"

"Very funny. Why don't you try that on, too?" He nodded in the direction of a black-and-blue-plaid flannel shirt. "It'll complete the whole lesbian lumberjack thing you've got going. Not that there's—"

"Anything wrong with that!" We laughed at the same time. "Great. Now I'm taking fashion advice from the Jerry Seinfeld of farming."

"So get 'em." He sighed. "But when you wake up tomorrow and realize you own a pair of boots an Italian war widow wouldn't wear, don't say I didn't warn you."

"Stop. You had me at lesbian lumberjack."

The long and short of it is, I didn't buy the boots. But what kind of brain fizz possessed me to put them on?

I've shown our rental houses in heels. Corralled cattle in heels. Fixed fence boards, fought off snakes, and shooed the goats out of the garden in heels. I've lifted hay bales, changed the hens' bedding, and chased a raccoon out of the chicken coop in heels. Platform, chunky, stiletto; I wear 'em and I work 'em. I like to think of it as "high yield in high heels."

Okay, I totally stole that quote from one of the T-shirts at Tractor Supply, but still.

The point is that I'm slowly but surely losing myself to this country stuff. It's fine for the rest of my family, but I liked the old me. This new chick who raises chicks and chows 'em down makes me nervous.

And the fact that I went back and bought those rose-colored gardening gloves plus a pair in lilac and, *shhhh*, the black-and-blue-plaid flannel shirt begs just one question: Can work boots be far behind?

Chapter Fifteen

THE MOTHER OF ALL REALITIES

$\mathcal{I}$f I knew then what I know now about being a mom, I would've had my tubes tied when I was ten.

Twenty years into marriage, and seventeen years into motherhood, it's official: I'm one of those women you don't want at a baby shower. While everyone else is cooing and gooing and telling the MTB[101] to "enjoy every moment" because "they grow, and they go," I want to haul her butt to a bar, get her a virgin colada, and give her a clue.

Make that a couple of clues.

I want to start by asking, "What the heck were you thinking, honey?" I won't give her time to answer, of course. I mean, what can she say? "Everyone else is doing it"? (So I guess if everyone else is jumping off a bridge into

_____

101. Mother to be.

a river of reeking Pampers, you'd do that, too?) "I've wanted to be a mom my whole life"? (You mean to tell me you spent your youth fantasizing about staying up all night and being barfed on? Might as well be a groupie for a rock band, babe. It's a whole lot more fun and easier on your figure, too.)

No, once you've reached the baby shower portion of the program, it's way too late to question the MTB's motivation. But still, she needs a reality check.

And who better to give it to her than the Reality Chick?

Hello, my name is Susan, and I'm a bitter blond crone with two kids who some days just wants to knock the blocks off everybody who didn't level with me before I embarked on this motherhood business.

Like today.

Today is the first day of summer vacation and already Cuyler has that "there's nothing to do" look on his handsome face.

Excuse me? You declined attending a dozen different camps because you said you couldn't wait to have fun on the farm. So go ahead: Milk a chicken; goose a goat; run with the bull calves. But please stop looking at me like I should be able to pull bunnies out of my butt to entertain you.

"I'm bored," he announces while I'm sitting at my desk trying to wrap up the copy for a Web site that's due by the end of the day.

"You're what?" I ask. I cannot possibly have heard him right. It's nine thirty in the morning. School let out yesterday. At twelve thirty. Not twenty-four hours later my son's run out of things to do? And he's *telling* me? If I'd so much as thought the phrase *I'm bored* within fifty miles of my mom, I'd still be polishing silver.

"You're kidding me, right?" I reply. "Get your fishing pole and head to the pond." He doesn't move. "Okay, okay. Grab your backpack and your bug book, and go collect creepy-crawlies." Still not moving. "All right, better idea: Go shoot BBs at Dad's collection of empty Budweiser cans."[102]

"Been there, did that," he responds, sighing and rolling his eyes. "What else have you got?"

"What else have *I* got? I've got the car keys, my friend, and, while I'm loath to use even a gallon of our overpriced gas to get you out of my sight, in five seconds I'm going to haul your hindquarters to the library and leave you there with a list of books you've got to read before you can return to the boring old farm. That's what I've got."

I didn't catch his reply; it was obscured by the pounding sound of his sneakers as he stampeded out the back door.

Maybe it's catching; earlier today Casey also left the house in a huff. Perhaps you heard him stomping around, slamming drawers, and generally throwing a tantrum the likes of which I haven't seen since he was a toddler. It was so bad, I actually stood there wondering how to soothe him. Dig out his "fluffy"? Find his "baba"? Dust off his "binky"?[103]

---

102. Heck, shoot 'em at the full ones; it'll do wonders for his waistline.

103. Special note to my pregnant pals: Do yourselves a solid and save that stuff.

His problem? His new workplace. Yes, today is the first day of my firstborn's first summer job. A job he doesn't want, and that he has sulked and moaned over, and cursed us for since we set it up. A job he's left us hate mail about, and threatened to run away over. Is he cleaning the public toilets in Central Park or picking up litter along the highway? No.[104] He's employed on a farm. In the fresh air. He's building fences and making hay and helping move cattle. All things he could do here, but he won't; heaven forbid he should work for his father.

He's also earning a whole lot more money than he would slinging burgers at McDonald's or Burger King or Taco Bell.[105] Those places were his first choices for employment. Why? Because they're filled with young people and he wants nothing more than to be one of the gang.

And that, of course, is the crux of the problem.

Every now and then the rumor goes 'round that there are Crips and Bloods making milk shakes and working the cash registers at the local fast-food restaurants. And why not? I'm sure Crips and Bloods have bills to pay, too.

But if that rumor turns out to be just the teensiest bit true, my kid can't work there. Why? Because in addition to being sweet and funny and easily as good a dancer as any of those young Disney movie stars, my big guy is also the very definition of gullible: an easy mark who has a

---

104. But if he keeps it up he could be enjoying both of those fun community-service experiences next summer!

105. Where he wouldn't sling burgers as much as burritos, and if he did for some reason actually try to sling a burrito, he'd make a mess, get fired, and we'd end up arguing about acceptable employment opportunities. Again.

heck of a time telling the good kids from the bad seeds. All he wants is to make friends. And that's very, *very* hard to do when you're autistic.

I'm no expert on autism, but I know how it's affected my kid. To be clear, Casey is high-functioning autistic, so he's luckier than most. But he still has a terrible time reading social situations. Body language is almost totally lost on him. And he literally cannot take a hint. But what's worse is that he assumes everyone, whether they're nice to him or not, is his friend.

Some days he's better than others. But most of the time he gravitates toward anyone who'll give him the time of day. So we can't just stick him someplace, cross our fingers, and hope he'll be okay. We have to be involved and make sure of it.

And no teenager, autistic or not, takes kindly to that.

Like I said, there are days, weeks, months, even entire quarters when I really want to bop everybody who didn't level with me about motherhood. Who didn't tell me that no matter what I did to make my kids' lives easier, happier, safer, more loving, and more fun, they were going to find fault with it. Who didn't try to make me see for even a second that the road to hell is paved with good intentions and untied fallopian tubes.

Kidding, of course. I love my sons. But that doesn't mean they're not making me nuts.

Right this instant, Casey—you know, the kid with the well-paying job during an economic downturn—is texting me from a cornfield: "How could u do this to me mom?" and "Soooo hot" and my absolute favorite, "Please, some-

body save me!" And my little guy? He keeps popping in
to pout and tell me—say it with me now, people—"There's
nothing to do!" I ask you: How can there be nothing to do?
The kid's got five hundred acres to play on. My brothers
and I had a patch the size of a place mat.

Ah, yes. We're one day into a ten-week break and already both my babies are miserable. That must be some
kind of record. From zero to suicidal in under a single
summer day! It takes most kids at least forty-eight hours
to get that glum. Which makes me wonder if there isn't
something really special about my parenting style. I mean,
maybe I should give classes and coach other moms. Then
I'll never have to shop for a baby shower present again. I
can simply give gift certificates to my seminars.

Or maybe I'll just shut the hell up and hit babyGap like
everybody else. Ignorance, after all, is bliss. And nothing
says bliss like a teeny, weeny leather bomber jacket, pants,
and matching booties.

Of course, it also screams, *Bitch to change the baby in!*
But nobody asked me, now, did they?

Chapter Sixteen

THERE OUGHTA BE A PILL

Remember Sea-Monkeys? They came in a packet and you put them in water and, supposedly, they came alive.

I was never really sure whether they did or not, because it seemed to take an awfully long time. I mean days and days of nothing happening and my mom saying, "Susan, throw that stinky stuff down the drain!" And then one day, when I was at a Girl Scout meeting pretending to give a Thin Mint about achieving a sash full of cooking, sewing, and babysitting badges, aka the original T.G.I. Friday's "flair," she seized her chance to chuck the whole thing in the toilet. I came home, spied the carnage, and thought, holy cannoli, we're going to hell.

I was certain we'd committed murder and, being a nice Irish-Italian Catholic kid, equally certain I was going to burn for all eternity with Hitler. And Stalin. And Mussolini.

Not to mention my mom.

"Susan, get your hair off your face. Benito, don't you think she looks better with her hair off her face? See, Susan? Even Mr. Mussolini agrees."

Just the thought of being trapped for the rest of time with Joanie jawing about my hair with the likes of killers, rapists, and whoever gave *The Blob* the green light was enough to send me straight to confession. The priest cleared me, then gave me two Hail Marys and one solid piece of advice: Sea-Monkeys are for chumps. But kill a Chia Pet, missy, and you'll never get a direct flight to the pearly gates.

All these years later, I still think of the Sea-Monkeys. The guilt's gone but I'm intrigued by the idea of a pet in a pill. Why not, right? We have pills for pain. Pills for depression. Pills that prevent my colon from seizing like somebody filled it with cement. Love those pills, and Ativan is awesome, too.

So why not pills that can do really cool things?

Here at Dr. Suzy's Fantasy Pharmaceuticals, the GlaxoSmithKline/Forest Labs/Merck–like conglomerate I have in my head, we've got several revolutionary pills in the pipeline.

For starters, there's Busy Bee. Designed for kids (like mine) whose favorite phrase is "I'm bored!" and parents (like me) who are sick of buying duct tape and ducking those nosy buddies from Family Services, Busy Bee banishes the "there's nothing to do!" blues in seconds. Simply sprinkle a touch on your little sprite's breakfast and say, "See ya at dinner, sweetie!" Dozens of ideas fill your kid's head and he (or she) is off and running. Building a tree fort, bathing a hen, even, believe it or not, reading a book. In an instant, your kid stops moaning and groaning and you don't need duct tape. Or an attorney. Oh, yeah. Busy Bee's gonna be big.

Next up there's Insta-Friend. We developed this one for my sweet firstborn and the millions of socially awkward kids just like him. If you met my boy, you'd love him, which would immediately identify you as an adult, because kids his own age would rather have their iPads nailed to their foreheads than be forced to sit with him at lunch. I'd cry about it, but when I do I can't see, because the protein clouds my contacts.[106]

Insta-Friend's great because it works for kids of all ages. And there's no worry if your child can't swallow a pill. Why? Because you take it for him! Simply pop it and *poof*, the perfect friend appears. Your child likes to ride his ATV all over creation? What a coincidence; so does Insta-Friend! Your little one's most comfortable coloring? Insta-Friend's packing a carton of Crayolas! And there's a free added bonus: Every Insta-Friend comes with a box of Kleenex, because you're going to cry when you see how happy your kid is.

And speaking of kids, if yours think bathing is something that should be done once a quarter whether they need it or not, you'll want to consider Clean Freak. Created with my dirt-loving duo in mind, Clean Freak dissolves instantly in junior's fruit juice, and works immediately upon consumption.

---

106. Yes, we're working on a pill for that, too. You take it with a bottle of wine and everything looks better. Or at least different. You know, from the floor.

That's right. Children who just seconds before thought nothing of working their earwax into their hair to hold it in place ("It's called bed head, Mom!") have been known to jump up, peek down their pants, and holler, "Holy cow! I've got grass stains on my groin!" Then, fast as Tug bringing a live chipmunk in the house, they race to the shower and actually *use soap*. I know; it's a miracle. I'd cry, but, well, we've already covered that.

Of course, all this began with the idea of a pill that can turn into a pet. And while we at Dr. Suzy's Fantasy Pharmaceuticals have yet to perfect growing a four-legged friend in a test tube, recent research indicates that a toilet bowl could be the ticket. At least as it pertains to certain kinds of dogs. We've had some major success growing mutts in this manner. Purebreds, on the other hand, won't perform in anything other than a Toto toilet and are thus more likely to be flushed.

Which, now that I think of it, is the exact same fate my Sea-Monkeys met.

So I guess I really am going to hell. I didn't kill a Chia Pet, but I still bet I'm going to burn. Or at least do a stint in the holding pen. Look for my next book, *The Counterfeit Farm Girl Goes to Purgatory*, in which I bug God to bring Busy Bee and Insta-Friend to fruition, manage to work the Big Guy's last nerve, and wind up sentenced to spend eternity with my mom and the Sea-Monkeys.

Yeah, they hatched. And they've got something to say about my hair.

Chapter Seventeen

DEATH BY FAMILY TIME

"Casey, you have *breath cancer*," hisses Cuy as his big brother burps right in the poor kid's face. We're in the car, on our way home from lunch after the little guy's final flag-football game. Hemingway's driving. I'm manning the iPod. And our two surly spawn are busting each other in the backseat.

"Yeah?" Casey taunts. "Well, your fingernails look like you gave up toilet paper for Lent. *Last year*." Oh, God, that's gonna do it, I think to myself.

"You are so disgusting," Cuyler shoots back. "It's just dirt!"

"That's *poop*, pipsqueak," Case responds, grabbing Cuy's right hand and shaking it so hard I fear that if it *is* poop, and it goes in my hair, I'll definitely do jail time for my unmotherly and murderous response. "So tell it to the marines, turd boy."

"I *am* the marine," Hemingway bellows. "So knock it off before you both need ventilators."

Isn't family time fabulous? And this is just us, in the car, not even in the restaurant, where they pelted each other with Sweet'n Low packets. Or in a major department store, where they began beating each other with shopping bags and attracted a crowd. Not to mention top management. *Oh, hello, Mr. Neiman. Nice to meet you, Mr. Marcus!*

And isn't it even more fabulous that we're smack-dab in the middle of family-time *season*, aka summer vacation? I barely survive the evenings and weekends with my wonder boys, and yet here we are enjoying (and I use the word loosely) ten—count 'em, *ten*—terrifying weeks together.

And, except for when Casey's at work and Cuy's doing a stint of indentured servitude for Hem,[107] we really are spending them together.

With the economy as it is, we canceled our annual pilgrimage to Myrtle "Please God, Let My Bathing Suit Fit" Beach and began a campaign of presidential proportions to get people to visit us. After all, we're on five hundred cattle-filled acres, so we have the room and the built-in entertainment options to keep guests happy.

We've got cow tipping, manure tossing, and goat goosing. We offer nightly power outages, rooster races, and sometimes the very special opportunity to find a black

---

107. Now, that'll teach the kid to cry boredom.

snake. In the shower.[108] We're also just an hour from D.C., so if you like monuments with your morning moos, you're certain to agree with Frommer's: Old McCorkindale's Farm, aka Nate's Place, is the vacation destination of the recession!

I'm kidding, of course. The budget travel tipsters don't review us till next week. So for now it's back to my boys.

I understand that brothers fight. I have three brothers, a million nightmarish memories, and the post-traumatic stress disorder to prove it. I know what I'm looking at here. I'm looking at sixty-plus days of board games that spiral into bodily fluid free-for-alls. Backyard campouts that result in bloodletting, burns, and a course of antibiotics.[109] Marathon matches of Halo, Star Wars, Nazi Zombies, and Conflict: Vietnam that end in tears, recriminations, and regurgitated food fights.

If we lived in a neighborhood, my sons wouldn't have to spend so much time together. There'd be other kids to hang out with. But we don't. And as of this writing, there isn't a single child in any of our tenant houses. So while Casey's at work moving cattle,[110] and Cuy's helping Hem do whatever it is that needs doing,[111] I spend much of the

---

108. Lather, rinse, reptile!

109. For me.

110. And doing his best to communicate with his coworkers, several of whom only speak Spanish. As Case has a tough enough time speaking English, you can only imagine how comical things can get. Not to mention dangerous. Hmm. Maybe McDonald's was the way to go.

111. Yesterday's task? Install what I call a pigeon eviction system in the equipment shed. It's actually a bird-cry simulator that looks like a cross between a huge Halloween decoration and a disco ball. Hem and Cuy hung it from the ceiling and set it up to shriek every half hour. I only wish they'd told me. Sure, the pigeons hate it. But the couple with the three kids did, too.

only quiet time I'll have all day (aka billable hours) doing the one thing I can't bill for: reminding all my friends, including several local school principals and my pastor, that "As of a certain date we'll have a house open. A nice house surrounded by pretty, rolling pastures that are perfect for four-wheeling! And paintball! And taking target practice! In short, a house that's perfect for a *family*!"

And if we don't get one soon, mine's going to kill me. Not to mention one another.

As far as I'm concerned, the phrase *summer vacation* is a misnomer. For parents, and teachers, too. Sure, they get a well-deserved break from my sons, but they still have to be home with their own kids. And while I'd never presume other people's children are as challenging as mine, I refuse to believe I'm the only mom in the free world who keeps Prozac in her purse. And threatens to give it to her kids.

Jeez. I'm just joking. That's what the muscle relaxants are for.

As for how the nail poop–slash–breath cancer business turned out, we made it home safe, sound, and without anyone needing life support. That may change shortly, as I just heard something about playing Halo. I give them twenty minutes before somebody cries foul, hocks a lugie, and all hell breaks loose. If you see them running down the road, beating each other with Xbox controllers and the like, let me know. I'll stop what I'm doing and drive over.

After Labor Day.

Chapter Eighteen

AH, THE WONDERS THAT
AWAIT ME IN MY WHIRLPOOL

It's been a few years since we sold our home in the suburbs and, quite literally, bought the farm. But there are still days, like laundry day, when I question the soundness of that decision.

Back when we lived in the land of sidewalks and neighbors we could actually see to wave to, the weirdest things I ever found in the washing machine were earrings, car keys, and the occasional cell phone. Oh, and money. Once I found a hundred-dollar bill. You bet I kept it; it's not my fault those 2T OshKosh B'Gosh pants have shallow pockets.

If you've always lived on a farm, you're probably immune to the wonders that await me in my Whirlpool. But if you're a city girl, suburbanite, or former suburbanite turned quasi–country girl like me, hold on to your delicates. Following is a rundown of just a few of the things I've found in my washing machine lately. The bad news? It includes goat teeth. The good news? Apparently they make Clorox "with tartar control!" Who knew?

I advocate brushing with bleach about as much as I advocate suffering through laundry duty without an adult beverage. Which is to say, not at all. My feeling is, wait till five, whip up a frozen margarita, and you'll be much better equipped to deal with such discoveries as . . .

An egg. Of course, by the time I found it, it was as if I used fabric softener made of mucus. You bet I went through a whole lot of Tide on that load.

A three-inch nipple. Can you say phallic? I know it's for the bottles Hem and Cuy use to feed the baby bulls, but my inner Bart Simpson still snickers.

Poultry bands. The ankle bracelets of the banty set. Made of brightly colored aluminum and numbered for quick and easy "future dinner" identification.

Range cubes. The dog biscuits of the bovine world. My better half keeps them in his pockets to feed the "girls" and then forgets they're there. They spill out into the wash, crumble, and coat the clothing like chicken cutlets. This usually inspires me to whip up a batch, which interestingly enough makes the herd very happy. Oh, my God. You think maybe they're manipulating me?

A hypodermic needle. No, no. I haven't taken to giving myself Botox injections. The needle's for medicating the cows. And since the "girls" don't get communicable diseases, thank God, there's no point in using a fresh needle for each stick. Of course, there's also no point in Hem's keeping the vet kit in his vest pocket, but he always forgets it's there. Hmm. Maybe it would help his memory if he got stuck. With laundry duty, of course.

Castration bands. They slip these on the bulls' you-know, and it makes them shrivel up and, well, you know. Only I didn't know. I thought, "Oh, looky! Hair bands at the bottom of the dryer!"

A deer bone. At first I thought it was a dog bone. You know, one of those flavored jobs you buy by the dozen, divvy up among the beasts, and spend the rest of the day watching them square off and steal from one another. But upon closer, and I mean *thisclosetocoronary* inspection, I realized it used to be a real, live bone. One somebody found and couldn't resist keeping. Is it any wonder I can't resist dunking my progeny in Purell?

Ammunition. That's right, a live round. In my washing machine. Talk about a nice, clean shot . . .

Ear tags. Like poultry bands, but for cattle. I no longer freak when I find them in the wash, unless there's a tidbit of ear still attached. That really gets my goat. And speaking of goats, I honestly don't know how Duke or

Willie lost two teeth, or how they wound up at the bottom of the washer (though I sense the presence of shallow pockets . . . again), but for the full ten seconds I stood there freaking out, I was certain they came from Cuy's mouth. They didn't, of course. They were way too white to be his. I love my son, but the kid can't brush worth a damn. And since they really don't make Clorox "with tartar control!" I can come to just three conclusions:

> One, these suckers definitely once belonged to one of
>   our billies.
> Two, my little man's plan was to try to trick the Tooth
>   Fairy.
> And three, if this is what he'll resort to, maybe it's time
>   I come clean. And give the kid back his Benjamin.

Chapter Nineteen

SUZY SOPRANO

"*F*resh meat!"

"What?" I couldn't hear Dee worth a damn. A reedy, souped-up cover of the Bee Gees' "You Should Be Dancing" was bouncing off the walls of the cavernous, blindingly white multipurpose room. Kim was calling moves in time with the music. And I was killing myself to win the "So You Think You Can Jazzercise" contest running through my mind.

"A warm body. By the door!"

Shit if she wasn't right. Leaning against the pale yellow wall was a pretty blond woman. She was watching us. She was smiling. And best of all, she appeared to be breathing.

"Suz, a live one at three o'clock." Wendy gulped her water and nudged me in the direction of Dee's blonde. "Go talk to her. See if she wants to be more than the audience."

An audience. Lord, I love an audience. Why? Because when I'm heel hopping and jazz handing, I'm consumed by a fantasy in which I'm the next Bebe Neuwirth in *Chicago*. Catherine Zeta-Jones and Renée Zellweger wouldn't be bad either, but ages ago I saw Bebe on Broadway and that babe kicked butt.

Of course, the closest I'll ever come is my Jazzercise class. Typical type A that I am, you'll always find me in the front row, furiously following the instructor, shvitzing like the field hand I'm slowly but surely becoming, and trying desperately not to fall down and make a fool of myself. Which I do pretty frequently, because in all honesty? I'm a colossal klutz.

But don't try to talk to me, see, because, as I've mentioned, I'm not there. In my mind I'm blinded by the footlights, rockin' my *rond de jambes*,[112] and jazz-squaring to within an inch of my life now . . . and forever . . . at the Winter Garden Theatre.

Oh, wait. That's *Cats*.

But you know what I mean. And you do this stuff, too, right? Stuff like stand in the shower and pretend you're Beyoncé or Barbra Streisand or Martina McBride. You just start singing to your Schick Slim Twin and in your head you're bringing the house down. That is, until you realize your kids are about to bring the bathroom door down with their pounding and pleading for you to shut the hell up.

---

112. I speak French about as well as I speak farm, but after three years of ballet lessons I can tell you this: *rond de jambe* means "half circle made by the pointed foot." And *spasmodique* means "pissing away your parents' money."

At least, that's what usually happens to me. And yeah, my kids curse. I'm one of those people who think a well-placed cuss adds color.

"What are you waiting for? She's gonna get away!" Wendy again, flick-kicking her way back to me and maneuvering me toward the door.

"Get her to join the class," Tracy chimed in from the back row.

"Screw that!" cried Court. "Get that mom in the Mafia!"

The Marshall Mafia, that is, aka the Claude Thompson Elementary School parent-teacher organization. PTO for short. Marshall Mafia for fun.

My henchwomen had spoken. It was time for the mob boss to make her pitch. Reluctantly, I left my place in line, grabbed my water, and ran out to say hi.

"You're missing a great class," I said, smiling and sticking my hand out and pulling it back just as fast. "Oh, sorry! I'm sweaty. I mean, I'm Susan. But I'm also sweaty." Smooth as sandpaper, Suz. Nice going.

"I'm Pam." She smiled back. "You guys set this up?"

"Uh-huh." I wiped my palms on my shorts and sipped my water, certain I was making a great impression: panting, sweating, and reeking like the aforementioned field hand. *Hi! I'm with the PTO and do my pits stink!* "It's a fundraiser. The fee goes toward class trips or new gym equipment. You know, whatever the kids need. And I happen to have spectacularly compromising pictures of Kim"—I paused and pointed to one of my best friends, aka Drill Instructor Petro, her headset and high ponytail bobbing up and down as she lunged across the stage, taking the class to whole new levels of pain—"that I keep threatening to post on the Internet, so she teaches for free."

"You're funny." She laughed.

"It's a defense mechanism. But thanks."

"Direct, too." She looked at me, surprised, but still smiling.

"I love to bullshit. Really. I can talk shopping and shoes all day. But not all the time, you know? Life's too short."

Of course, right this second I didn't feel like getting all existential or shooting the breeze. I wanted to ask her quickly about the board and get back to class. Just wham, bam, come to a meeting, ma'am. But something in her response rang my bell.

"You're right, you know," she said. "Most people just take it for granted, but life really is too short."

Hmm. What had we here?

I cooled my jets and considered her. She was perfectly put together. Dark jeans. White man-tailored blouse. Sparkly gemstone earrings. She looked like a woman who felt fabulous. Yet something told me she felt anything but. An aura of exhaustion hung on her like a mismatched accessory, and while her eyes smiled sapphire blue and beautiful, they were edged with an unmistakable trace of sorrow I'd seen before.

In my mirror.

We stood there and watched as the class rolled out their mats, got their weights, and guzzled water like they were in the Sahara and not a teensy-weensy elementary school in Marshall, Virginia. It was impossible to keep the room, which functions as both an auditorium and a cafeteria, cool, and now it was thick with body heat and the smell of perfume and perspiration. Some folks find it offensive. But for me, it's practically a mating call. Not for sex, but for sanity. Exercise helps keep my depression at a distance. And as far as I'm concerned, a little body odor beats the hell out of the bouquet of Black Angus I'm surrounded by at home.

"Want to try the last ten minutes? I have weights you can use." Say yes, I thought to myself. Say yes, and I promise to tell my stupid intuition to take a hike.

"Not tonight." She laughed a little and shifted her bag on her shoulder. "Maybe next week."

"You sure?"

She nodded and fished out her keys. "Well, nice to meet you."

Oh, boy. She was leaving and I hadn't even asked her about being on the board. My capos were going to kill me. Worse than that, my "been there" buzzer was going berserk. My new friend Pam and I were cut from the same cloth. I was certain of it.

And I was equally certain Wendy, Tracy, Court, and Dee were the best natural antidepressants around. I had to convince her to come back.

"You know, we do other fun stuff. Besides Jazzercise," I said, scrambling and gesturing toward the fifteen or so moms, teachers, even the school principal hip-lifting their way to cardiovascular health (not to mention a cold one, if I knew my crew). "You should join the PTO. Really, we have a great time."

She walked toward the front doors and stopped next to a commanding oil painting of Mr. Claude Thompson, the school's namesake and the county's first African-American principal. It was a captivating memorial of a man who'd been beloved by his staff, the students, and their parents. I'd never met him, but I'd heard the tales, wistfully told, of how he ran a tight ship but was all for having fun.

"Honestly. We do lots of neat stuff, like spirit days and family movie nights, when we show such four-star Academy Award winners as *Kung Fu Panda* and *Alvin and the Chipmunks*. It'll give you an aneurysm, but the little ones like it."

She laughed. Bingo. Time to take it up a notch. "And, um, we hold dances, too. Not pole dances—the administration put the kibosh on those—but disco dances. We teach the kids the Hustle and the Electric Slide and the Macarena. You know the Macarena, right?"

Feel free at this moment to picture me, belly sweat–stained and mascara streaked, not just doing the Macarena in the middle of the painfully fluorescent lit hall of my son's elementary school and in front of the venerable visage of its sweet, dearly departed former principal, but humming the musical accompaniment as well. Not the most traditional recruitment technique, but it got her attention.

"You're a nut. You know that? Okay, say I join, but"— she hesitated—"well, I can't promise I'll make all the meetings."

My radar raced. Words formed and died on my lips. I didn't want to risk offending her, but I couldn't ignore the feeling that she was trying to tell me what I sensed the moment I met her.

It drives me crazy when I do this. I meet a person for the first time and suddenly, inexplicably, know something about them that they didn't share. Like the fact that they play the piano. Or that they're a Pisces. Or that they're the middle child. You know, some detail I've no business knowing.

And it doesn't matter where I am or who I'm talking to. Or not talking to.

One night, Hemingway and I were out to dinner and the waiter, whom we met five minutes earlier for thirty whole seconds, came to deliver our drinks. He put them down, my handsome farmer said thank-you, and I said, "Fray fan?"

"Excuse me?" The waiter looked at me, startled.

"You like the Fray, right?" I was kind of startled myself. I mean, where the hell did that come from?

He clutched his pen and order pad to his chest, inadvertently dotting the pleats of his white tuxedo shirt with little pinpricks of black ink, and backed away like I might bite him. "How'd you know that?"

I shook my head and glanced at my wine. I had no idea how I knew it.[113]

"Suz, what've I told you about scaring the staff?" Hemingway sipped his Stoli and tonic and did his best to calm our wigged-out waiter. "Please excuse my wife. She

---

113. To be clear, I know only one song by the Fray. Their single "How to Save a Life" is one of my all-time favorites. And to be equally clear? I have no clue how I knew the waiter was a fan. I just did.

has gumball-machine mouth. Whatever she thinks comes right out."

"Huh," he said, eyeing me suspiciously. "I'll be back in a sec to tell you the specials."

Needless to say, we never saw him again.

This bizarre talent of mine is no less true of my depression radar, or what I typically call my "been there" buzzer. It's a blessing and a curse. A blessing because I instantly empathize with and am ready to befriend whomever I'm talking to, and a curse because it's a heck of a lot more acceptable to blurt out, "You're an Aries, aren't you?" than it is to lead with, "My gut says you're a Lexapro girl."

Shooting from the hip has its place. But here, in the hallway, with Pam, was not it.

"Don't worry about getting to all the meetings," I insisted. "I don't make all the meetings, and I'm the president."

She raised her brows and burst out laughing. My stomach flipped; I'd read her wrong. Oh, my God. How mortifying. "I'm so sorry, Pam. I didn't mean to . . ."

"To what, sound like the guy in the old Hair Club for Men commercials? Remember them? 'I'm not just the president. I'm also a client!' "

A kindred spirit. And sarcastic to boot. I had to get this mom in the Mafia.

"A wiseass. Good. You'll fit right in." I paused. "So what do you say?"

Her hand was on the door. "It might be fun to be part of the . . . What do you guys call yourselves?"

"The Marshall Mafia. It's what you get when you make a Jersey girl president. Just call me Suzy Soprano."

"Well, Suzy Soprano, I'll probably miss the winter stuff."

"But not because you're a ski buff, right?"

She didn't say anything. She didn't have to. "Well, if it makes you feel any better, I'm no ski buff either," I offered. "In fact, from, like, December to March I'm more of a covers-up-to-my-nose, hide-in-bed buff."

"You?"

I nodded.

"No way. You're, like, Mrs. Happy."

"Mrs. Happy. Mrs. Sad. Mrs. Up. Mrs. Down. I've been a missus my whole life. And that's a long time to be married."

She laughed, and nodded her head in the direction of the class. "And now you're married to the mob."[114]

"They're a great group." I looked over to see Dee watching us and waving and smiling as if it were ice-cream-sundae night at the asylum. Wendy joined her and suddenly I felt the need to introduce them. From a distance, of course. "That's Wendy and Dee doing the Howdy Doody routine," I said, pointing. "Tracy's in the back, and Court's over there, the redhead in the corner. Terri and Stef aren't here tonight, sloths that they are. If I can't make a meeting, one of them runs it and it's fine."

I had to get her to join. Not just because I needed another body, but because I knew how good it was for my

---

114. Anybody else remember *Married to the Mob*? Michelle Pfeiffer was so funny and gorgeous, and quite possibly the only person in the world to look hot in big hair.

body—and my head—to have to get up, dress up, and show up, especially on those days I'd much rather buy a one-way ticket right down the proverbial rabbit hole. "Really. No one'll mind. Hell, we hold most of the meetings at my house, and we drink so much chardonnay we don't know who's there and who's not."

"You're joking."

"You got me. We drink merlot."

"You're funny."

"And you're in, right?"

She was about to reply when suddenly the music stopped, the chatter started, and the Jazzercise class came to a close. Damn, now I'd have to wait until next week to kick Bebe out of her spot on Broadway.

"So what time does Miss Kim in there commence the torture?"

"Seven o'clock. Sharp."

"And if I'm late . . . ?"

I raised my eyebrows. "You like lunges? Just joshin'. Kim's more of a jumping-jack kind of girl."

She pushed open the door. The crisp fall breeze consumed the humid hallway, and I shivered. "Next Tuesday, then," she called over her shoulder. "Seven o'clock."

"Sharp!" I shouted. And she was gone.

I peeked in at my pals and gave them the thumbs-up sign. The Marshall Mafia had a new member.

Suzy Soprano strikes again.

Make Mine a Hemingway

· · · · · · · · · · · · · · · · · · ·

A Hemingway Daiquiri, that is. The sophisticated ladies of the Solomon Schechter Day School book club in New Milford, New Jersey, had this yummy cocktail created in honor of my honey. I thought it was particularly prescient of them to realize that not only does my man need a drink; he deserves one in his name, if for no other reason than that he puts up with a woman who actually refers to herself as Suzy Soprano.

It's a tad more complicated than a Tennessee Snow Cone, but it won't leave you with Jack Daniel's breath. You know, the kind that makes your spouse blanch, dogs cower, and kids flee the house should you utter a single syllable before you brush.

Ingredients:
—1½ oz. Appleton White Rum
—½ oz. Luxardo Maraschino
—juice of 1 lime
—juice of ¼ pink grapefruit
—teaspoon simple syrup

Mix everything in a cocktail shaker with ice and strain into a chilled cocktail glass. Then sip and say, "To Hemingway. God help you!"

Chapter Twenty

STAR OF STAGE, SCREEN, AND LIVESTOCK EXCHANGE

As I've mentioned several times before, either because I'm getting old and can't recall I've already said it, or because I still, after all these many years, can't believe it, I am a star of neither stage nor screen.[115]

I am, however, pretty popular at our local livestock exchange. For the uninitiated, a livestock exchange is where folks go to buy and sell—hold on to your hat now—livestock. I know; I've become a real font of farming information.

To be clear, I'm talking about the Livestock Grill, inside the Fauquier Livestock Exchange. Maybe you've been there? My friend Kevin's usually in the kitchen, and there's

---

115. For ages, I also wanted to be a game-show hostess. While my classmates aspired to being men and women of letters, I wanted to turn them. I'm sure my educator parents were very proud.

typically eight to ten good-size gentlemen camped out around the lunch counter talking business, kidding one another, and clearly enjoying the succulent rib eyes, sizzling burgers, and mouthwatering honey-dipped chicken that make a diet addict like me seriously consider saying, "*Sayonara*, salad."

But I won't. Kevin makes a mighty good salad. And if I could just get him to deep-fry it, it would be really delicious.

Anyway, around lunchtime a few weeks ago, I raced in and commandeered four seats: one for each of my three men, and one for me.

I was alternately checking my watch and covertly coveting a massive serving of french fries and the aforementioned honey-dipped creation being devoured way too close for my caloric comfort by one of three large cattlemen to my left, when out of the blue, their behemoth buddy in the middle addressed me.

"Excuse me, ma'am, but are you that woman from the paper?"

You know the work talk, chatter, and general merriment I mentioned earlier? It halted faster than that old E. F. Hutton commercial: "When E. F. Hutton talks, people listen." And *I* was E. F. Hutton. Only I wasn't being asked for financial advice. I simply had to 'fess up, or not, to being "that woman" from the newspaper. And I had to do it with half the lunch crowd and a sweet young waitress watching me.

My brain raced through my recent columns. Oh, dear, what had I said? Had I complained yet again about the

cows fornicating in my front yard? Implored the fashion
police to crack down on anyone wearing riding pants in
public? Moaned about the lack of nightlife in Marshall?
Made snide comments about bolo ties and tiny plastic
cowboy hats, like the kind on the heads of my hulking in-
quisitors, and how men the size of Michael Strahan shouldn't
wear either? I couldn't recall, and all I could think was,
Why, oh, why did I have to be a writer? Why couldn't I
have a nice, safe job, like bounty hunter or inner-city
schoolteacher?

"Well, that depends," I replied, smiling, and trying to
soften my Fran Drescher–meets–Valerie Harper honk so
as not to add "damn Yankee" to their list of reasons to dis-
like me, if indeed they were keeping such a list. "If you
don't like the woman from the paper, then nope, it's not
me. But if you do . . ."

"It's her!" exclaimed the man on the end.

"I told you!" said the man in the middle.

"You got that Mustang outside?" asked the man next
to me.

Oh, my. They read the piece about the day my Mustang died in the Marshall Shopping Center. Right in front
of Anthony's Pizza and the Movie Gallery. Boy, I miss
Movie Gallery. The Redbox in Bloom is nice but the selection's so slim. Netflix is fine, but my demanding duo
needs instant gratification. ("Wait a week? But all our
friends saw *Borat* yesterday!") Sure, I could drive the
twenty minutes to Blockbuster, but by the time I pay for
gas and the rental fee, I could buy two one-way tickets to
Kazakhstan for my kids.

Clearly the lack of a local video store (and the fact that living in the sticks means we can't stream squat yet) is something I really could rant about. And maybe I will. But right this second it's back to my moment of stardom at the Livestock Exchange.

"Nope, the Mustang's home," I replied. "But it's all fixed, in case you were worried." I smiled, and was just starting to thank him for reading my column when suddenly the conversation around the counter recommenced.

"Figured it was her from her picture."

"Which paper? The *Democrat*?"

"Yeah, the weekend one."

"I read that article. It was pretty funny."

"She writes mostly girl stuff, right?"

"You callin' me a girl?"

At that slightly testy second Hemingway arrived with Casey and Cuyler in tow, and someone on the other side of the counter spilled a soda. My kids took their seats, the waitress took our drink orders, and Kevin stopped cooking long enough to clean up the mess and tease the guy who made it. Was I saddened that my fifteen seconds of celebrity had come to a close? Absolutely not. I want as few people as possible watching when I ask for a salad. And a side of fries.

Chapter Twenty-one

MY BIRTHDAY MEANS JACK

"Any birthday is preferable to the alternative, dear daughter."

This from my mother, paraphrasing Maurice Chevalier,[116] of all people, when I called her to bellyache about my upcoming "big day." I'd hoped for a virtual hug or a shoulder to cry on. A little of the sweetly superfluous "now, now, don't go threatening suicide over a number, Suzy" flattery she typically offers and that I've come to count on. Just a teeny-tiny, itsy-bitsy bit of sympathy, since I'm turning forty . . . *plus*. Big plus.

But no. She didn't utter a single, "Darling, you don't

---

116. A popular French actor and singer with a thing for chorus girls. It's funny my mom should quote him and the French beauty philosophy. Particularly since Dame Joan, as she's affectionately known, is generally more Anglophile than Francophile. Or even American.

look a day over thirty!" or even a, "How can you call yourself old? You hold your liquor better than any college
coed!" (Which I don't, but I'd still like her to lie to me.) Instead, she took a hard line when I complained about my
smile lines and demanded I consider my crow's-feet from
the French perspective.

The French, for those of you who've yet to be treated to
this fountain-of-youth factoid, consider forty the old age
of youth, and fifty the youth of old age. *Puhleeze.*

Desperate to forget my crinkly eyes, pouchy lower lids,
and the parentheses punctuating my mouth, my disap-
pearing upper lip, slowly but stealthily spreading snout,
slowly but stealthily descending derriere, age spots, and
the fact that both my forehead and neck can now double
as sheets of loose-leaf paper, I raced into my morning
Jazzercise class. I would not go gently into that good night.
I would disco, disco against the dying of the light!

At least, that was the plan until the class manager[117]
greeted me with the words, "Susan, you expired yesterday."

So that accounts for my sudden, overwhelming urge to
lie prone in something pine.

Ninety-two bucks later my membership was renewed,
delaying, by the miracle of modern checking, my expira-
tion by muscle atrophy, not to mention Botox, Restylane,
and Juvéderm overdose, for another two months, and I
dashed from the Jazzercise center to the eye doctor. Some-

---

117. Every class has a class manager who takes attendance, collects membership fees,
and harasses people into wearing Santa caps and doing Jazzercise routines down Main
Street in twenty-six-degree weather. Of course I participate. Nothing says "Merry
Christmas!" like a head cold.

thing was wrong. Very wrong. Things were fuzzy, out of focus. I actually had trouble writing out my check—not an affliction I've ever suffered from, no matter how many no-venas Hemingway has begged my mother to make.

I was in mega panic mode when I plopped down in the big chair, eyeballed the big E, and cried, "Doc, I think it's the big C." To which my wonderful optometrist, who just happens to have a whole Owen Wilson in *You, Me, and Dupree* thing happening, replied, "Relax, Susan, it's not cataracts. You're just ready for readers."

What's next? A spot in assisted living?

Oh, no, way worse: a birthday greeting from the AARP.[118] That's right. The American Association of Retired Persons. Oh, my God, the fogies have found me. Let life on the lamb[119] begin.

I returned from Dr. Dupree's still crying over the bright blue Peepers stuffed in my pocketbook, only to discover I needed them to read my mail. There, placed squarely in the center of the kitchen table by the thoughtful old man I married, and complemented by a jumbo-size bottle of Benefiber, a fifty-four pack of Depend Adjustable Underwear,[120] and a box of gingko biloba tablets,[121] was a postcard

---

118. At the time of this writing, it was about a month before my birthday. I wasn't too happy about it, but then, I never am. My birthday is in the late winter, it's usually freezing, and I'm usually in bed recovering from the flu. Or something really special, like surgery.

119. And I really do mean lamb. If I buy one of the big suckers I saw at the Fauquier Livestock Exchange, I can make a nice, comfy escape. And maybe Jenn will make us a couple of scarves!

120. With Super Plus Absorbency, should I overdo it in the fiber department, I guess.

121. Because we can't have me forgetting to take that fiber, now, can we?

and an introductory issue of the one publication no one willingly subscribes to: *AARP the Magazine.* Who's on the cover? Jack Nicholson. Like the prospect of turning fifty isn't frightening enough.

Of course, the really scary thing is that I actually don't hit the big five-oh for . . . a little while longer. And yet all of this stuff is happening now.

Wrinkles, readers, achy knees, and patches of gray hair (on my head, too). Forgetfulness, confusion, and a brand-new fear of falling, breaking a hip, and finding myself in the hospital. Without a sweater.

And that's not the worst of it.

Late-night hot flashes that leave me so drenched that Hemingway swears it's like sleeping with a soaker hose. Bizarre life insurance solicitations that scream, "Don't Leave Your Loved Ones in the Lurch!" and slick, four-color brochures pitching gated golf course communities (with on-site nursing care, no less) make me wonder: Is the universe trying to tell me something?

And if it is, maybe I should simply go deaf. It works when Hem's moaning about the MasterCard bill, so it should do the trick on the bullies from the AARP.

They can't have me. Not now, and not in the future. I don't care if they send me moisturizer and sunblock samples, free pedometers, or packets of trail mix. I don't care if they send me discount coupons for movie matinees and early bird dinners at Cracker Barrel, cases of BOOST, or a six-month supply of Centrum Silver. I don't care if they send me boxes of Osteoflex and more Grecian Formula than the Gray Panthers can use in a year. Hell, I don't care if they send me ruby-encrusted reading-glass chains, cash-mere cardigans, or a complimentary Prada purse. *(Please don't send a Prada purse. Please don't send a Prada purse. Please don't send a Prada purse.)*

No, I'll never capitulate, not even to couture. Unless, of course, they come across with a pair of the only pumps I'd give a kidney (and maybe a kid) for. And then my birthday will really mean Jack. Not to mention Manolo.

How Do I Love Thee?
Let Me Count the Stitches

· · · · · · · · · · · · · · · · · · · ·

TO: Friends and family

FR: Suzy@stuckinthesticks.com

Date: Sunday, 11:01 a.m.

Subject: Operation: Romance

So, what are you doing for Valentine's Day? Running to the store for a special card for that special someone and hoping like hell the pickings won't be especially slim? I've been there. In fact, I just got back. That was me in my messy ponytail, mascara-smudged eyes, smelly sweats, and rykäs stinking up Wal-Mart's card aisle at eight this morning. I passed on those with hearts and rainbows, teddy bears and butterflies, puppies and kittens, but picked up one with a sweet elderly couple holding hands in a field. They look like they've been married since before Minuit bought Manhattan, and the expression on the old lady's face is a cross between love and longing ... for a pickax. Something about her just spoke to me. Though I wonder what she'll have to say to Hemingway.

And what about Valentine's Day night? Are you going to a party? A favorite restaurant? A movie? Or maybe you're headed to a hotel with a heart-shaped tub, scented candles, and a bottle of bubbly. Personally, I'm thinking of making a romantic batch of chicken cutlets. Or maybe a meat loaf. The McMen really like meat loaf. And to me, nothing says "I love you" like a meal consumed without kvetching.

If you're wondering if I'll get flowers, chocolates, or any other gifts for this month's Hallmark holiday, the answer is no. I don't want flowers. They die, and that makes me sad. I don't want chocolate. I eat it, and that makes me fat. And getting the little silver wrappers out of the weave in my sea-grass rug[122] ticks me off, too. Sad, fat, and angry. Not exactly the perfect mix for amour.

As for other presents? Well, any Valentine's Day that doesn't involve a surgical procedure is gift enough for this girl. Yes, twenty years ago this Valentine's Day I celebrated this most romantic of holidays in the hospital. I was married six whole months at the time, and I can still hear my brand-spanking-new husband hollering, "I knew I should have gotten the extended warranty!" as they whisked me off to the OR to remove my spleen.

Every year since, I've sent my surgeon a card. I always ask to visit my dearly departed vital, and he always asks how things are going with my therapy.

Of course the one trip I am making right this moment is back to the store. I picked out a love note for my true love, but I

---

122. You'd think I'd have chucked this thing by now. Not only does it have patches of Tug's dried poop and vomit stains from Grundy's consumption of a dead something that so didn't agree with him that he had to have surgery—two thousand dollars' worth of surgery—it's also where Duke left a housewarming gift the first time he got in. Oh, and it feels awful on bare feet.

completely forgot the stash of red Swedish Fish and two-pound bag of Twizzlers I always give him. Yes, he gets candy. But no flowers. And definitely no surgical procedures. The only one who's operating on my man is me.

Love,

Susan

Chapter Twenty-two

AIN'T NO WAY TO TREAT THE LADIES

*F*acebook. Twitter. Instant messaging. E-mail. All this advanced technology. And still they've got to totally flatten my ta-tas to make sure they're tumor-free. Priorities, people. Priorities!

I remember my first mammogram. I stood there, pressed against the machine and thinking, My God. This contraption's like something out of *The Crucible*. Did having teeny-weeny breasts make me a witch?

I know it makes me a bitch; I kvetch pretty regularly about being last in line when God handed out hooters. Of course, on Double Dose of Big Fat Butt Day I was the first one through the door, but again, that's something I'll address in *The Counterfeit Farm Girl Goes to Purgatory: Like My*

Life Here Hasn't Been Hell.[123] But really, I hadn't cast any spells, chanted, or even levitated Hemingway's sweat socks into my bra. And yet there I was, feeling as if I were about to be pressed to death, one ta-ta at a time.

Anyway, I recall the nice technician telling me to put my arm this way, and lean my shoulder that way, and please stay still while she compressed my minuscule mammary into the shape and—sadly—size of a silver dollar. Then she actually asked me to hold my breath.

I looked at her like, People breathe during this procedure? Then she flipped a switch, and boom. It was over. Until we had to do it again. And again. How the mosquito bites that masquerade as breasts on my chest managed to cast a shadow I'll never know. But they did. Twice. Each.

Ouch.

Can you imagine if men had to endure this to protect the health of their . . . *you know*? We'd need to have curbside pickup for the number of guys dropping like flies from all manner of you-know maladies. There's no way they'd go for protecting the family jewels by crushing the crown. No, the you-knowgram would be much more pleasant than the mammogram. For starters, it would probably be done in a sports bar with a couple of pitchers of beer and a football game blaring.[124] And it would in no way, shape, or form involve squishing the little sports fan.

All this is not to say I don't get my annual mammo-

---

123. Yeah, I added a subtitle. It's the copywriter's equivalent of a double tap. Ready, aim, *Roget's*!

124. Or maybe a NASCAR race. But definitely not baseball or golf. Any sport that involves hitting balls would hit too close to home.

gram. I do. Sometime right after my birthday I celebrate the fact that I'm one year closer to death by trying to prevent it. And afterward they usually send me for an ultrasound; seems I'm so filled with fibroids my virtually nonexistent jugs are tough to judge. My favorite part of that particular procedure is when I'm lying on the table and the tech walks in and asks if there have been any new developments. I lift the sheet, glance down at the girls, and reply, "Nope. Still flat as a four-year-old."

But I digress.

I guess I just don't understand why, in order to protect a woman's breasts, we have to practically pancake them. Is no one working on correcting this situation? Sure, it's a little more pleasant since my first visit with the vise; some hospitals give you fluffy robes and slippers, bottled water and chocolates, soft music, a million magazines, and the occasional chair massage. But they're not fooling anyone. This isn't some spa appointment and I just happened to select "mammogram" off the menu. The hell with that.

When I get pampered I want a hot-stone massage and a mineral mud body wrap at Salon Emage,[125] thank you very much. Not twenty minutes in a hyperclean trash compactor.

No, it's not fun, but it's a necessary evil. One I've learned to follow with two other necessary evils: shopping and wine. I schedule my appointment just late enough in the afternoon so that when I'm finished, there's still time to treat myself to something sparkly, usually a new pair of

---

125. On Lee Street, in Warrenton. I like to think of it as a little slice of heaven in the hinterland.

earrings. Nothing expensive. Just something fun to draw attention up and away from my poor, beat-up bosom. I tend to gravitate toward hoops. Really, really big hoops. Hoops so huge I can slip them over my head and hula. Which I don't do, because they'd probably get caught around my throat, and God knows what kind of nifty medical equipment the hospital would employ to free me.

> **Doctor:** *Looks like we'll need the larynx crusher for this one.*
> **Nurse:** *But, Doctor, she just had a mammogram. Hasn't she been flattened enough for one day?*

Once I've shopped, it's on to chardonnay. Sometimes I meet my girlfriends at a restaurant. Other times I come home and have a glass with my honey. And yes, there are times when I sit my sofa and say a prayer. Of course, I thank God for my good health. But I harangue Him, too.

We've got the iPhone. And Kindle. And Skype. And yet the mammogram remains the Model T of medical technology. I'm not asking for a sunroof, Lord. But shock absorbers sure would be swell.

Of course, God has bigger fish to fry, so I've decided to take matters into my own hands. The next time I go, I'm videotaping the entire experience and putting it on YouTube. And I'm getting my films and loading them on Facebook. If I have to flash the masses to improve mammography, I will.

Care to join me?

Write your congresswoman, the American Medical Association, or President Obama. Hell, write to Michelle. Go for your mammogram and demand a better mousetrap. Together we can effect change, spark a revolution, and maybe even force the geeks who gave us Google and Twitter to use their brainpower for the titters.

If it works, it'll be the biggest thing my tiny breasts have ever done. And then I'll have to decide: Do I want a medal or a chest to pin it on? Believe it or not, I'm thinking medal. All of a sudden I'm jonesing for a new piece of jewelry.

Cupcakes Got Your Goat?

· · · · · · · · · · · · · · · · · · · ·

TO: Friends and family

FR: Suzy@stuckinthesticks.com

Date: Thursday, 8:17 a.m.

Subject: Suzy's Snow Day Science Experiment

We're having a wild snowstorm here in the hinterland, so the boys are home. Hemingway and Cuy are out feeding the cows, and the dogs are literally soaking themselves in the white stuff. Casey is demonstrating that he's the true brains of the bunch by staying in bed. And I've secured my spot on the other end of the spectrum by washing the kitchen floor. What is wrong with me?

The worst part of today's snow day is not that the kids are certain to kill each other over what game to play on the Xbox or that the kitchen floor and the bathrooms—yes, I made the mistake of cleaning those, too—will soon be filthy again, or even that in about ten minutes Hemingway's going to run in and drag Casey kicking and screaming out into a snowdrift.

No, the worst part of today's snow day is that there are forty-eight cupcakes sitting on my dining room table. They were supposed to be delivered to Cuyler's school this morning for a bake sale or a class party or some such nonsense I signed up for. Only now, of course, that nonsense, whatever it was, is postponed due to precipitation. Sure. I can bring them in tomorrow and the kids can eat them then. But I fear there'll be none left. Already they're calling my name. *Suzy... Suzy...You're too old for bathing suits and sundresses...CAVE and CONSUME US!!!!*

In an effort to fight back and not have to live on water with lemon and the occasional can of soup for what's left of my life, I brought a few out to the cows. I thought of it as a sort of snow day science experiment. I wasn't sure cupcakes would rank up there with range cubes, but if they did, I'd have forty-eight fewer things to worry about.

So I traipsed outside with my Giants cap barely protecting my blowout,[126] carrying a couple of yummy yellow-cake-buttercream-and-sprinkle-covered confections. And the cows? They decide to stay hidden in the hog pen. Guess they can't risk ruining their precious tresses. Their loss. As it turns out, Willie and Duke, our two rather bovine billy goats, were only too happy to breakfast on some of Betty Crocker's best.

I say *some* because, well, I just couldn't part with all of them. Forget bathing suit season. My main concern at the moment is whether or not I've got enough milk.

    Love,
    Susan

---

126. Oh, the stuff I'll do in the name of semistarvation.

Chapter Twenty-three

IT'S OKAY, PHIL. YOU'LL GET MY BILL.

I have a confession to make. I'm pretty peeved at Punxsutawney Phil. If that damn groundhog had looked left instead of right, I wouldn't have six more weeks of winter to suffer through. And trust me, I'm suffering.

My skin? Flaking like a shot-with-sugar, bursting-with-butter, overbaked piecrust, people. My hair? Suffice it to say I've seen hay bales sporting healthier, more lustrous-looking locks. My nails and toes? Poster appendages for the Mitten and Sock Society. And my body? As flushed as a sheet of matte picture paper, and achy like somebody beat me with a bat.

Hmm. A bat. Could make the perfect accessory for my visit to Gobbler's Knob next February. Kidding. Just kidding. I'd never in a million years harm the world's smallest, furriest weather forecaster. But if I could just get a little face time with Master Phil, I'm certain he'd see, by the pimples and red patches, lusterlessness, fine lines, and flaking (oh, the flaking!) of my complexion why February second is none too soon to declare spring.

Ah, spring. The season of renewal and rejuvenation, rebirth and restoration, invigoration, revitalization, and the terrifying realization that if I don't have my legs waxed from ankles to ass without any further ado, I'll be able to rent myself out as a fur coat by fall. And once I do have my legs waxed, which this year could involve bringing in a Bush Hog, because, honestly, that's how overgrown they've gotten, I can't run from the pasty, pale truth: Winter leaves me as ashen as a cotton ball. A cloud. A Q-tip. A snowdrift unchristened by the goats, cows, chickens, dogs, and deer that traipse across our pastures like they own the place.

If you're getting the sense that I look sickly, *sickly* doesn't begin to describe it. *Walking corpse*, on the other hand, comes close. So is it any surprise that I book myself a hydrating facial and a full-body bronzing session with the first sign of spring? I do. It makes me feel healthy, sexy, and pumped to put my sweaters, as well as my home-made dartboard of press clips and pictures of that wretched rodent prognosticator from Pennsylvania, in storage, and break out my T-shirts and shorts, skorts, sundresses, and sandals.

Of course, before I can actually *wear* sandals I need to do something to salvage my feet. They're not pretty any time of year, but winter brings out their worst. For starters, my toenails typically fall off and head to Florida, I think. And then the entire area surrounding my toes gets dry and rough and calloused, and while it's nice that I can save money on steel wool and sandpaper, emery boards and Brillo pads (you'd be stunned how many household scrubbing tasks I can handle with my heels), it's even nicer that my egregious extremities can be made glitter-wedge, peep-toe-platform, and flirty-mule fabulous by the miracle of the modern sea-salt pedicure.

So I get one of those, too.

Of course, I haven't as yet, and thus have no business being in open-toed shoes. Right this second, two of my toenails on my left foot have gone to the great shoe store in the sky (or maybe Miami), and a third is threatening hoofer hara-kiri as well. Both the nails on my big toes are long enough to pick my teeth with, and the remaining five are stained with what's left of the Red-y for Anything red I selected at my last pedicure. (And if that's not what's on them, then what I really need is a podiatrist.)

Sure, I could've stuck with boots. But with the temperature beginning to climb a bit, my poor piggies would have sweated, not to mention stunk. And I couldn't bear to add odor to an already offensive situation.

So here I sit, *Glamour* "don't" digits on display in my gynecologist's waiting room,[127] trying to avoid the stares of the perfectly pedicured. How did they know? What primal female instinct in the midst of thirty-eight-degree days propelled them to say, "True, I'm still wearing two long-sleeved T-shirts, a sweater, long underwear, jeans, and a down vest, and yes, I had to defrost my car again

---

127. I do all my annual checkups right around my birthday. I know; it's a weird way to celebrate. But it's a good way to get a read on whether I'm having another.

this morning, but something tells me it's time for Conga-Line Coral!"

And how did I not get this essential girl gene?

In a few minutes, my evil extremities are going to be in stirrups, and then I'm really going to be embarrassed. Maybe my doctor won't notice. I mean, feet aren't her focal point anyway. Today it's all about the plumbing. And I am so ready. I've tracked my cycle! I've showered! I've shaved!

Shit. I think I shaved. Or did I just use my Slim Twin to smooth my calluses? Oh, that would be just like me. Attack the hoofers. Forget the hay bale.

I've lost my mind, and obviously dumped a whole lot of girl DNA, too. Staring at my sad toes now, I can't decide which would be best: the aforementioned sea-salt pedicure, or simple amputation. Maybe I'll discuss it with my doctor. Or maybe I'll just shut the hell up. The hay bale business is bad enough to make her triple my copay. If I mention my freak-show feet, we just might have to refinance.

Beyond my feet, my list of spring spruce-ups is more than a dozen lines long. Which I guess makes sense, as I'm doing my utmost to limit such maintenance to once every six months.[128] That's why, in addition to all the other indulgences I've detailed here, I get massaged and manicured,

---

128. The twice-yearly beautification business is part of my halfhearted attempt not to plow through my 401(k), our checking account, and the kids' college fund in order to delay looking like a leather handbag for as long as possible, and I have to say, it sucks. No, I don't miss being a hotshot marketing pro. But I pine for, crave, dream about, long for, and miss more than words can say the money that let me invest in these indulgences. Sure, I was burned out. But, God, I looked good. Now, on the other hand, if the leather handbag I resembled was a Louboutin . . .

cut, highlighted, and deep-conditioned. I get my lashes tinted, my brows waxed, and my eye zone zapped. I get power-peeled, cocooned in seaweed, and green-coffee contoured. I do it all in keeping with my mantra—which just happens to be the famous L'Oréal tagline, "Because I'm Worth It"—because I *am* worth it.

And because I survived the long, snowy weeks of winter. Thanks, Phil.

I survived the short, dark days, the cabin fever, and the bitter cold. I rose above the urgent "storm stock-up" trips to the supermarket, the sudden squalls, and the school closings. I bested the black ice, the heavy boots,[129] and looking for the dogs in nine-degree weather. I carried on despite frozen pipes, forty-mile-per-hour winds, furnace failure, power outages, and an impressive attempt by all six of Cuyler's barnyard beasts, which include Willie and Duke, the aforementioned grossly overweight Boer wether billy goats, and four growing bulls, Eli, Fido, Ky, and Charlie, to push their way onto the mud porch (like I said, it was nine degrees). I made it to the end of the doom, gloom, and "don't drive without snow tires, a blanket, a case of bottled water, and a couple of leftover cupcakes in the glove compartment!" season with no help from that heartless groundhog. And so did you.

So don't delay a moment more. Pick a treatment and treat yourself. Book a bikini wax, a manicure, or a deep-tissue massage. Schedule some raindrop therapy, a relaxing foot rub, or a European exfoliating facial. Lock in a

---

129. But not work boots. Yet.

honey wrap, a salt scrub, a pore-purifying steam in the sauna, and a soak in a mineral spring. Hell, flip open the menu at your favorite salon and spa and reserve the entire right side. And don't give a moment's thought to the bill. It's on Phil. After all, he made us wait for spring. Now it's his turn to do the springing.

Chapter Twenty-four

JUST ANOTHER BLUE-GENED BOY

"Why won't she write him a love song?"

Cuyler and I were on our way to school: him to learn, me to try to learn how to teach PE, which is what I'd suddenly, surprisingly, found myself employed to do. I don't know if other PTO presidents get "promoted" to teacher, but when I got the chance to hang out all day with the kids I love fund-raising for, I took it.[130] Sometimes Cuy and I talk during the ten-minute ride; sometimes we listen to music. On this warm, blue-skied spring morning we were doing a little bit of both, which was kind of tough, as we had the Mustang top down and the iPod blaring.

---

130. The kids are cute and they're actually happy when I finally, ultimately, get so confused ("You can have two runners on a base, right?") I stop whatever we're doing, put on "The Cha Cha Slide," "Cupid Shuffle," and Soulja Boy, and call it a class. An aerobics class, but a class nonetheless.

"What?" I hollered into the wind.

"The girl in the song!" he shouted. "She keeps saying she's not going to write a love song for somebody!"

I nodded.

"But why? Why won't she write it?"

I had to think. Despite the fact that "Love Song" by Sara Bareilles was blaring in our ears, I hadn't really heard it. I'd been lost in thought, trying to recall the rules to dodgeball. I'm sure there are loftier pursuits, but this was mine at the moment, and I intended to figure it out. That, or ask a fourth grader.

"I think it's 'cause he doesn't love her." No response; total silence, in fact, except for Sara's beautiful mezzo-soprano voice wafting through the honeysuckle-scented breeze. I leaned over and lowered the volume. "Listen to the words," I urged. "She's talking about someone, a boy, probably, who says they need a love song, but *she* needs a better reason than that. Like, she needs to know he loves her. And then she'll write the song."

He considers this for a few seconds. "But she's kind of already written it, hasn't she?"

The kid doesn't miss a trick. "Yeah, she kinda has." I steal a quick look at my son. In his jet-black Jack Bauer T-shirt and just-this-side-of-acceptable blue jeans that I shouldn't have let him wear but couldn't resist because he makes them look good, his long, dark hair whipping in the wind, he looks like a fourth Jonas Brother, a fifth Bea-tle, or the next Bon Jovi. Basically, some teenybopping heartthrob I couldn't possibly have given birth to. "Nice catch."

"I wish you had a job like that."

"A job like what? As a singer?" I laughed.

He nodded.

"You have to be able to sing, Cuy, to get a job as a singer."

"Well, you got a job teaching gym and you don't even know how to play flag football."

Guess I wasn't asking for his help with the dodgeball business. "Well, there are some things you can learn on the job, as they say. But other things you really have to have a talent for."

"Well, I know your talent then."

Of course he did. I'm a writer. And sometimes when he reads something I wrote, he laughs. So I'm a funny writer. *That's* my talent.

"You know how to find good shrinks."

I nearly missed the turn into the school parking lot.

"My talent is finding good shrinks?" Where the hell did that come from?

"You found Dr. Mann," he replied, simultaneously popping his seat belt and slipping into his backpack as I screeched into a spot. "Whoa, Mom. Slow down."

I grabbed his knee before he could do a *Dukes of Hazzard* and hop out of the car. "Cuy, are you kidding?"

He shook his head. "I don't always like talking to her 'cause, like, just sometimes I don't feel like talking. But you found her. And she made me feel better. So that's a talent, right?"

He was serious. I was speechless. But not for long.

"I found her 'cause I love you. Not because I have a

thing for finding therapists." He laughed. For a ten-year-old my son has a terrific sense of humor. "Seriously, Cuy, I would have gone to the moon and back to make you feel better."

"Whatever." He leaned toward me with his head bent, the universal signal for "yes, you may kiss me good-bye, but only on the head, and only here, in the car, where no one can see you," then opened the door and dashed up the steps ahead of me.

God forbid he should be seen with the shrink finder.

It wasn't that long ago that I'd sat talking with Dr. Mann (aka "the good shrink"), in her happy, comfy office with the Fisher Price knights and the big gray castle that Cuy finds so comforting during his sessions, about the differences between clonidine, Seroquel, and Abilify, and which would work fastest to stop my burgeoning cattle farmer from gnawing the insides of his mouth into chopped meat.

The mouth-chewing business was the latest in self-mutilating techniques my younger son had been employing to ease his ever-increasing anxiety and anger. He denied doing it, of course, but when your kid walks around looking like a blowfish with his cheeks puffed out to relieve the pain, there are only two conclusions you can draw: one, he's been biting himself, or two, he's morphing into the aforementioned sea creature.

Since I didn't see gills, I went with the mouth-destruction diagnosis.

When he first began displaying the anxiety I'm certain he was born with, because even in utero Cuy bucked around the clock like the bull calves he so lovingly cares for, he simply scratched at his arms and legs. And then his face. And neck. And chest. And knees. And tush. It's not an exaggeration to say that at one point, he was so streaked with scratches, he looked striped.

We went through dozens of shirts, finally settling on long-sleeved black and midnight blue polos because they hid the bloodstains best, changed laundry detergent seven times in a fruitless quest to find one that actually fulfilled its claim to soften clothes,[131] and discovered that three-pairs-for-a-dollar ankle-length sweat socks do a darn good job of absorbing blood before it drips into seventy-five-dollar Nikes.

We also endured a lot of stares from folks who looked as if they were ready to report us to Family Services. And I'm really not complaining; those people have their place. But it's an awful, sickening feeling when you realize the grandmotherly type making small talk with your kid in the local Sears is really trying to determine whether you're hurting him, when you're desperate to figure out how to help him.

Prescription eczema creams? We tried several and finally came to the conclusion that a cheapie tube of Aquaphor, applied head to toe atop a nice, thick coating of equally cheap Burt's Bees Body Butter, worked as well if not better. Plus it didn't cost us the equivalent of a mortgage payment every month.

---

131. In fairness to the manufacturers of fabric softener, many of which do actually live up to their hype, what I really wanted was something that would give my kid's clothes the consistency of mashed potatoes.

For a few wonderful weeks, Cuy went to bed each night slick as a used-car salesman, and we all slept like babies. And then one day I awoke to the sound of crying coming from the bathroom. I raced in and found him sitting on the floor, his tear-streaked face filled with pain, trying to apply Neosporin and Band-Aids to two bloody thumbs. The anxiety had returned full throttle and his response was to rip apart his nail beds.

Enter the kiddie shrink and Prozac and endless applications of SolarOil, Solar Butter, aloe, and vitamin E. Enter gauze pads and adhesive tape, Vaseline and white gloves, and the kind of bribery never before seen this side of a political campaign.

"Leave the bandages alone and you can have Conflict: Vietnam Four Thousand Two Hundred and Twelve for the PlayStation."[132] No response. It's late Saturday afternoon. I've done my best to distract him all day. We've read. Played Aggravation and Monopoly and made chocolate-chip muffins. We've watched *Elf*. Twice. We've eaten Drumstick ice cream and frozen cookie dough directly out of the container. We've done almost anything he wanted and everything I could think of. But it's akin to trying to ignore an abscessed tooth. You can take it for only so long before you flip.

He's staring at his thumbs. They're covered in cream, wrapped in gauze, and taped from wrist to tip in a desperate effort to help them heal. His need to get to them, tear at

132. I have a confession to make. My sons have an Xbox, a PlayStation, a PlayStation 2, a PlayStation 3, and, at this writing, are campaigning hard for a Wii. Hey, it's a poor family that can't raise two princes.

them with his teeth, scissors, the corner of his sea-foam green iPod is palpable. I've got thirty seconds, a minute tops, before his anxiety and the itch of his recovering cuticles crests at the same time. I do the only thing I can think of: I sweeten the deal.

"And the PSP. You can have it for the PSP, too. Okay?"

He snaps his head around horror-film fast and hisses, "They don't make it for the PSP. And besides," he adds, sticking his tiny, mummified fingers in my face, "I certainly can't play like this!"

Clearly the powers of Prozac never did manifest for my young man.

Unlike some people,[133] I'm a big fan of today's pharmaceutical companies[134] and the myriad medications that have given millions back their lives. To the gang at Forest Laboratories, Bristol-Myers Squibb, and my personal favorite, GlaxoSmithKline,[135] thank you from the depths of my much less frequently depressed heart.

When I'm not busy blaming myself for my son's anxiety disorder, which I do nearly every day, much to the dismay of my own therapist, I'm thanking God for having given him to me. I'm lucky to have him, and I think, in a weird, cosmic way, he's lucky to have me, too. At least I understand what he's going through, and I know what to do to help.

By the time Cuy's anxiety appeared, I was the dean of

---

133. Tom Cruise comes to mind.

134. The real ones, of course. Which are second only to the one I have in my head.

135. Way to go with the Wellbutrin!

antidepressants and president of the talk-therapy fan club. I knew what to look and listen for in myself and others.

And when I heard and saw the signs in my son, it broke my heart.

But you know what's funny? After all those years of second-guessing myself when he was a baby, after all those days and nights of his inconsolable crying and fussing and my not knowing what the hell to do because the "how to" pamphlet they promised me did not pass with the placenta, after all those hours of asking God why I didn't get the mom gene that the women in the park and at the pool and in the playgroups and in the parenting magazines obviously got in spades, because they were so cool and confident in caring for their kids when I was about as calm as a crack addict in caring for mine, I finally, totally trusted myself to make the right calls.

As he mentioned, Cuy doesn't particularly like the talking part of the process. Having the castle and knights to play with makes it less uncomfortable, but still, he's far from a fan. Mainly it's because he's shy. But it's also because he's like most people who suffer bouts of anxiety and depression: He's afraid he'll find out he's a freak, the only one in the world to ever feel the way he does. And he thinks if he stuffs the sadness and the agitation that run like a freight train through his body, it will go away.

Unfortunately and fortunately for him, I know it doesn't work that way.

My job is to get him to talk, and, as I've already confessed, I'm not beyond bribery to do so. In fact, Cuy and I

have had some of our best conversations on our way to
Wal-Mart for some video game I promised if he'd just 'fess
up to his feelings. So what if it costs me twenty-five or
thirty bucks?[136] It's a small price to pay to convince my kid
that the monster under the bed will go away only if you
pull him out, hold him up to the light, and look him right
in the eye. Telling yourself he's wearing diapers doesn't
hurt either.

Yes, my son is mature. But it's been my experience that
potty humor has its place. And it's waaaaay up there on
the depression-tool totem pole.

At this point Cuy's thumbnails are so pitted he can use
them as soup spoons. But that's okay. He no longer picks,
chews, rubs, or stabs at them. Why? Because he no longer
wants to. His cuticles have healed, and even though they're
as thick as Fredo Corleone's skull, he has no problem cap-
turing Viet Cong in Combat: Vietnam Four Thousand Two
Hundred and Twelve, or playing any other video game, for
that matter.

He's stopped tearing at his skin, too, and these days
the only time he scratches is when he picks up poison ivy
from racing around the fields on his ATV, or has a mosquito bite.

Speaking of biting, we went with the Abilify. It takes a
good-size chunk out of our checking account each month
(without prescription coverage, thirty five-milligram tablets cost just under four hundred and fifty dollars; with coverage, which we're lucky enough to have, it's a "measly"

136. I know I'm full of shit. The games cost, like, sixty bucks a pop. But still.

one hundred and thirty-four), but it stopped his mouth chewing immediately.

In addition, his teeth grinding, nightmares, and panic attacks are things of the past. My younger son wakes up in a good mood, happily feeds his baby bulls their bottles, and occasionally even smiles when I take him to school.

Which is exactly what he was doing right this second: standing by the front door, smiling, and, could it be, waiting for the shrink finder?

"What's up?" I asked. "Why didn't you go in?"

"I was just wondering what we're doing later."

"Maybe dodgeball."

He rolled his eyes and tugged on the straps of his backpack. "Do you even know how to *play* dodgeball?"

"No. But I bet you do."

"So that's my talent?" he asked, feigning indignation. "Teaching you how to teach PE?"

"Cuy, you have a million talents. You know all kinds of stuff about history. You're a great free safety. You're—"

"Good at deciphering love songs," he cut me off sweetly. He was beaming. Those little blue pills were worth every penny.

"Yes, you're good at deciphering love songs. And you're going to be really good at helping me again today, right?"

He shook his head. "You know, Mom," he said, pulling the door open and stepping aside so I could enter, "you're lucky to have me."

My sentiments exactly, sweetheart.

It's Father's Day on the Farm: Do You Know Where the Duct Tape Is?

. . . .

TO: Friends and family

FR: Suzy@stuckinthesticks.com

Date: Sunday, 12:09 p.m.

Subject: The wife from hell

That's me, the wife from hell.

Why?

Because it's Father's Day, and instead of letting my man sleep till noon, which he totally deserves, as he's up early every day tending to cattle, chickens, broken fence boards, aggressive goats, and all manner of farm matters, I awakened him at four in the morning.

Why?

Because I got up to work, made the mistake of checking my e-mail, and discovered one of my columns running on NBC-Washington.com. And then I needed someone to celebrate with. And it couldn't be just anyone. It had to be my better half. The one who puts up with my myriad neuroses, my non-stop neediness, and my spectacular lack of self-esteem.

"What if I'm never funny again? I mean, that piece? That piece could be the last piece that makes anybody laugh. Seriously. I'm committing suicide."

"Does the Mustang make my butt look big? Be honest. I've got no business being in a car that hot, old crone that I've become. Right?"

"What about boobs? You think I should get boobs? Maybe just one boob, on the right, to even 'em out. You'd like that, yes?"

"Oh, my God. Only I could f*!#k up frozen fish sticks. Give 'em to the dogs; I'll make mac and cheese. Oh, my God. The milk's bad. What kind of mother lets the milk go bad?"

Yeah, I'm a delight to live with, and even more wonderful to be awakened by before sunrise. But for some reason, he puts up with me. It's been more than twenty years, and I still don't know why. And you know what's really crazy? Even in the wee dark hours, he's pretty happy to see me. Yup. His exact words were, "Great, Suz. Proud of you. Now get the hell out of my face before I duct-tape your mouth. It's Father's Day, dammit."

That's right, it's Father's Day. So, hon, your hammock's out, your Budweiser's on ice, and nobody's going to bother you all day.

Nobody but the wife from hell, that is. But you're good with that, right?

Right?

Love,
Susan

Chapter Twenty-five

JAMMIN' WITH THE JONAS BROTHERS

It's official: My dear friend and favorite Jazzercise instructor Kim is the world's best mom. I am the world's second best.

Why does Kim beat me for top honors? Because when tickets for the summer's hottest concert—the Jonas Brothers at Nissan Pavilion, for those of you lucky ducks[137] who don't have the words to "Burnin' Up" burned into your brain—went on sale, she didn't hesitate to buy a bunch. Why am I happy to be, quite literally, second banana in this rockin' produce department? Because when Kim wound up with two extra tickets to the sold-out show, I didn't stop

---

137. Speaking of ducks, have I mentioned my campaign for waterfowl? It's part of my ongoing quest to give this place a little Central Park style. Of course, I got Hem's okay to add ducks and swans to our ponds. But I've decided to surprise him with the ice-cream parlor. And the pot dealer.

and think and wait and wonder like I did when they first
went on sale. I offered her double on the spot and called it
a day.

Or, to be accurate, I called it a date. With Casey.

See, both Case and Cuy are learning to play electric
guitar, and every afternoon they jack up their amps and
jam with the Jonas boys. It's an interesting sound, rather
akin to the noise a cat might make if you put it in a blender.[138] But at least they're practicing. And I'm certain that at
some point they'll get good, or at least less painful to listen
to, and then the dogs will stop whimpering and trying to
hide between my legs, and Hemingway will stop charging
around the house, palms pressed to his ears, hollering,
"Susan, what *is* that sound?"

The fact that there were only two tickets wasn't too
troublesome. Why? Because the day of the concert was
also the first day of Cuyler's four-day stay at shooting
camp. Hallelujah for the nice folks at 4-H! Wonderful of
them to coordinate with the people at the Nissan Pavilion,
don't you think? Yes, at the very moment my little guy
would be taking target practice, Casey and I would be taking the opportunity to stock up on Jonas Brothers T-shirts.
And CDs. And posters of Kevin, Nick, and Joe in all manner of "aren't we cool?" and "moody is our middle name"
poses, and one of a perky little brunette with a whole
Punky Brewster–meets–Debbie Gibson thing going on
named Demi Lovato.

"Who?" I asked my son.

---

138. But you wouldn't, because there isn't a margarita recipe in the world that calls for
tequila, margarita mix, crushed ice, and half a cup of cat.

"Their opening act, Mom."

"Demi Moore?"

"Demi Lovato, Mom. From *Camp Rock*. C'mon, Mom. Keep up."

I try to stay current. Really I do. But sometimes I miss the boat. I mean the band. Or at least their opening act.

In any case, on the morning of the concert, a few crucial details had to be dealt with. First, I needed to decide what we'd bring. A blanket, because, hey, lawn seats are tough on the tush; two pairs of binoculars; and money to feed my eternally hungry escort.

Note to self: Never again permit perpetual eating machine to "help" shop supermarket snack aisle. A hundred bucks on Tostitos, Cheez-Its, and Chips Ahoy! is a shameful waste of money. Particularly since most of it was consumed before it went in the cart.[139]

Then I had to decide what to wear. I threw open my closet and looked at my clothes. The last time I went to a concert was before I had kids. Was my Jackson Browne at the Beacon Theatre belly shirt appropriate? Or maybe my Bob Seger at Madison Square Garden sweatshirt? I could wear both; it might get chilly. Or better yet, something Springsteen. My "No Nukes" tank top would be perfect.

I reached in and started rifling. Then rifling turned to ransacking. They were here the last time I looked! But when had I last looked? Nineteen eighty-nine? I had the gnawing sense that my cute Jackson Browne top had long ago been demoted to dust-rag duty, a memory so painful I

---

139. And the rest was consumed before daybreak. But you already knew that.

practically need an epidural to endure it, and my Seger and Springsteen stuff had most likely met a similar fate.

"Casey!" I shouted. "We can't go." My lanky (and slightly alarmed) heartbreaker was across the hall in a heartbeat.[140]

"Why not?"

"I have nothing to wear," I whined.

He looked at the pile of clothes at my feet and on the bed, spilling out of the drawers, and draped over the chair. And he started to laugh. "Mom, we can't go 'cause I'm grounding you for this room."

"I know, I know," I replied, embarrassed at behaving like a child in front of my suddenly very mature firstborn child. "All this stuff and no concert T-shirts!"

I looked up to see him looking down at me, slowly shaking his head, and pulling at his shirt. His New York Giants shirt. "Mom," he said quietly, "I don't have a concert T-shirt to wear, either. This is *my* first concert."

Earth to Susan. It might have been all about you and your "No Nukes" tank top twenty-five years ago, but once the plus sign turned pink, that show closed forever. Now it's all about Facebook, and iTunes, and Nazi Zombies, and some singer named Avril Lavigne whose first name I'm totally convinced is a typo, and of course Kevin, Nick, and Joe. Snap out of it, woman, and get your kid to the concert!

He was still standing there, staring at me. "Mom," he prodded, "you're being ridiculous. We gotta get going."

---

140. Isn't it astonishing how fast kids can move when there are no chores involved?

No, no, I thought. I am not being ridiculous. I am getting dressed and I am taking my son to see the Jonas Brothers, to experience the magic of live, loud music, to begin his descent, like his mother and father before him, into rock-'n'-roll-induced deafness. And to purchase his first shamefully overpriced concert T-shirt.

I am not being ridiculous. I am being the world's second-best mom. And I'm buying myself a little something to celebrate that fact when I get there.

At my age, it won't be a belly shirt or a tank top. But if anybody's hawking Jonas Brothers burkas, I'm so stocking up.

Chapter Twenty-six

SWAN LAKE? NOT SO MUCH.
BUT SWAN POND SOUNDS ABOUT RIGHT.

Crazy, isn't it? I mean, why would a woman who has a hate/hate relationship with hens suddenly have a hankering for waterfowl? My guess is that it has everything to do with the water portion of the word *waterfowl*. I love the water. For starters, I'm a Pisces. You know, the sign with the two fish swimming in different directions. I like to think one is headed toward the Jersey shore,[141] the other to a lake somewhere. And if there were a third, I swear it would be pointed toward a pond. Sure, there are other kinds of bodies of water, but since ponds[142] are all I've got here at Nate's Place, ponds are what I'm going with.[143]

---

141. Specifically Martell's Tiki Bar in Point Pleasant.

142. Or, as we occasionally call them, overgrown mud puddles.

143. And it's a damn good thing we have overgrown mud puddles—I mean ponds. I don't think I'd have lasted five minutes being landlocked among livestock.

Both our ponds are filled with fish and box turtles and toads, and complemented with an impressive assortment of bugs and, of course, black snakes.[144] So as far as I'm concerned, they're primed for water poultry, pretty water poultry like swans and ducks, and the geese that'll probably swoop in and poop all over the place[145] once word gets out it's "game on" for water game here at our house.

Of course, just because I want swans and ducks and am okay with geese doesn't mean they'll be okay with me. In fact, if they call ahead to the hens and run a reference check, they might choose not to waddle around here at all. And that means that, of late, I've tried to get a little chummier with the chickens.

The other day I braved the humidity to give them fresh hay in their favorite laying box (you know, the planter on my front porch where they continue to blow me away with their mind-boggling output of barely an egg a week each). Then I combed the garden and the crisper drawer[146] for dead and nearly dead veggies, which I cut up (along with a little roast beef and salami so they'd see whose side I'm *really* on) and topped off with a sprinkling of Craisins, crumbled Triscuits and Cheez-Its, and bits of yummy French bread. And then, as if this gourmet creation weren't already worthy of a Twenty-one Feed Bags of Scratch salute, I served it with a nice big bowl of ice-

144. Isn't it nice they have someplace to hang out when they're not in the house? Yeah, I thought so, too.

145. Is it just me, or do Canada geese shit more than any animal known to man?

146. And the spot under the fridge where food collects when the kids kick it around playing "keep away" with the dogs.

cold FIJI water. That's right. None of that crap out of the hose for my hens!

Did I gain their trust? Win them over to the Suzy side? Are you insane? It was like throwing pearls before poultry. Not five minutes after I served the meal of the year to our snotty bunch of banties, I overheard one of the fetid brats on her cell ranting about how you just can't trust "the one with the yellow head and the high heels." That does it. No more designer water for that little diva, and I'm taking *all* of our fowl off our family plan, too.

Of course, if she convinced the two trumpeter swans and four white-crested ducks I ordered to do their swimming someplace else, I'm really going to be ticked (and she's going to be teriyaki-ed[147]). I was joking about the ice-cream parlor and the pot dealer, but I was serious about wanting to give the ponds a sort of Central Park–meets–Washington Square feel. If the waterfowl don't show, what am I going to tell the homeless guys I bused in to play chess and drink gin out of brown bags all day? I can't expect them to make do with just the mime.

And I can't make do with just black snakes, toads, big fish, and little guppies in my overgrown mud puddles. I need elegant, long-necked swans and ducks with fluffy white plumes, and yes, even perpetually crapping Canada geese, and if I have to step up the sucking up to get them, then so be it.

So, hens, here's the deal. I'm bringing in a Sabrett stand and a pretzel vendor, and I've reconsidered my position

---

147. Stunning, isn't it? I can now make six different dinners, most of them with chicken. Geez. I hope I'm not becoming Wade Boggs.

on the ice-cream parlor,[148] too. You're going to be fat, happy, and high from brain freeze. And that's because you're going to be bunking with the waterfowl in a veritable amusement park for poultry.

Beats the heck out of that window box, huh?

There's just one catch. You need to pick up the phone and take back all that smack you said about me. I want those ducks and swans here stat. And believe me, you want them, too.

Get in the way of my Washington Square–ing and Central Park–ing this place up, and I'll have to find something else to do. I already exercise and read, tickle the ivories, scrapbook, and occasionally play with my camera. So to my way of thinking, that leaves finally learning to speak Italian,[149] or learning to cook Italian. After all, I'm just one meal away from being able to go a whole week without doubles. And I'd be happy to practice on every last one of you malcontents if it means eventually making the perfect chicken marsala.[150]

---

148. I can't exactly open a Häagen-Dazs, but a Mister Softee should suffice.

149. And not just curse in it.

150. Wade Boggs wouldn't give me his recipe, but Dame Joan's will do the trick. And once it does, my fowl friends, it's on to chicken Francaise.

Tell Me You're Kidding with the Cankles

. . . .

TO: Friends and family

FR: Suzy@stuckinthesticks.com

Date: Wednesday, 3:15 p.m.

Subject: Fit to be tied

I have a confession to make. I may inflict bodily harm on whoever came up with "Cankle Awareness Month."

To the best of my knowledge, it originated at Gold's Gym, and my guess is that it was the brainchild of some promotion-seeking sycophant in the marketing department. And I know promotion-seeking sycophants. Hell, I *was* a promotion-seeking sycophant. In several marketing departments.

And I can just imagine how the meeting went.

"Okay. We've maxed out the muffin top and moob scare stuff, and Dimpled Thigh Days don't start until September. Third-quarter membership sales are slumping. We need to do something now! I hate to say it, people, but the situation calls ... for the *cankle*."

Thanks, Gold's. That's just what we women need. Yet another body part to pick at, obsess over, and feel inferior for.

"It's so unfair, Francine. I've got chunky ankles *and* a flat chest. Do you think standing on my head would help?"

No, but a smack to the skull of the guy who gave us this campaign would work wonders. And it had *better* be a guy. Because, ladies, if we're helping perpetuate this self-loathing in any way, we're lost.

Look, I'm not anti-Gold's, and having spent the better part of my career as an advertising copywriter, I'm the first person who'll try to sell you something.[151] But I'm tired of these ploys that play on body image. I already know I'll never have legs like Elizabeth Hurley, Catherine Zeta-Jones, or even Maggy and Molly, the two purebred Clydesdales that call Nate's Place home and that could give the Rockettes a run for their money. But up until I logged on to the Internet this morning, I was okay with it. I could wear a skirt, or shorts, or go barefoot on the beach without a shot of liquid courage with my lunch. Or breakfast.

But now?

Now I'm considering a pair of Frye Billy Pull Ons or Ugg Classic Talls to hide my tree trunks. And that makes me wonder: Maybe Gold's is in cahoots with boot manufacturers. You know, I *have* seen an awful lot of women pairing winter footwear with sundresses this season.

Of course, the most fitting thing about Cankle Awareness Month is that there's nothing Gold's or any fitness center can do to cure the condition. In fact, the only exercise that really

---

151. Anybody wanna buy a book?

works is one you can do wherever there's a stair. Simply dip your heels, then come up onto the balls of your feet. It's easy, fabulously convenient, and best of all, it's free.

So why join the gym, particularly one that woos you by making fun of your full ankles? Take the fee and put it toward boxing gloves and a bag. That's what I'm going to do. It's a great way to get in shape and work out my anger issues. Which makes it cheaper than (more) therapy, and a whole lot safer for that promotion-seeking sycophant in Gold's marketing department.

Love,
Susan

Chapter Twenty-seven

FORBIDDEN IN FAUQUIER

"I have bursts of being a lady, but it doesn't last long."

— SHELLEY WINTERS

Knowing what I do now, it was bound to happen. And if I'd kept my eyes open and truly been the observant, opinionated chronicler of life in the backcountry that I claim to be, I would have seen it coming. But I didn't. I never saw the signs or read the tea leaves. Never noticed the writing on the barn wall or that my local library, while bursting with every single book on today's bestseller lists as well as the latest issues of *Newsweek, Time, Psychology Today, Popular Science,* and *Better Homes and Gardens,* had just one old (I'm talking Christie Brinkley–on-the-cover-and-actual-cigarette-ads-inside old) copy of *Cosmopolitan* on its magazine rack, and that torn, dog-eared tome was available only occasionally. Where it would disappear to, I don't know. Maybe they'd loan it to one of the other two libraries in the county, or maybe somebody writing a tell-all about the cast of *The Breakfast Club* or a thesis on the rise and fall of Love's Baby Soft and Bonne Bell Lip Smackers borrowed it for research purposes. All I know is that sometimes it was there, and sometimes it wasn't. If I'd given it a moment's thought, it might have dawned on me that a lone, decrepit copy of *Cosmo* most likely meant folks found its content crude, distasteful, even downright vulgar. And if I'd realized that, I'd have known without a doubt that my days as a local columnist were numbered. Because frankly, if you're not a fan of Helen Gurley Brown's baby, it's almost guaranteed you're going to hate my stuff.

But, busy as I was tracking the here-today, hidden-tomorrow routine of the aforementioned ancient copy of my favorite racy read, I never did stop to consider its deeper meaning. And as a result, the counterfeit farm girl has real embarrassing news. I've been banned in Boston. Or, more accurately, forbidden in Fauquier.

Time was when my column ran in the Fauquier County weekend paper almost every weekend. And then every other weekend. And then every three weekends. And then once a month. And then, maybe, every six weeks or so. And then, well, not at all.

In fact, one weekend there was a column in the paper *about* me penned by my dear friend Jenn, the aforementioned twenty-first-century Renaissance woman who sews, knits, gardens, cans, cooks from scratch, owns her own set of Craftsman tools, shops all year for Christmas gifts, which means that while the rest of us are still running around, she's done wrapping, fixes her own car (with the Craftsman stuff, of course), changes her own blown fuses, air-conditioning filters, and stripped washers (while doing the wash, I should add), and oh, yes, just happens to be a wonderful writer. But to my way of thinking, it's just not the same as seeing a piece *by* me.

"Suz, who cares? It's the local paper," said Hem, adding insult to injury by staying glued to a copy while giving me his little pep talk.

"I care," I whined. I sipped my coffee and glanced at Jenn's sweet, smiling face staring up at me from her hysterical story about a birthday dinner she and several of my girlfriends gave me. It was such a great night. We laughed and ate and drank mojitos and too much wine. Okay, I drank too much wine and then behaved questionably with a huge barbecue fork. I was lucky it didn't make the paper I can't seem to make. Oh, wait; it did. Damn.

"They used to like me," I moaned. "Why don't they like me?"

"Maybe they're giving other people a shot. Relax. I'm sure they'll run your stuff again."

"They haven't run anything in ages! Why didn't you tell me my new stuff sucks?"

Hem stopped reading and looked at me over his glasses. "And now it's my fault."

"No. It's just—"

He cut me off. "Your new stuff's fine. It's funny." He paused. "It's not you, okay? It's not personal. It's business. Remember business?"

I shrugged. "The editor doesn't even respond to my e-mails."

"Don't do it, Suz."

"Don't do what?"

"Don't let this paralyze you." He folded up the paper, added it to the pile on the porch, and put on his Giants cap. "It doesn't matter what I say," he continued, bending to give me a quick kiss. "You're going to do it anyway, aren't you? Thousands of dollars and hundreds of hours of therapy, Suz, and you still rival Richard Lewis for who has less self-esteem."

"I only *wish* I had as little self-esteem as Richard Lewis," I replied, half laughing, half crying. "Look at how successful he is! Seriously. I'm a published author and I can't get picked up in my own paper? It means I suck. Right? I knew it. I suck."

"Paralyze, paralyze, paralyze." Hem teased, shaking his head and walking out the back door toward the tractor and a day spent blissfully Bush Hogging and not wondering why the hay has it in for him.

"That's not going to happen," I shouted, knowing full well it already had. Even as I said the words, I felt that big pause button in my little blond brain go off and that was it.

You know the expression "Pride comes before a fall"? It's true. And right before pride comes crippling insecurity and the fervent hope that when you fall, you're killed on impact. 'Cause writer's block is a bitch to live with.

It's been at least four weeks now and I still cannot string two words together, let alone two sentences. And nothing, I repeat, nothing I write is the least bit funny.

At this point I have tried several methods to bust my block. For starters, I stopped reading the local paper. This resulted in my not knowing about a terrific sale at one of my favorite shops; the opening of a new restaurant that I intend to try on my next birthday, as I understand that 1) the house chardonnay is J. Lohr and 2) there isn't a barbecue fork within fifteen miles; and the fact that the kids' schools were closed on a day I sent them, or at least I thought they went, so where they spent seven hours and ate lunch is something I really must look into. And I will. As soon as I write something funny.

I also tried changing when and where I write. For a while, instead of writing at five in the morning at my desk, I was writing—or, more accurately, attempting to write—at four in the afternoon in one of the Adirondack chairs we have in our backyard. But writing in the company of the chickens and the goats and the "girls" in the great outdoors, at the end of the day, made me want a drink. Which in turn made me drunk. This was great because for a short while I was sure I was Jerry Seinfeld, Larry David, *and* Richard Lewis funny until one morning when I reread what I wrote. And then I cracked open a fresh bottle of Baileys, put two shots in my coffee, sucked it down, and chased it with two more. Not good. And definitely not funny.

I also bought several books of prompts: ideas designed to help writers get the creative juices, and hopefully words, flowing. "Write about lust," one said. I'm a wife, mom, advertising copywriter, columnist (at least, I used to be), PTO president, and unlikely gym teacher. I have laundry to do, a house to clean, dinner to make, and homework to oversee. I have ads to write, clients to call, pieces to post, and lesson plans to convince Cuyler to come up with (for a fee, of course). Unless they mean lust for sleep, servants, or a little cottage on the water to which only I have a key, I'm unsure I have any experience with the topic.

"Write about a phone call that never came," said another. Ah, this could work! I could write about the motor vehicle department in New Jersey that refuses to respond to my calls inquiring whether my check for a whopping parking ticket I got while visiting the Garden State arrived or if it didn't and they're issuing a warrant for my arrest. Now, that would be something for someone to write about. But not me. I have writer's block.

"Write twenty-five hundred to three thousand words on anything, anything that comes to mind, however insignificant, and go for quantity, not quality," said still another. Are they insane? All that comes to mind is that nothing comes to mind, followed by the sinking feeling that it's distinctly possible nothing will ever come to mind again, and if, by some lucky chance, something does pop into my head to write about, there's no way I'll eke out twenty-five hundred to three thousand words, and the only thing funny will be watching me pull my hair out in tufts while I try.

My dad keeps telling me not to worry; it'll break. I'll get inspired and *wham!* I'll be writing. But what if it doesn't? What if I can never again poke fun at our farm and the chickens that refuse to stay cooped in their coop and instead stroll my front porch with impunity, burrowing into my window boxes, laying, like, one egg a week, and brutalizing my poor petunias? What if I start wearing T-shirts that read COWS ARE FRIENDS, NOT FOOD, instead of running out into the pasture, scouring our herd of beef cattle, and bellowing, "Ninety-five sure would be great for our barbecue, hon!" What if I stop kicking our goat Duke out of the Mustang and instead slap a diaper and a pair of Ray-Bans on him and let him sit on my lap like a dog while I do errands? What if, God forbid, my fast mouth fails me forever? What if I can no longer be Her Royal Highness the Most Petulant Princess of the Pastures, the Ranter in Residence, or, and this is the kids' new favorite nickname for their miserable mom, Little Miss Nasty of Nate's Place?

Riddled with self-doubt, tired of memorizing synonyms for *hack* and *loser* on Thesaurus.com,[152] and unable to complete even the suicide note I started, I realized I had to do something. Something radical. Something totally out of character. Something I usually avoid at all costs. Something I fear more than the return of the striped leg warmer or the poncho. Something that frightens me more than the collapse of the California chardonnay industry, the complete and total failure of the fake-bake and false-eyelash businesses, the discontinuation of Victoria's Secret's "butt lift" jeans and Sally Hansen's Navy Baby nail color, or the prohibition of the push-up bra, Spanx panties, and do-it-yourself face-lift kits. (Okay, they don't exist. But someday they will and I'll be addicted to them and then the bastards at the Food and Drug Administration will pull them

---

152. Which happens to be my all-time favorite Web site, right after DailyCandy and the Fauquier County Public Schools site, which I really should visit more often so I don't send my kids when it's not in session.

and I'll wind up racing around the country scouring drug-
store shelves, buying whatever's left and then hoarding
them like Elaine Benes's contraceptive sponges and asking myself every single day for the rest of my life if a wrin-
kle is lift-worthy or if I should wait until it becomes a
crevasse so deep it sucks in an eye.)

I had to muster up all my Jersey and confront the situation head-on.

I popped an Ativan, put on my big-girl pants, and
picked up the phone.

"Hello!" I blurted when the newspaper's managing
editor answered. "How have you been, and where have I
been?"[153]

Her response? The dark side. At least as far as folks in the
community are concerned. Readers have complained I'm a
bit bawdy, rather ribald, even risqué. Seems my pining for
bigger breasts and a smaller butt, my unabashed enthusi-
asm for high heels, tattoos,[154] and margaritas, my desire for
well-behaved kids who love family vacations and don't
mind taking them with other families so I can stay home
and break in a new blender, even my reminiscences about
high school boyfriends and the days when I could wear a
two-piece bathing suit without wishing everyone on the
beach would go blind are inappropriate. Verboten. Taboo.

Who knew?

---

153. Clearly another shining, mature moment for needy Suzy.

154. I have a pretty little orange-and-yellow butterfly tattoo on my right shoulder.
Hem's not too happy about it. He thinks it shows a "distinct lack of breeding." I think it
shows I'm more of a redneck than I realize. Oh, dear. I think we're thinking the same
thing.

Hmm. I would've if I'd paid any attention to my *Cosmo Girl*–less library.

"Let me get this straight. I can't write about boobs, and Miracle Bras, and implants, right?" I asked. "Not a problem. But how about man boobs? You know, moobs? That usually leaves 'em laughing. No, huh? Maybe cow udders? They crack me right up. Don't they just look like one big boob with lots of long nipples hanging off them? What's that? Okay, okay, no boobs of any kind. But maybe I could still write about the two I gave birth to?"

Not a chance, *chiquita*.

And so I've been banished, blackballed, cut off, cast out, shown the door—dumped is what it comes down to—for columnists who'd never write about wanting to sell their kids,[155] or how they once spent five, maybe ten, but no more than fifteen seconds tops, I swear, trying to figure out how to trade their husband for a Birkin bag.

I hung up the phone feeling awful that I'd offended people. I mean, I'm the type who apologizes when the waitress gets my order wrong ("Oh, I'm so sorry. I wanted the roast beef, but it's okay; tuna's great. Sure, sometimes I break out in hives or get a little short of breath, but as long as my throat doesn't close, it's cool"), or because someone lost an earring ("It was your grandmother's? It has three diamonds? And it fell off right here, in the ER, while you were taking care of me? Oh, I'm so sorry. Forget my gush-

---

155. But that's only because they can't figure out how to price them. Here's a hint: If the kid's first word was *Budweiser* or the name of the quarterback on your favorite pro football team, start high. Casey used to stand in front of the TV, an empty can of the King of Beers in one hand, and the full diaper he just pulled off in the other, screaming "Simms! Simms!" Trust me when I tell you I could get twenty-five, fifty bucks for that boy.

ing head wound. I'll help you find that sucker. And maybe you'll let me keep a carat?"). I take on responsibility for everything. The war in Iraq? You have no idea how bad I feel about that. The crappy spaghetti sauce selection in the supermarket? What can I do to make it up to you? The stain on your pretty silk blouse? Let's trade. Mine was doomed come cocktail hour anyway. No matter what it is, I'm sorry for it. In fact, if there were any money to be made as a professional apologizer,[156] believe me, I'd pursue it. But there isn't. And for that, I'm really, well, you know.

The long and short of it is, I was pretty pained I'd put people off. When Hem came in, I told him what happened, and then I called my mom, and my shrink, and when I was finished crying (you'd cry, too: She charges fifty bucks for a phone session, which is a bargain compared with the seventy-five big ones my mom bills me), it hit me: I was okay with it. In fact, I felt fine. Incredible. Formidable. Like a force to be reckoned with. I'm not happy the reckoning went the way it did, but you know what? By being banned, I'd finally arrived.

Right this moment I feel Mae West, Madonna, Cher, Shelley Winters, Helen Gurley Brown, and Bonnie Raitt great.

I'm too risqué.

But I'm not shit-tay.

Good-bye, local paper. Good-bye, guest columnist gig. Don't let my writer's block hit you in your ample butt or tacky tattoo on the way out!

---

156. With a subspecialty in guilt carrying, of course.

Chapter Twenty-eight

CHRISTMAS IN COW COUNTRY

*(OR, SUBURBANITES DECK THE HALLS, FARM FOLK
DECK THE HEIFERS)*

*H*ard to believe, but this will be our fourth Christmas on the farm. I really thought we'd have run screaming back to suburbia by now (or at least I would have), but no. Here we are. Still in cow country. And we've got several new family traditions to show for it.

Number one is my favorite, although all five are fun. Feel free to take 'em and tweak 'em. No cow? Light up the cat. No chicken to chase? Free the kids' ferret. There's no more magical way to make merry than by releasing your inner redneck.

So don't wait a moment more. Deep-fry your turkey, stick chewing tobacco in your sweetie's stocking, and absolutely, positively go for the gusto and give your whole gang—yes, even the baby—new double-barrel black-powder shotguns.

They're eleven hundred bucks a pop, but it's the holidays. What's a lung shot for the ones you love?

Oh, and while you're at it? Don't forget to have your Christmas picture taken with a camo-clad Santa. You haven't lived until you've celebrated at least one holiday season sticks style.

#5. Annual "Plug in the Porch Lights ('Cause They're Up Year-round)" Ritual

Time was when we spent Black Friday at the mall. Now that we're farm folk and a trip to the stores means packing a lunch, we spend it on the porch. We gather the dogs, the kids, and the camera, and watch as dear Hemingway plugs in the outside lights. Once the sole province of the trailer-park set, leaving the lights up year-round makes seasonal exterior adornment a snap. Plus it's frozen-hands- and four-letter-words-free!

#4. Cattle Lighting Ceremony

We're unsure whether other farmers light up their livestock, but we've been doing so since our first holiday here. Each year Casey and Cuyler select the most docile and beautiful (i.e., least covered in crap) of our bovines, and then together we affix battery-operated Christmas-tree pins to their ear tags, and tiny holiday lights to their horns. Suburbanites deck the halls. We deck the heifers.

#3. Holiday Hog Day

Once we've bedecked the beasts and trimmed the tree, the kids know it's time . . . to select the holiday swine! It's not easy, since the little fatties are so darn cute, but on Holiday Hog Day we stiffen our resolve, head to a friend's pigpen, and pick out Christmas dinner. There's nothing like the taste of a home-grown, all-natural, country-cured ham. If you can forget it was once called Kirby.

#2. Catch and Wrap a Live Chicken Contest

The first one to catch a chicken, wrap it in a burlap sack, and tie it with a big red bow wins a fifty-dollar gift card to the retailer of his choice. Yes, it's a weird tradition, but for ten minutes a year we get to see our sons interested in a real game and not video games. Happy holidays to us!

#1. New Year's Naked Hayride

The ball drops, we toast, and we send the boys to bed. Then it's just me and my handsome honey in the hay. We don't actually ride around the farm, but that doesn't mean we don't get anywhere.

Chapter Twenty-nine

YOU SAY YOU WANT A RESOLUTION

I've been thinking a lot about New Year's resolutions. Like most people, every year I make them. And every year I break them. Fast, too. Despite the fact that I exercise just about every day, on January first, I'm training for a triathlon. On January second, I'm icing shin splints so severe it's as if I've been a sloth since the invention of the wheel. A bag of frozen peas strapped to each calf works well. Two pints of Peanut Butter Swirl and a spoon work better.

Of course, even before I ratchet up my personal boot camp, while others are still nibbling and toasting, I go Gandhi. And I don't simply cut back. I abstain. I fast. I seek a deeper level of purity. A higher level of consciousness. The corkscrew I had Hemingway hide. Why? Because by dinnertime I'm delirious; Mahatma could subsist on water, but this woman needs wine.

Maybe I can't sustain my patented Delay Death Program because I start out too gung ho. Boost my immune system and crinkling complexion by drinking eight glasses of water a day? Please, only sissies drink less than sixteen. Good thing Santa brought me a bedpan. Sleeping on the toilet is tough.

And then there are the resolutions that get broken not by me, but by those I've given birth to. If I vow to be more involved in the lives of both my boys, and then offer to, say, help Cuyler finish the fort he's been building, his response is quick and incredulous.

> *Cuy, peering at me from beneath bangs that would blind a Jonas Brother:* "Mom, does Dad know you're sick?"
> *Me:* "I'm not sick. Who said anything about being sick?"
> *Cuy, shouting up the stairs:* "Dad? Mom's offering to help me fix the fort."
> *Hemingway, shouting down at them:* "Stay back! She could be contagious!"

So much for familial support.

To be frank, I'm tired of the same old declarations. Doesn't a new year deserve new resolutions? Or barring that, at least a little variation to the ones I love to break?

For instance, I don't always eat right every day. But what if I vow to do so every *other* day? Ah. Just that little tweak's made the prospect more palatable. In fact, I'm so enamored with the day-on/day-off tack, I think I'll take it with all my resolutions. One day I'll exercise; the next I'll use my dumbbells as bookends. One day I'll look for real, paying work. The next I'll revel in this writer/slacker/gym-teacher gig I've got going. One day I'll stop at nothing to put "color" on my family's plates; the next I'll resume my quest to have corn dogs reclassified as a vegetable.

I have to confess that for a true type A, this rather type B approach is a little off-putting. But in the interest of not declaring myself a loser by, say, January second, I think I'll try it. I like the kinder, gentler concept, and the idea of feeling halfway successful instead of like a full-on failure is pretty appealing, too.

Thanks to this revolution in resolutions, this could be the first New Year in years that I actually stick to my self-improvement plans. One day I'll floss. The next I'll forget I have teeth. One day I'll toss the chickens some scratch. The next, they can go scratch. One day I'll drink nothing but water. The next day nothing but wine. I won't be able to work, exercise, or make dinner, but as long as it's slacker-bookend–corn dog day, it should be fine.

A Note from Suzy, Princess of the Pastures

. . . .

Remember the old Tareyton cigarette ads, the ones that featured people sporting black eyes and the slogan "I'd Rather Fight than Switch"? I hadn't thought of that line in years. But the other day, as I watched a nurse access Hemingway's mediport to start his chemotherapy, it popped into my head. With just a slight tweak, I made it *"We'd* Rather Fight than Switch"; it was suddenly the perfect description of the way in which we're struggling to hold on to our identity as a couple since he was diagnosed with pancreatic cancer.

Sorry to spring that on you. There's really no easy way to tell people. And trust me, there's no easy way to be told, either.

Now, it goes without saying that there's a whole lot to hate about cancer. For starters, there's the fact that it's, well, cancer, and it's having its way with someone you love. But there are dozens of other little stupid and not-so-stupid reasons cancer's completely reprehensible. Like the fact that it's not satisfied with trying to take a life. Oh, no. It has to try to take your way of life, too.

Consider for a second a simple argument between husband and wife. You can hardly have one. You know it's foolish to fight. One of you has *cancer,* for

God's sake. Why spend what little time you may have left locked in a battle over whether to add more Rhode Island Reds or Barred Rocks to your supply of egg layers? Or whether to buy another half dozen Holstein bull calves that have to be bottle-fed twice a day, every day, for twelve weeks, no matter what the weather?[157] Or whether white or colored Christmas lights should glisten on the porch this holiday?[158]

Or—and this is our favorite thing to feud over—what we'd do if we hit the lottery.

We love this game. We pretend we just won ninety-five million dollars, then take turns describing how we'd spend it. Why his stadium-size custom train layout trumps my three-thousand-square-foot shoe closet, I don't know. But I do know we've agreed on at least one thing: We'd definitely build a brand-new house.

The fact that I want it on a beach and he wants it on a lake[159] is why things usually get a little loud.

I know. We shouldn't fuss. But to us it's fun. We enjoy the verbal jousting. The running word circles around each other. The poking. The prodding. The "kiss me and I'll forgive you" expression Hem uses to cap each of our "energetic conversations" that makes me want to put a pillow over his face while he's sleeping.

---

157. I'm talking so cold the cows' drool freezes on their face, and so hot the smell of steaming manure makes your eyes tear.

158. We keep white and colored lights up, then argue over which to plug in.

159. This alone tells me my man is going to get better. He still wants to live on a lake and raise salmon. All that fresh fish sounds good to me, but Nemo's definitely not going to like it.

Or while he's awake. Unfortunately, these days I could totally take my skinny former marine.

Heated, passionate exchanges are just how we do things. Or at least it was until cancer came along and cramped our style. Now, just as we're making our approach to the rip-roaring debate runway—about, not to beat a dead decoration, the Christmas lights, which I think should impart a lovely Helmsley Palace–like sophistication rather than an Evening at the Tractor Pull–type ambience, *sweetheart*—we both stop. Simultaneously. And apologize. And give in to the other's request.

Yick. Blech. Boring.

I won't do it, you know. We won't do it. We're going to let it rip and get rowdy over whether John Deere or New Holland takes the gold in the tractor games,[160] whether mashed potatoes beat macaroni and cheese on the comfort-food food chain, whether Dave Matthews should be killed or simply have his vocal cords cut out, or whether Marshall Faulk or Tiki Barber was the better running back. We're going to debate train layouts and lake houses, shoe closets and shore property, and we are going to enjoy every single strident second of it.

We're not going to capitulate to cancer's crap. You hear me, *cancer*? You can't have my husband's life, or one iota of the way we live our life. And you're certainly not invited for Christmas. I don't care how much you like white lights.

---

160. I have a confession to make: I now know enough about this stuff to argue both sides. And don't even get me started on who makes the better bat-wing Bush Hog.

Part Three

WILL FARM FOR LOVE

"If you can't make it better, you can laugh at it."

—ERMA BOMBECK

Chapter Thirty

WILL FARM FOR LOVE

L've come to the conclusion that God has quite the sense of humor. That or He's really ticked off at me. Why? Because in the past few months, since Hemingway got sick, I have taken charge of the farm.

That's right. Me. The city chick who still prefers calling a taxi (especially the Takeout Taxi) to driving a pickup truck, and who'd still much rather be surrounded by people than poultry any day.

Trust me, it's not a promotion I wanted or worked for or ever showed any interest in receiving. It was thrust upon me when Hem had emergency gallbladder surgery that ultimately unmasked a much more serious condition.

Specifically, stage-four pancreatic cancer, with metastases to his liver and lymph nodes.

In his moment of need and fear, what could I do? Kick

the hens in their heinies and suggest they apply at Perdue? Sell his goats, Willie and Duke, just because they keep coming into the kitchen? Neglect the vegetable garden he gave his heart and soul to, even though it had to be harvested at the same time I needed to be in the hospital with him? Take the steer he and Cuyler bottle-fed, nursed through "the scours,"[161] and love like pets to the livestock exchange?

No. I couldn't dismantle his life in the name of saving it.

Instead, I tiptoed up to the plate, stared at it long and hard, and flashed on "What I Did for Love" from *A Chorus Line*. And then, very quietly, so as not to attract the attention of those only too eager to see me fall face-first into a cow pie, I slipped into a pair of work boots. Yes, you read that right. I not only own but wear the cutest pair Tractor Supply had in stock. I even almost like them, but not with shorts; our Boer wether billy goats have better legs than I do.

If I told Hem it was just too much to care for the farm on top of caring for him, the house, the kids, and our three crazy canines, we'd be out of here faster than Susan Boyle's stint in the spotlight. But it's not too much. We have wonderful friends who pitch in and help cut the fields and corral escaped cattle and fix fence boards and cart our boys to school and work and football practice and who show up with dinner piping hot and so delicious that it's painfully clear my cooking's about as good as my farming.

---

161. Bovine speak for—sorry—loose bowels.

But I'm getting better, and Hemingway will, too. And when he does, he's going to want his farm back. Believe it or not, I hope he'll still let me help. Not only have I finally gotten the hang of some of this stuff; I'm sort of starting to enjoy it.

And yes, I do believe that's God I hear giggling.

Chapter Thirty-one

I'D LIKE TO HAVE A WORD WITH JOHN WAYNE*

*Disclaimer: No animals were hurt during the writing of this chapter. The author, however, sustained a sprained wrist and a couple of contusions. But she had it coming.

When I was a kid, my three younger brothers and I played tag and manhunt and war and, yes, I confess, cowboys and Indians. We didn't know it was politically incorrect. We thought it was fun, what with all the scalping that occasionally resulted in somebody needing one of those Band-Aids that could double as a diaper, stabbing one another with spears fashioned from tree branches that occasionally resulted in somebody needing a tetanus shot, and hopping on one another's backs and hollering, "Giddy up, bitch!" that years later resulted in the bitch (aka me) needing panties made with the kind of steel girders typically reserved for suspension bridges and definitely not sold by Victoria's Secret.

We also watched our share of John Wayne movies. I'm unsure what David, Nick, and Dan liked best about them— maybe it was the cattle drives, the fact that everyone was filthy and no one was threatening to take away their Tonka trucks if they didn't take a bath, or the characters' ability to get shot and then, in the next shot, smoke a cigarette— but for me, anytime some bad guy jumped on a horse bareback and rode it into the sunset, I was smitten.

Not with the bad guy, mind you, but rather the whole bareback business. It just looked so freeing. So fun.

So easy.

I tell you this not to excuse my stupidity, but in an attempt to explain why, one day, when Hemingway was sleeping, the boys were in school, and I was at my desk trying to write but in reality just staring at the computer screen wondering whether I would ever again string together a complete sentence that didn't have to do with doctors, Doug Ross and Derek Shepherd[162] not included, of course, I decided I needed to clear my head.

So I stood up.

And walked to the door.

And went outside. A move that's still so unusual for me, I sometimes expect my skin to glisten and glow and get all translucent, like that Edward guy.

If I may digress for just a second, I happen to think Hot Fangs and I would get along famously. He doesn't like

---

162. Because I'd happily write about George Clooney and Patrick Dempsey all day.

wine, so that would leave more for me, and if one of the cows, or hens, or goats (or even dogs, God love 'em) got out of hand, he could drink it. Not your typical farm-management technique, but then, I'm not your typical farm manager.

In any case, I found myself out on the porch and I stood there for a moment because, truthfully, unless there's a task I have to tackle, like shooing a cow out of the road and back into the pasture, watering Hem's insatiable fruit trees, feeding the chickens, forcing the goats out of the garage, or making one of our tenant houses presentable for showing to a potential renter, I don't know what to do outside.

And honestly? I don't understand the appeal of the place.[163]

But on this particular day inspiration struck. Suddenly I was seized by the desire to embrace country life, commune with nature, befriend a hen.

And ride one of the two massive, beautiful, Budweiser-commercial-worthy Clydesdales that reside on our farm.

Bareback.

Hey, blame it on Hem. Usually, when he's not sleeping, he's watching films that could give narcolepsy to an insomniac. But recently he'd been watching Westerns. Some with John Wayne, and others with a whole lot of "Let's poach that pony and ride 'im bareback to the brothel!"–type stuff and, well, I'd been watching with him.

---

163. Let me be clear about this. I'm an indoor girl. I love nothing more than a day spent sitting at my desk, staring out my window, working on ad copy, a column, or a post for my blog. And if I do decide to go out and enjoy the sunshine, I'm a million times more likely to drop the top on the Mustang and hit Lou Lou than I am to take a walk in the woods. It's just not my thing. And besides, I hate bugs.

And once again, I was smitten.

"I could do that, you know." I pointed with the stub of my Bachman pretzel rod at the old black-and-white film flickering on our new flat-screen TV.

"Work in a whorehouse?" Hem looked at me out of the corner of his eye and kept munching. The two of us are totally addicted to pretzels. In fact, they're the only carbohydrate I eat. I can go for weeks on salad and the occasional piece of chicken, but if I sit down to watch TV or a movie, it's *auf wiedersehen*, Atkins.

"No, silly. Ride bareback."

"Naked, like Lady Godiva?"

"I'm serious."

"Me, too." Tug hopped up onto the couch, and Mr. It's a Dog's World, We're Just Living in It scooted over to give him room. To give him room on the butter-soft, chocolate leather, designer-name couch that cost, like, six trillion dollars. And I thought the pet beds at L.L. Bean were pricey.

"It's all about sex for you, isn't it?"

"You know what they say. Men think about sex every seven seconds. Unless you're a man with cancer." He snatched the bag from my hand, pulled out a bunch of broken pretzel pieces, and plopped them on his chest.[164] "Then it's every four. Sometimes three. We have a lot more time on our hands, what with chemo and bone scans and MRIs and all that time spent lying around being poked and prodded."

---

164. I'd get him a paper plate or a bowl or even a napkin, but he wouldn't use it. My husband adheres to the "human as serving dish" school of thought. And I adhere to the belief that whoever came up with the DustBuster should be canonized.

"I'm guessing you're particularly fond of the poked—or I should say poking—part."

"I've taught you well, young Skywalker."

Great. Now I was sitting with the dog and Darth Vader.[165] "I really could ride bareback, you know."

"Something tells me you're not referring to poking."

"You're incorrigible."

"And you're nuts." He sneaked a hunk of pretzel to Grundy, who thinks he's a throw rug and resides permanently under my husband's feet. "You'd break your neck."

"First of all, I saw that. And second of all, I would not. I'd squeeze my knees really tight, and hold on to the horse's hair."

"Mane. It's called a mane."

"Details, details."

"You know they're stuntmen, right?" Hem pointed at the television.

"And you know they learned from the Indians, right? I mean, *they* didn't learn from the Indians"—now we were both pointing at the television—"but that's where it all started. Before there were saddles, people rode bareback."

"Suz, whatever you're thinking, please stop thinking it."

"I'm not thinking anything, handsome. Just making conversation." I sank back into our huge, and hugely overpriced, dog-hair-covered couch, and popped another piece of pretzel in my mouth. "Besides, I can't do anything crazy. I have a husband to take care of."

And I would go back to taking care of him. Just as soon as he woke up.

---

165. Darth Vader. Can you even imagine how bad his breath had to be under that black helmet head thing?

In the interim, I was going to pay the aforementioned Clydesdales, Molly and Maggy, a visit.

If you're thinking I'm a rookie, a neophyte, a green-horn when it comes to horses, you're wrong. I'm practically a master equestrian. Once, I fed and watered Maggy and Molly for a whole week. By myself. In fact, I got so good at it, I could write a book. Okay, maybe not a book. But definitely a short list, like this:

How to Feed a Horse, Counterfeit Farm Girl Style

1. Approach the stall while craning your head from side to side surveying the pasture. If you don't see the horses, stop and shout, "Here, horsey, horsey, horsey! Time to eat, horsey, horsey, horsey!" Don't worry about embarrassing yourself. You're wearing a low-cut, skintight tank top, a pair of short shorts, and open-toed platform wedges. I'd say that ship has sailed.

2. Step inside the stall, keeping an eye out for anything long, black, and slithery, or small, black, and sporting whiskers. Should you spy a creature such as I've described, scream. No one will hear you, or help you, but you'll feel better. Then proceed to the garbage can[166] containing the feed.

---

166. The rumor that Secretariat's feed holder was Waterford is false. He got Rubbermaid, just like the rest of 'em.

3. Slowly lift the lid, keeping any eye out for anything long, black, and slithery, or small, black, and sporting whiskers. Should you spy a creature such as I've described, scream, slam the lid down, and hightail it out of there while telling yourself in no uncertain terms, The horses can eat dog food or diet. It's their call.

4. Should you not discover anything long, black, and slithery, or small, black, and sporting whiskers, scoop lots and lots of food (because you want the horses to like you, right?) into the red plastic Hook-n-Feed[167] containers sitting next to the garbage cans.

5. Step out of the stall carrying said containers. Startle yourself silly upon discovering both breathtaking, massive mares at the fence, whinnying loudly for their food, and promptly drop the buckets. Shove the feed back in quickly, though not so quickly that you lose your balance, topple off your shoes, and take a few pointy pieces of hay, a discarded Gatorade top, a shell from your kid's cap gun, a wheel from what had to be a Hot Wheels car, a couple of BBs, and some gravel to the knee. Not that this has ever happened to me, but I can imagine. And I'd feel guilty if I didn't warn you.

---

167. Look at that: lingo. And you doubted my master equestrian status. (Not to mention my talent for perusing the Tractor Supply Web site.)

6. Carry the containers to the fence, hook them to the top board, and stand back. You'll know the horses are finished with their meal when one or both feeders land at your feet.

7. Return the feeders to the stall and close the door. You don't want anything getting in (or anything you might have missed getting out) while you're giving the horses water.

8. Lift the latch for the water and wait. And wait. And wait. Entire seasons, elected officials, and OPI nail color collections can change while you wait for the water, which I've a strong suspicion is piped in from the Pacific via Mother Russia and then routed through at least a hundred thousand miles of hose and a couple of colons before it comes out the other end and into the horses' trough. To fight boredom, multitask: Catch up on your reading, wonder what people who live in places where there are other people are doing right now, or clip your nails. (And now you can appreciate the brilliance behind my choice of open-toed footwear.)

So I really am almost a master equestrian. A self-taught, almost master equestrian who's watched way too many Westerns (and a little *Lone Ranger*, you know, in reruns).[168]

---

168. I'm old, but I'm not that old.

And there's really no reason a self-taught, almost master equestrian who's watched way too many Westerns and a little *Lone Ranger* can't ride a six-foot-tall, two-thousand-pound Clydesdale bareback.

Except for the fact that it's a spectacularly bad idea.

Now, I know what you're thinking. You're thinking, Susan, have you missed your medication? Wake up, woman! You could be killed or suffer (additional) brain damage. Or worse, you could lose one of your brand-new Steve Madden sandals. Sandals you were lucky to find in a size seven. I mean, every woman in the free world is a size seven! And you got them on sale online, no less. This is no time to go 'round the bend, blondie. No good can come of this. Your husband is sick. He needs you healthy to take care of him. And your children! If you're hurt, who will keep your children in cheese puffs, Chips Ahoy!, and the rest of their favorite breakfast foods? Be strong and tell yourself, I will not give in to this insane fascination. There's too much at stake.

Ooh, steak. With broccoli sautéed in olive oil and a nice tossed salad. Beats the hell out of the hot dogs we ended up having that night. But I find it's best to make something simple when you've got a migraine.

And ringing in your ears.

And a bruised hip.

And a wrist so painful you should probably have it X-rayed. Right after they rule out internal bleeding and arrange a psych consult.

But to do that you'd have to be in a hospital. And to be in a hospital, you'd have to confess to having done something as stupid as cajoling a couple of horses to come to you by proffering carrots and apples and a squished Almond Joy that you actually didn't share because animals should eat chocolate about as frequently as they should find hyper blond women with impulse-control issues on their backs, and then scaling a four-board fence and climbing atop the smaller[169] of two huge horses. Just to see if you could.

Which as it turns out, I could. And I did. And I'll tell you how, but only if you promise not to try this on anything other than a carousel or rocking horse, or maybe one of those stick horses preschoolers love (and people like me should be limited to).

I dropped the snacks to the ground and the horses bent to eat them. Maggy, the more diminutive of the duo, was, most conveniently, pressed up against the fence. It was like a sign from God saying, "Go for it, girl!" Thinking I'd better move fast before God changed His mind or somebody showed up to question my sanity (or simply cart me off to an asylum), I scaled the boards as quickly as my platform wedges would allow. And then, just as I swung my vampire-white leg over the horse's expansive, chestnut brown back, I stopped.

Something was missing.

Something more than a saddle and the good sense not to try a stunt like this.

Something like . . . reins.

Oh, shitty, shit, shit, shitties, I thought. Where did I get

---

169. Because I'm not a complete idiot.

the cockamamie idea that I'd ride bareback holding on to the horse's hair—I mean mane? And how did I miss the fact that good guys, bad guys, cowboys, and Indians alike used them in the film Hem and I watched the other night—not to mention the John Wayne Westerns and the *Lone Ranger* reruns my brothers and I couldn't get enough of as kids?

Not being a detail girl was going to get me killed.

Quickly, I revised my plan. No reins, no riding bareback. I'd simply *sit* bareback, for just a second, and climb off. I'd come this far, and I couldn't bring myself to just give up, chicken out, walk away.

Oh, no. I was lucky to limp away.

Maggy let me sit on her for about a tenth of a second before she said, and I quote, "Yo, Daisy Duke, what the hell do you think you're doing?" and took off like a shot. To be honest, I think that's what she said. I really couldn't hear over the whole pleading and praying thing I had going on.

"Maggy, please stop. Oh, God, please make her stop. If you make her stop, I promise not to do anything this dumb ever again. And that includes putting collars on Cuy's bull calves. Or at least not pink ones. Really, Mag, there's no reason to run. You can get just . . . as much . . . exercise . . . walking. And it's easier on the joints. It would certainly be easier on mine right this moment. What the . . . ? Was that . . . ? Oh, my God, I think I got a bug in my eye. What if it's a mosquito? Or a bee? I'll go blind! Blind because I *had* to ride bareback! Oh, sweet Jesus, please make her stop running. Or maybe she's galloping.

That's it, she's galloping! God, I'm good. Sorry. That just slipped out."

And then I slipped off. Definitely not the kind of graceful dismount I've seen in the movies. But then, those riders had reins.

Not to mention brains.

I was lucky, though. A whopping pile of decomposing cow poop smack in the middle of a nice, stagnant mud puddle and occupied by a big old lumpy toad who was none too happy to have me, quite literally, drop in, broke my fall, and neither Maggy nor Molly gave me the good, swift kick I so deserved. In fact, when I staggered to my feet, wincing at the pain in my hip and wrist, both horses seemed to shake their heads and sigh as if I were trying their patience.

And then I remembered my patient and set the record for the two-hundred-yard dash in four-inch, mud-soaked, broken-strapped, bought-for-a-song, impossible-to-find but now ruined-beyond-recognition, size-seven Steve Madden sandals.

"What are we watching tonight?" Hem asked while the kids finished their hot dogs, I took another two Excedrin with another vodka tonic, and he made himself a vanilla milk shake. "We got a whole bunch of Netflix today. *Sherlock Holmes, Zombieland, True Grit.*" He added one more scoop of ice cream, hit "blend," and I thought my brain would bleed right out onto the table. He didn't notice, which is nothing new and is certainly fine with me. He can miss my aneurysms anytime, as long as it means missing my shopping bags every time. "John Wayne, babe," he prodded, raising his eyebrows, tucking his chin, and giving me the thumbs-up.

"I was thinking we could save *True Grit* for tomorrow night—"

"And watch your boy Robert Downey Jr. tonight," Hem teased. Then he finally, mercifully, stopped the blender, poured the shake in a glass, and rifled through the pantry for a bag of pretzels. "You got it. *Sherlock Holmes* it is. Come on, Tug," he added, giving the dog the high sign and heading for the den, "let's go fire up Mommy's detective movie."

Whew. At least for the time being I was safe from Westerns and John Wayne. And that probably saved my life. I mean, any more inspiration from the Duke, and I might just win myself a Darwin Award.[170]

---

170. And I quote directly from www.darwinawards.com: "The Darwin Awards salute the improvement of the human genome by honoring those who accidentally remove themselves from it. . . ." Oh, yes, I'm bound to be a recipient.

Chapter Thirty-two

FAILING CAREGIVING 101

I've failed Caregiving 101. True, final grades aren't out yet, but my interim progress report is piss-poor.

It all started when I miscounted Hemingway's pain medication and instead of making it through the weekend, we ran out on Sunday at the start of the Giants game.

"Guess we'd better pray they win, right, Mom?" Cuy whispered as I ripped through the bottom shelf of the kitchen cabinet that once held my favorite coffee cups, my honey's massive, and I mean birdbath big, Bucknell University tea mug, and an assortment of Twinings teas no one drank but which smelled so sweet I just couldn't throw them out. These days it's home to the McPharmacy. Open the door and the happy scent of Orange Spice still spills out, followed by about four hundred prescription pill bottles, powdered medications, liquid medications, aspirin, Advil, Motrin, and empty sample packs of stuff that worked and we may want again but, dammit, no Dilaudid.

"You bet, bud," I replied. Where the hell was the Dilaudid? *Take eight milligrams every four hours and you won't feel a thing and you won't care if the G men beat the Bucs.*

But, of course, he did care, and he could feel a thing. He could feel *the* thing, the burning, throbbing sensation in his stomach that hasn't subsided since it started in the summer.

Luckily for me, the Giants trounced Tampa Bay twenty-four–zero. This provided a nice, natural high for all the McMen, and gave me time to dig out the stash of Vicodin I keep tucked deep in the back of my nightstand drawer for just such emergencies.

Yeah, my trucker handle is "House."

Of course, I don't take the stuff; I just keep what's left over every time it's prescribed. I had a bunch from when Casey had his wisdom teeth pulled and decided he'd rather tough it out on Tylenol. And I had about half a bottle from Hem's gallbladder surgery. He said it really didn't do anything, so he stopped taking it. He was just doing the whole bite-the-bullet, be-a-marine thing, I thought as I grabbed the bottle and ran back to the kitchen, which I'm willing to bet bore more than a passing resemblance to Elvis Presley's bathroom. I gave Hem one Vicodin with a glass of water and prayed he was wrong, and I was right.

You know, like usual.

Come Monday I restocked the Dilaudid. Lest you think this is a no-brainer, permit me to shine a little light on the lunacy of prescription narcotics. Thanks to uzi-carrying drug lords and the losers who love them, honest, hard-working, pain-stricken people must present a physical, written prescription to the pharmacist. It cannot be called in. It cannot be faxed in. It must be handed to the man or woman behind the counter.

This isn't too much of a problem when the doctor writing the scrip is close by. But it's a whole different kettle of decomposing fish when he or she is ninety minutes away. Ninety minutes out and ninety minutes back. Three hours round-trip. One hundred and eighty minutes just to retrieve a three-by-five-size piece of paper. Tack on another ten for my favorite pharmacist to fill the prescription, and ten for me to get home with it, and you can understand why, when I read a headline like, THIRTEEN GUNNED DOWN IN ESCALATING DRUG TURF WAR, my immediate response is, "Kill 'em all, and let God sort 'em out."

Ultimately, it took a three-woman tag team to get the job done. My sister-in-law Nancy lives near the hospital, so she retrieved the prescription. She then handed it off to her friend Karen, who was headed out our way for a meeting. Karen and I met on the main street in Middleburg to make the exchange.[171] I got the prescription. She got a hug. And I hightailed it outta there. Fast, but not fast enough.

Pain, we were about to learn, is like a train: Once it's left the station, it's very tough to catch and almost impossible to get ahead of. Unless you're Superman. Mere mortals require assistance. From morphine.

---

171. It felt like something out of *Traffic*, minus the piercing yellow lighting and Benicio del Toro's smoldering stare, of course.

Who knew?

I raced in from the pharmacy with a bottle of water and the Dilaudid and gave Hem four two-milligram pills before I peed or even put my bag down. In fact, I think I peed holding my bag. And then I ran back to our bedroom and stood there like a crazy woman, willing the drug to work. Twenty minutes passed. Thirty. Forty-five.

"Hon," I whispered, like I did back in the days when a bad hangover was the worst pain either of us had ever felt (not including contractions, of course, and believe me, we both felt them. What? I should deny him the joy of what it feels like to poop a pumpkin? Sorry, I'm just not that selfish, and if you think I was letting go of "little" Hem before big Hem hollered for the anesthesiologist, you're, pardon the play on words, nuts), "how ya doin'? On a scale of one to ten, how's the pain?"

"Ten."

Ten?

I gave it fifteen more minutes, and asked again. "Ten. *Still* ten." Eight milligrams of Dilaudid, which usually knocks his socks off, and nothing? What the hell was happening? Or, better question, why the hell wasn't anything happening? I called the physician's assistant. With her okay, I gave him a second dose. Another hour and a "Still ten, Sue. Stop asking!" later, I called again. You know that train I mentioned earlier? It was long gone. (And yes, I do believe that was the Vicodin I saw sitting in the club car.)

Monday night was bad. Hem didn't sleep, again. So I didn't sleep, again. It was like having a newborn in the house. You're delirious with exhaustion. You feel hung-over, yet you haven't had a drop to drink. Yes, you're the perfect person to be dispensing medication.

Tuesday I added Extra Strength Tylenol, Advil, and Motrin to the mix. All are perfectly good pain relievers if you have a fever, headache, or sore throat. As Hem didn't have any of that stuff, I have no idea why I thought they'd help. Needless to say, nobody slept Tuesday night, either.

But then Wednesday rolled around. Whew! We made it. Time for Hem's two-week postop[172] follow-up. Off to Georgetown we went. We saw the surgeon. And we saw Hem's favorite gastroenterologist, too. And they both said the same thing: "You're in this much pain? You're not eating or drinking? And you haven't left the house since you left the hospital? We're admitting you."

To which my frighteningly skinny, suffering, yet unceasingly stubborn farmer replied, "No, thanks. But I'll take some stronger pain meds."

They prescribed them, the whole time looking at me like, Yo, caregiver, you're cool with this?

Of course I wasn't cool with it. Couldn't somebody overrule Mr. I Hate Hospitals? Oh, wait, that's supposed to be me. I could just see the teacher dropping my star in caregiver class. My brain was screaming, C'mon, Suz. Speak! Get a spine, woman! Stamp your foot and say, "Dude, motion denied. You're staying put."

But I didn't. I couldn't. He was scared he'd never leave

---

172. Two weeks earlier, Hem went in for Whipple surgery or, in medical speak, a pancreaticoduodenectomy. It's the most commonly performed operation to treat pancreatic cancer, but it's done only if the cancer hasn't spread. All of Hem's presurgery test results pointed to his being a good candidate but, when they opened him up, they found it was too late. The cancer had metastasized to his liver and lymph nodes.

the hospital. I was scared I wouldn't be able to keep him comfortable at home. Trust me when I tell you, fear really fucks up your judgment.[173]

The long and short of it is, I brought him home, and right then and there, if it hadn't already done so, my caregiving grade dropped to a D.

It didn't matter that I surrounded him with fluffy pillows, lifted Tug onto the bed to snuggle in next to him, fed him his favorite lemon Jell-O, and, of course, plied him full of painkillers. Nothing helped. And so, after another night in the seventh circle of hell, I did what I should have done the day before: I checked him into the hospital.

Within twenty minutes Superman showed up wearing scrubs and wielding morphine. The needle went in, Hem almost immediately, mercifully, passed out, and I did my best not to become a puddle right there in the emergency room.

In the end, I got points for not crying like a ninny, but it's not enough to save my grade. For that, I'll need extra credit. Maybe I'll learn to access Hem's port or start his chemo. Or maybe, if I really want an A in caregiving, I'll finally learn to count.

---

173. And being sleep-deprived doesn't help.

Now I Lay Me Down to Sleep, A Portable Phone within My Reach. If the Power Should Blow Before I Wake, Get Me Up, Dammit, and Let's Celebrate!

. . . .

TO: Friends and family

FR: Suzy@stuckinthesticks.com

Date: Thursday, 10:18 p.m.

Subject: Rikki, don't use that number

Every single time I turn around, the power is out. It's just one of the realities of rural living, along with the fact that every time I open the back of the Durango, Grundy and Tug hop in, lie down, and look at me like, "See? We're good boys. Now take us to visit Daddy, *darn it!*" I don't like when the power goes out, or when I'm forced to take the Mustang because the Durango's filled with dog hair, but I'm learning to relax and go with the flow. I live in a pretty much people-free environment, and when the power goes out, I can't call anyone either. No electricity, no phones. And forget our cell phones; they get even worse reception than the Salahis at that White House dinner.

Clearly, the inability to communicate makes me crazy. But ever since news of Hemingway's diagnosis got out, I pray nightly for just two things: a cure for pancreatic cancer, and a good old-fashioned power outage.

Why? Because for some reason we haven't had one, and I'm exhausted from fielding eight million phone calls a day from folks who are worried sick and want to know how we're doing.

"We're fine. He has cancer, and I'm losing my mind trying to not to think about the fact that he has cancer. But other than that, it's all good."

And the five million phone calls from those who want to know if there's anything they can do.

No, there really isn't. Unless you have the magic cure and, if not, could you take a break from calling every thirty seconds? I appreciate your concern; I really do. But I've got nothing new to tell you. If that changes, I'll send out smoke signals. I swear.

And the two million phone calls from people who want me to know it's okay to feel helpless and to call them if I want to cry.

But I don't feel helpless. And I don't want to cry. For starters, I don't have the time. I have calls to make and appointments to schedule and doctors to bug and prescriptions to pick up and dinner to make and homework to oversee and dogs to wash and pain medication to dispense and bills to pay and laundry to fold and eggs to gather and chickens to feed and goats to shoo from the equipment shed and really, really, truly, I don't want to cry. Except for when the phone rings and I stop, on a dime, to answer it because ... because how can I let it ring when I know you're calling because you love my husband and our kids and me, and you're worried? How can I let it ring knowing you'll wonder where we are and if we're on our way back to the hospital at two hundred miles per hour because he spiked a temperature or started vomiting or passed out or whatever? I have to answer the phone because I can't add to your worry.

I know, I sound so ungrateful. But I'm not, and I love you from the bottom of my heart for loving us. Thank you for your prayers and concern and calls. Now please, Rikki, step away from the phone. I probably am helpless, and I probably should give in and cry. But there's no time for that today, and tomorrow, as they say, is not looking good, either.

Chapter Thirty-three

DRAWING THE LINE AT THE LEECH

Sometimes I wonder just how dumb supposedly dumb animals really are. Our three hundred or so cattle have acres and acres of pasture at their disposal, yet they haven't left the spot closest to our house in days. There can't be much grass left, but still they stay there, like they're stuck in one of those interminable sales meetings I used to have to sit through. They venture only as far as the springhouse for a drink in the streams that feed it, and then they're back, staring through the fence, a group of future steaks on a stakeout. What are they waiting for? I wondered. And then it hit me: It's not what they're waiting for; it's who. Hemingway. He hasn't been out talking to them and feeding them range cubes. He hasn't been working in the garden and tossing mushy tomatoes and cucumbers in their direction. They sense something's wrong. They're looking for him.

And they're not the only ones.

Duke and Willie would like to find Hem, too. Only they're not nearly as polite and passive as the cows. While the "girls" are content mooing in the direction of the house, the goats content themselves by trying to get into it. And sometimes succeeding. It's true, this is their usual shtick, but lately they've stepped it up a notch. Twice they've both gotten onto the mud porch, and once they got into the kitchen.

Sure, the bad news is that Hem is sick. But the worse news is that the goats keep trying to pay him a get-well visit.

Of course, we did get some good news recently. Gemcitabine, the drug of choice for pancreatic cancer, is not just very powerful but very highly tolerated. This means Hem shouldn't be nauseated, and he shouldn't lose his hair. Not that he cares. As long as he doesn't lose his head and can wear his Giants cap, he's cool.

According to some site I found on the Internet,[174] visualizing the gemcitabine (aka our best chance for growing old together and arguing about whose turn it is to make margaritas) kicking ass, taking names, and vaporizing those vile cancer cells as it courses through Hemingway's veins could make him (and me) feel better, more proactive, and less powerless. So you can bet we'll be trying that trick.

We've also decided to augment the best modern medicine has available with one or more of today's alternative

---

174. And, as you can imagine, there are thousands of them, so check with your doctor before acting on anything you read.

cancer remedies. Don't scowl. Some of this stuff actually works. There are people who were told they had a month to live three years ago who firmly believe they're still here thanks to a combination of chemotherapy and flaxseed-infused cottage cheese.

Yes, regular old cottage cheese with a heaping helping of flaxseed mixed in. Who'd'a thunk it?

And that's not the only alternative out there. There are dozens of them.[175] Oxy E, coenzyme Q10, OxyDHQ. The list is endless and we may try a few. But Hemingway and I agree: Under absolutely, positively no circumstances will we ever resort to the lowly leech.

"I'm not going to Mexico for any of that *Man on the Moon* stuff, Sue," he says, referring to the Jim Carrey movie about comedian Andy Kaufman.

"After all I've done for you, you'd deny me the pleasure of watching some witch doctor pretend to pull leeches out of your belly button? You ingrate!"

"I think it's enough I've agreed to eat that cottage cheese concoction." He pauses and pretends to put his finger down his throat. "Start pushing stuff like leeches, eye of newt, or green eggs and ham, and somebody's gonna get hurt."

Hmm. Green eggs and ham. I hadn't thought of that. It doesn't sound too good, but in all honesty, none of this stuff does. Not the visualization. Not the natural supplements. And certainly not the chemo. It all screams, My husband is sick. And that simply makes me want to scream.

---

175. Sorry to repeat myself, but *please* don't do, take, or try anything you discover on your own before running it past your doctor.

Any such outburst is going to have to wait, of course, until we're on the other side of this thing and he's insisting it's my turn to fire up the blender. It won't be, you should know. My man is a terrible turn taker, with a tendency to prefer drinks made by his favorite blond bartender.

I, on the other hand, would prefer if one of our not so dumb animals could be taught to make margaritas. This rules out Grundy, Tug, and Pete, for obvious reasons, and don't even think of suggesting Coca and Cola. The last time those two "helped," I caught them licking the cap to the Cuervo. They didn't get sick, but I did. One bottle costs thirty-two bucks! That leaves the hens, the cows, and the goats. As I don't like feathers or big green doody flies in my drink, I'm leaning toward Duke and Willie. They already know their way around the kitchen, and frankly, I've always wanted a cabana boy named Billy.

Chapter Thirty-four

PLEASE DON'T SQUEEZE THE STINKBUGS

This just in: Stinkbugs have hit New Jersey.

And for that, I blame my mother.[176]

My mother—or, as I like to call her, Dame Joan—recently paid a visit to the stinkbug capital of the country—or, as it's more commonly known, our house—and when she left for her little slice of the Garden State, she apparently gave a lift to an entire colony of the only bugs with a built-in attack aroma.[177]

Unknowingly, of course. But still.

I tried to stop her. I didn't want her to go home. I wanted her to stay and help me do fun things like chase

---

176. I'm pretty ticked at her for the whole global-warming thing, too.

177. Step on 'em, squeeze 'em, touch 'em in any way and the aroma they release will make your eyes water. Better to vacuum 'em up and burn the bag. And maybe your Bissell.

down prescriptions and run to the pharmacy, take the trash to the recycling center, clean the gutters, weed, and, most important, guard the garden from the goats, which, truthfully, she did better than Hemingway or I ever have. Of course, my mom is an elementary school principal. She has a BA and a master's degree in pest control. And she's pretty good with kids, too.

Seriously, though, you should've seen her standing between the hundreds of cherry tomatoes, cucumbers, and the exceedingly long (phallic-looking, frankly) red jalapeño peppers we planted by mistake, puffing away on a Misty Ultra Light, and lecturing (in an English accent, no less) the goats and any cows, chickens, or dogs that dared approach about how they were going to spend eternity pushing up carrots if they came any closer.

The poor beasts looked at one another like, Who's the Brit? But they left the produce alone.

Of course, she didn't just pull scarecrow duty before she left and the stink about the stinkbugs started. We got in some really good gossip time, too. Juicy stuff I can't share, because if I tell you, I'll have to kill you. And maybe even use you as mulch.

In fact, about the only thing we didn't get to rehash was my absolute favorite family memory. No, not the one about the night my brother David, who today is a total hunk but at the age of four was a big old Baby Huey, sneaked a jumbo-size bag of minipretzels into his bed and was busy stuffing himself with them when, of course, one lodged in his windpipe. He started gagging and clutching his throat and making all these disgusting Chiller Theatre scary choking sounds, and I, Super Big Sister, flew into action. I jumped out of bed, screamed for my parents, and raced to his side. Then I whipped off his covers, pulled his pillow from behind his head, and put it over his face.

(Let this be a lesson to little brothers everywhere: Tease and torture your big sister all day, every day and she just might think your middle-of-the-night retching is yet another ruse to make her life miserable. And try to kill you.)

And no, I'm not referring to the incredible Christmas party my brother Nick threw when he was in high school. There was food and drink and a dozen girls dressed as elves plying a kid in a Santa suit with big, red Solo cups of beer, which they got from kegs in the kitchen that had "Feliz Navidad!" and "Let it Snow!" written down the side. There was a beautifully decorated tree in the living room. Even a gigantic blowup sled and reindeer on the lawn, wreaths on the double doors, and hundreds of blinking, colored lights all over the front of the house. Hands down, it's still the best holiday party I've ever attended. In August.

And no, I'm not talking about my baby brother, Dan, who as a toddler had a habit of covering himself in Band-Aids. I can still see him in his blue plaid OshKosh B'Gosh shortalls[178] sitting on the steps of our bungalow in Chadwick Beach, New Jersey, peeling the strips and sticking them on his legs, knees, belly, chest, elbows, even smack in the center of his forehead. We all thought it was cute until one day he covered the cat in them, too. Wearing a sweatshirt, David's football helmet, and two oven mitts on each hand, I watched

---

178. Shortalls: short for short bib overalls and clearly a clue to my future. Why, since he was the one wearing them, I don't know. But damn you anyway, Dan.

in horror as my mom held that pussy and pulled. And now you know why I've never been a fan of the Brazilian.

No, my favorite family memory and the one I wanted most to relive, belabor, and bust a gut laughing over—again—is about my dad. A tale nobody tells better than my mom.

And she was going to—right up until the moment she remembered promising to babysit for Mr. Let's Make a Bikini Top out of Band-Aids![179] and my sister-in-law, Saint Dawn. *That night.* "Susan," she said, "I'd love to spend the day doing a number on your dad, but I've got a train to New Jersey to catch."

While I raced to put Hem's meds, the phone, his reading glasses, a bottle of water, and his book by the bed, get my keys, chain the dogs up outside so they could relieve themselves without risking their lives,[180] and check the garden for errant goats, my mom tossed a half dozen cartons of Misty Ultra Lights[181] and, of course, her clothes into her big red Liz Claiborne bag.

Among her things was a navy blue sweatshirt emblazoned with the words "World's Best Grandma," and a long-sleeved white tee that announced, "#1 Bubby," which I read as "#1 Booby" and wondered, Which one? She brought them in a striped canvas tote that told the world "When the Going Gets Tough, the Tough Go to Grand-

179. Dave taught him to ride a bike. Nick taught him how to make a milk shake. I had to make some kind of contribution to Dan's "education."

180. Because I'm really tired of trying to clean the living room rug.

181. In New Jersey, buying a carton of cigarettes practically requires refinancing. In Virginia, they're so cheap they come with a free tin of chewing tobacco. And a list of local hospices.

ma's" (a trip I've considered taking several times since Hem got sick), but she hadn't worn them.

"Darling daughter," she said, when I offered to run in and get the sweatshirt one night when it was nippy and we were outside, once again, relieving Tug of his manure-and-mud frosting, "a sophisticated woman would sooner freeze to death than wear clothes with captions."[182]

The long and short of it is that the bag and its contents sat untouched near a window in the guest room for her entire stay. And my guess is that that carryall carried the *Halyomorpha halys*[183] home to her house.

Why? Because the window near which it sat is adorned with thick, pleated drapes that, days after my mom's departure, I discovered crawling with the ugly shield-shaped insects. In the folds, the hem, and clumped inside the tassels. Obviously when the going got tough, the bugs got going. Right into Dame Joan's unworn but well-traveled duds. Had I thought to help her pack, I might have discovered them.

And had I begged and pleaded and promised to never again wear my "Mommy Needs a Cocktail" tank top,[184] I might have convinced her to stay. And tell me my favorite story.

It was midmorning on Christmas Eve, and my dad,

---

182. Oh, I see. Better to just lug the stuff around, like a traveling tourist trap, instead of throwing it out, giving it away, or (and I really like this idea) opening a thrift shop with the shit!

183. The Latin name for the brown marmorated stinkbug.

184. A cute little number I usually follow the next day with my "Mommy Needs a Latte" tee and two aspirin. Check out the whole line of fun tanks and T-shirts at www .babybrewing.com.

who'd yet to get anything for Dame Joan,[185] suddenly hit
on the perfect gift. He'd give her something she'd wanted
forever, or at least since last December. Something he
hadn't had the time, inclination, or motivation to address.
Something she probably thought he'd forgotten or hadn't
heard her ask for in the first place. But surprise, surprise!
He had heard, and he hadn't forgotten. And now the time
was right. He was ready and this year he'd really put the
"merry" in her Christmas.

Quietly, he gathered his tools and brought them up
from the basement. He made a quick trip to the store for a
few final supplies and changed his clothes.

And then he commenced the gift giving.

It was all going pretty well (read: My mom didn't have
a flipping clue what my dad was doing) until she suddenly said, "Susan, what do I smell?"

She and I were in the kitchen. She was chopping, I was
stirring, and things were simmering. It was a little noisy,
so I acted like I didn't hear her.

"Susan," she insisted, sniffing. "I smell something."

I lifted the lid on the tomato sauce and practically put
my face in, pretending to check it. "It might be Dad," I
mumbled. "He's—"

"He's what?" She looked at me, then bent over and
started sniffing things. The broccoli-and-cheese casserole
she'd just made. The provolone, tomatoes, and mozzarella

---

185. Who, at that time, was known simply as Mom. The *dame* title was bestowed years
later after, having read one too many British murder mysteries, she threatened to buy a
cottage in the Cotswolds but didn't because she deemed it "too dear." (And we deemed
her in need of a doctor.)

I was getting ready to slice, place on a platter, and wrap in Saran wrap.

"He thought he'd surprise you. . . ."

Dame Joan stood straight up, turned an interesting shade of Oh, Shit, and rushed out of the room. Seconds later, she let out a scream that would've put Janet Leigh and Jamie Lee Curtis out of work.

When I reached her, she was standing just a few feet away from my dad. And my dad was standing on a ladder, lovingly applying a coat of primer to the one room my mom had been on him about all year.

The living room.

You know, the room with the *tree* in it: the focal point of the festivities. The room where the thirteen guests we had coming the next day would kiss and hug, squeal as they exchanged brightly wrapped packages, take pictures, and drink Asti Spumante and chablis, whiskey sours and Cutty and water. Until it was time for kickoff.

And then, much to my mom's dismay and despite her threats to burn dinner, pour the rest of the liquor down the drain, hide the ball, *blah, blah, blah*, we would commence our annual family touch football game, aka the Costantino Cup, in our spacious indoor arena, aka the living room. Which this year management had seen fit to paint. Could we be getting new uniforms, too?

But back to my dad.

After recovering from my mom's response to his thoughtful but poorly timed present, he painted the ceiling red and the walls white. It looked incredible. Even my mom, who retreated to the kitchen in an effort not to hyperventilate, said so.

But my dad wasn't sure. Being a really creative guy with a knack for color, composition, and making my mom crazy, something about the room didn't feel right to him. It felt off. Unfinished. Flat.

And so he flipped it.

In no time, the walls were red and the ceiling was white. The effect was stunning. And again, my mom, who was still rather stunned herself, said so.

But it was getting late. The walls needed to dry, the room needed to be put back together, and we had to do something to get the paint smell out of the house. Forty years later, we could have resorted to stinkbugs. But in 1973, our only option was to lower the heat, open the windows, and pray we didn't freeze to death during the night.

"Gene," my mom said, "I love it. I really do. But it's late. You're tired. I'm tired. Please finish."

And he wanted to finish. Really he did. But something was wrong. Something was lacking. The room needed to be livelier.

Richer.

Redder.

And so he covered the ceiling in it, too.

The result was jaw-dropping. *House Beautiful* beautiful. Like a room in a designer show house. Or a palace. Maybe even Buckingham Palace.

Dame Joan, who'd been through at least a carton of Benson & Hedges[186] as she cooked, set the dining room table, made ice, and alternately pleaded with God for

---

186. Her preferred poison pre–Misty Ultra Lights.

a) patience and b) the savvy to escape capture should she suddenly snap and kill my dad, was delighted.

My dad, on the other hand, *still* wasn't so sure. Because, well, while he liked the red, he couldn't decide: Maybe white was the way to go.

At midnight, when he knocked off to watch *A Christmas Carol*, the room was indeed white. The walls, the ceiling, the woodwork: all an interesting complement to my mom's increasingly glacial complexion.

But somewhere, between the time he fell asleep on the couch in his paint-covered clothes and the time my brothers and I came running downstairs to count the number of presents under the tree, divide by four, then pummel the sibling with the most packages, the whole room turned what we still fondly refer to as "I'm Gonna Puke Pink."

Which is almost as funny as "I Pink I'll Kill Him," the name my mom gave it when she raced in hollering, "No fighting on baby Jesus' birthday!" and discovered her favorite room the color of a sick salmon.

As if the nauseating hue weren't enough, there was the mess. The mess that my brothers and I ultimately broke out into two levels:

1. The mundane, run-of-the-mill, anybody-can-make-it mess: paint cans, pans, and drop cloths congealing in the corners. Flecks of paint on the furniture and smeared on the floor, and, of course, several long, decorative drips down the curtains. Pfff! Pedestrian!

2. The classic, Only Dad Could Wreak This Kind of Havoc without Help mess: This included the aforementioned run-of-the-mill stuff, plus such very special touches as dried paint stirrers poking out of Christmas stockings, baby Jesus' swaddling clothes bedecked with red polka dots (and now you know where Target and babyGap got the idea from), and many, *many* tree branches sporting white specks ("But Joan, it looks like snow!").

In case you're wondering, freezing our asses off hadn't helped the walls, which were still tacky, but it had done wonders for Dad's brushes, which had frozen solid while he slept and therefore had to be soaked. We didn't have a slop sink, so they went where they always went: in the kitchen sink. In turpentine. With my mom's tomato sauce warming up on the stove, six inches away.

Tomato sauce and turpentine: a bouquet surpassed only by that of—yes, we're back to the bastards—stinkbugs.

Oh, my scarred sinuses. Isn't it enough my beloved Garden State has to put up with people talking trash about the turnpike—the factories, the smell, and the huge white oil and gas tanks that look like oversize aspirin?

Honestly. New Jersey needs the stinkbug like Lady Gaga needs to come out of her shell.

And the worst part is, it's my fault.

Sure, I blame my mom. That's what daughters do.[187]

---

187. Can't parallel park, balance your checkbook, or attract a boyfriend who's never made the police blotter? Look no further than the woman who gave birth to you!

But the fact of the matter is, if my mom hadn't been at our house helping me manage, and I use the word loosely, the five hundred acres I'm now responsible for, none of this would have happened.

So, Jersey, my sincere apologies and this promise: to never again have my mom here during anything other than butterfly season.

Or at least check her bag before she leaves.

Chapter Thirty-five

THE GUILT IS IN THE MAIL(BOX)

In all the time we've lived on our farm, we've never had a mailbox. We've had a post office box. This meant that if we wanted to get our mail, which is typically comprised of catalogs, credit card solicitations, Costco coupon circulars, the *Ridgewood News*—which we stopped subscribing to ages ago but they still insist on sending us—bills, and, these days, "explanation of benefits" statements from our health insurance company telling us what tests, procedures, prescriptions, and specialists they're not covering, which isn't really a benefit unless you like knowing you're about to get calls from collection agencies, we had to go to the post office.

Of course, we're not the only people with a post office box. In fact, around here, having one is practically de rigueur: common as camo-print shorts and pajamas and

T-shirts that proudly proclaim, "Will Trade Husband for Tractor."

(And yes, I own each of the aforementioned articles of clothing. Tractor Supply is closer than Kohl's, not to mention Nordstrom, and sometimes I just don't feel like doing laundry. A girl can get tired of finding chicken feathers and animal fur floating around with her undies, you know?) A post office box is one of those things that identify folks in these parts as cattle farmers, horse people, and, most important, locals. From the minute we moved to northern Virginia, Hem insisted it was post office box over mailbox.

"It'll force me to get off the farm every day," he said. I agreed. God knows I'd have no trouble finding excuses to flee our beautiful but basically people-free slice of heaven. But my honey? He'd need a really compelling reason to leave the cows and the hens, the goats and the garden. Having to run to the post office to get his latest Netflix selections and the new issues of *The Progressive Farmer* and *Hobby Farms* and, of course, *Backyard Poultry* provided the perfect pretext.

These days, though, running to the post office provides nothing but additional angst.

With Hem sick, I'm the only driver, and having to go into town to get the mail is just one more thing on my never-ending list of things to do. There are days, sometimes two, three, even four days in a row, that I don't get there at all. Sure, I can ask a friend for help, and I frequently do. But more often than not, I forget. And then, usually when we're crossing the Key Bridge on our way back from the hospital and it's late and cold, and I'm tired and I already have a half dozen other stops I need to make before we can head home, I remember the mail. And how it's been fermenting in our box for about a week. And how it probably contains the bill for our health insurance premium, or worse, the DIRECTV bill, which, if I don't pay on time, they'll cut off, and then the next trip to the hospital will be for me.

And I start to cry.

So recently I began to contemplate getting a mailbox. I kept my musings to myself, because I felt guilty about racking up yet another failure in the farm-wife department.

See, right around the time my mom went home (and quite possibly infected the entire Garden State with stinkbugs), Hem went back into the hospital and I neglected to harvest the remainder of his vegetable garden. Tomatoes, cucumbers, carrots, peppers—much of it went to pot. I feel awful about wasting food. Children all over the world are starving. But the children in my house were starving, too. For comfort, clarification, quiet time with Mom. When I raced in at night from Georgetown, I didn't want to run back out again, even if it was just into the garden. I wanted to snuggle up with my guys, check on their homework, and ask how their day was. I wanted to sniff their sweet, sweaty heads, give them the supertight hugs Hem sent them, kiss their dirt-streaked cheeks, and throw them in the shower. I wanted to keep things as normal as possible. And I did. I just lost a lot of produce in the process.

And then, of course, there are the chickens. If you

know anything about me, you know there's no love lost between those birds and this blonde. But every day I made sure they got plenty of water and food. My downfall was in egg collection. I was simply too rushed to do it. I kept thinking, Sure, sure, I'll get to it later, and if by chance some hatch? What's the harm? What're a few more hens to hate me? Hell, they don't lay a lot of eggs anyway! Well, by the time I got around to it, the chickens had developed a yen for their yummy brown orbs, and that was it. Game over in the organic egg game. Not only would there be no new pullets, but I was back to buying eggs at Bloom.

So you can see why wanting a mailbox makes me feel so bad. Going to the post office is one of the last vestiges of the farm life Hemingway loves, and I can't manage to maintain it. But he loves me, too, and when I finally mustered the nerve to bring it up, he simply said, "Suz, how long have you been considering this?" Then he took me in the garage, where he had a brand-new black mailbox just waiting to be put to good use.

"I'm sorry I didn't think of this sooner," he said, handing it to me.

"And I'm so sorry you had to," I replied.

It'll probably go up this week, but when I can finally delete "take Hem for chemo" from my list, it's coming down. I may not be a great farm wife, but I know that as soon as he's feeling better, my husband will need to go back to making his daily mail run. And I'll need to make a trip to Tractor Supply. All their new stuff's in stock, and there's a "Keep Your John Deere Tractor Drivin' Hands off My Honey" tee I just have to have.

Chapter Thirty-six

NAILING THE NEW NORMAL

Cuyler peers at me from beneath his thick brown bangs, bites off a whopping hunk of his sausage McGriddle, and mumbles, "You think Dad will ever be normal again?"

"I hope so," I respond, surprised at both the directness of his question and my own stupidity for ordering a sausage-egg-and-bacon biscuit. Breakfasting at McDonald's is a new thing for us. I don't really enjoy it, but since it usually tricks Cuy into talking to me—for a whole lot less than the sixty-plus bucks I usually spend on video games to get the same result—we try to go once a week, whether my stomach can stand it or not.

"You *hope* so?" he snaps, flipping his bangs out of his eyes so fast his head bounces against the wall behind our booth. *Ooh.* Even with all his hair, that had to hurt.

"You okay?"

"Yes. No. I want Dad to be normal again." He rubs the back of his head, annoyed. "I want everything to be normal again."

"Me, too," I reply, refraining from offering to get him ice, lest he inadvertently injure another body part in response to such a "babyish" suggestion. "But you know, Cuy," I continue cautiously, "normal is a relative term."

A world-class, Bart Simpson–wicked smile spreads slowly across his handsome face. "You said we don't have any normal relatives."

"Nice one, wise guy. I've taught you well. But seriously. Normal can change. Remember when you had really long hair?" About a year ago, my kid was vying with Troy Polamalu[188] for who could stuff more hair into a football helmet. Troy's is curlier and longer, so he won. But Cuy came close.

"Having really long hair was normal for you, right?" He nods. "And then one day, you got tired of it and cut it. And then short hair became your new normal. See what I mean?"

He considers his greasy hash brown for a moment and then, much to my relief, returns it to its equally greasy wrapper. Whew. Pepcid Complete I keep in the car. Imodium A-D? Not so much.

"So if Dad can't farm," he asks quietly, "you think he'll just do work on his computer?"

"That's the plan. He'll do less physical stuff, and more management."

---

188. The Pittsburgh Steelers safety with the superlong, curly hair. Perhaps you've seen his Head & Shoulders commercials?

He picks at his place mat. I sip my coffee and watch his sweet freckled cheeks turn pink. I've learned to wait to acknowledge my younger son's crying, a true achievement for the woman whose picture graces the Urban Dictionary entries for both "oral diarrhea" and "emotional martyr."

"So that's the new normal then, right?" He rolls his wet eyes and shoots me the trademark 'tude it seems all fifth graders eventually master. "Cancer takes my outside dad, and makes him an inside dad. Just like that."

Just like that, I think to myself, and nod.

"Cancer sucks."

I take a breath so deep it feels like I've inhaled the whole left side of the breakfast menu. The glare of the fluorescent lights and the eau de deep fryer "fragrance" McDonald's is known for are making me nauseated. But what's worse is watching as a single, perfect tear slides down my son's left cheek, and then as he wipes it away with a swipe so fierce it actually leaves a scratch.

"You might want to think about cutting your nails," I offer, handing him a tissue.

Clutching the Kleenex, he considers his fingers for a moment. "Me, with short fingernails?"

"You, with short, clean fingernails," I suggest.

He cocks his head and gives me a small smile, the scratch filling and highlighting the red in his Marine Corps hoodie. "Could be a whole new normal for me."

"Could be, dude." I reach out and brush his bangs out of his eyes. "And who knows? Maybe you'll even get another haircut."

The words hang there as he ever so slowly places my

empty coffee cup, his drained container of chocolate milk, all our napkins, wrappers, and the receipt on the tray. "You know, Mom," he says, before turning to walk to the trash, "there're only so many new normals a person can take at one time."

Now it's my turn to try not to cry. He gives me an inch and I, typical mom, go for a mile. Of course he can have his hair. Hell, I don't care if it's butt-length by next football season. I don't care if he highlights it, perms it, sticks hot-pink extensions in it, or has it done up in dreads. If it makes him happy, I'm happy.

"I was just kidding, Cuy," I whisper, slipping into my coat as we walk out the door. "Long nails and long hair are the way to go." He looks at me like, "Yeah, right." "Really. I think you should give Troy Polamalu a run for his money."

"You do?"

I nod, and he hops in the car, happy.

He's right, of course. Too many new normals will make you nuts. Not to mention desperate for a good antacid, and a much better place to have breakfast.

Top 25 Things I've Learned
in the Past Few Months

· · · · · · · · · · · · · · · · · · · ·

25. A "Whipple" has nothing to do with toilet paper. Unless, of course, you have only Charmin
on hand to wipe your eyes, blow your nose,
and hyperventilate into when the surgeon
gives you the news that it's too late to perform
the one procedure—called a Whipple—that
could truly prolong your husband's life. I was
lucky. I had Kleenex and a shoulder to cry on.
My sister-in-law Nancy's. And she's down
one really cute Three Dots tee because of it.
Waterproof mascara, my ass.

24. When your kid says, "Mom, Dad's lying on
the bed funny," you're going to the hospital.

23. You can make a ninety-minute trip in forty-
five minutes. But only if you've had enough
chardonnay.

22. As soon as you notice a fence board's come
down, get up off your exhausted ass and fix
it. Otherwise you'll find both goats and a

steer out in the road, and a sheriff's deputy at your front door. Eventually the cow will make its way back, but the goats will require rescuing by a good-size Good Samaritan who'll *carry* them—one under each arm— back to the goat pen, then offer to put you and your husband on his church prayer list.

21. If you're on one prayer list, you're on them all. Now, that's a blessing.

20. The only thing tougher than being told your husband is sick is telling your kids. (And breaking the news to your folks is no fun either. Trust me, you will say, "I'm so sorry for having to tell you this," at least six times in the course of the conversation.)

19. If you can run out of pain medication over the weekend, you will. Check your supply on Thursday, Friday at the latest, and get refills. An empty bottle is never a good discovery, and making it on a Sunday, when you may or may not find an open pharmacy, just means you'd better have enough bourbon.

18. Four Tylenol PM will buy you six hours of peace. And one hour of vomiting.

17. Not even a top-of-the-line—I'm talking two hundred dollars from the Frontgate catalog—hammock can hold a heifer. And it wouldn't have had to if I'd fixed the damn fence board.

16. If you tell your kids they're babysitting Dad, and tell your husband he's babysitting the kids, you can go out with the girls and get back before anyone's the wiser. Of course, they'll all still be up, each having refused to be ordered to bed by the other. But hey, if you've had enough baked Brie and Carr's Table Water crackers, it won't matter.

15. People who tell me my husband looks good are lying. But it's only because they love me. And I love them, too.

14. A certain voice mail system can hold over one hundred messages. And you have to delete them one at a friggin' time. What, you people can't come up with a "clear all" option?

13. "It must be tough taking care of Dad twenty-four/seven" is code for, "I need you, too, Mom."

12. Waking up to the sound of footsteps on your roof does not mean you've slept straight

through to Christmas and Santa Claus is real, but rather that the nice people who've called once and stopped by twice offering to fix and clean your gutters before half fall down and the other half become full-fledged tree farms have decided to ignore your "Oh, you're so sweet but really, it's okay; I'll get to it" response. And that means that last night was the wrong night to decide putting on pajamas wasn't worth the effort.

11. Sometimes you've just got to nap.

10. I could never be an IV drug user. It took the nice visiting nurse more than sixty minutes to teach me how to "administer hydration" (which, you should know, is a euphemism for Suzy Gets to Stick Needles in Hemingway), and another ten to convince me to do it with my eyes open.

9. You can actually forget which friend has your child. That's why God invented cell phones.

8. Reading really funny books and laughing out loud in the chemotherapy infusion center is perfectly fine. If you're the patient. Caregivers should stick with Nicholas Sparks novels, reference manuals, and those twenty-six-page treatises that come with prescriptions.

7. Campbell's Chunky beef soup poured over rice can suffice as dinner. It's more gross than gourmet, but you have to like a meal that goes from can to consumption in under eight minutes. The kids love it, and it leaves me more time to drink. Which leads me to . . .

6. Wine poured over ice can suffice as dinner. And if you've ever spoken to me at six thirty in the evening, you know it has.

5. The medical personnel coming in and out of Hemingway's room saying cancer this and cancer that really are talking to us.

4. Being too tired to run out and close the chicken coop will result in unwanted guests. And wake-up calls from raccoons, not roosters.

3. The kindness in Fauquier County is immeasurable.

2. Nurses rock.

1. When all else fails, laugh.

Chapter Thirty-seven

LOOKING FOR DICK IN
ALL THE WRONG PLACES

This is what happens when the elderly attempt to text. Or at least it's what happened when I tried, in my advancing age, to read a text without my reading glasses, in the car, cruising 66 at sixty-five on the way home from the hospital on the Tuesday before spring break.

I heard the phone do its little chime jingle thing, and I scrambled to find it in my bag. My cavernous, bronze metallic Michael Kors bag in which I could carry at least six chickens and a rooster if, you know, they couldn't walk and wouldn't mind helping me find my cell from time to time.

Hem was next to me, in the passenger seat, napping, and I didn't want to wake him. He was worn out from the long trip, his treatment, and the news that his latest CT scan had revealed a spot on his spine that would require further investigation.[189] I was exhausted from the long trip, his treatment, and the news about the spot[190] that meant more trips and more treatments, not to mention more opportunity for him to continue torturing me with his plans, God bless him, to add turkeys to our flock of ill-humored hens.

"We'll just buy a few, Suz," he cajoled sleepily. "Three, maybe four, tops." He yawned, put his seat back, and pulled his Giants cap over his face. "We'll do the organic, free-range routine, and then, in the fall, we can butcher the biggest one and have it for Thanksgiving."

"*We* can butcher?" I repeated, turning so quickly to look at him the car lurched into the left lane, missing a bright green-and-white Lawn Doctor van by about a blade of grass. "*We?*"

We wouldn't be butchering anything. Rip Van Winkle here would be too tired, and I'd wind up standing in the coop alone, freezing, and wondering if it was possible to talk a turkey to death. 'Cause that I could do. But wield an ax? No way.

My stupid cell jingled again and I flipped it open. I know I should get one of those Bluetooth thingies with a headset, but the fact is they scare me. They look like bugs, for Pete's sake. Every time someone walks by wearing one, I have to stop myself from running up, throwing the person to the ground, and screaming, "Cicada!" and, "I'll save you!"

---

189. *Further investigation* is medical speak for tests, tests, lots of worry, and more tests.

190. In the world of cancer, everything's a spot. It's like we're all rugs someone's spilled wine on. "We've found a spot. It looks like cabernet, or maybe merlot, but we can't be sure. The radiologist will look at it, and probably lick it, and we'll get back to you."

In any case, I didn't recognize the number attached to the text, but I figured it had to be a friend. Why? Because, from what I could see—and I couldn't see much without holding the phone right in front of my face, which, as you can imagine, makes it pretty tough to drive and is probably the number one reason they came up with the whole Bluetooth thing in the first place[191]—the note mentioned Cuyler and the possibility of his dog-sitting one Saturday.

A Saturday at our house, with no racing back and forth to the hospital? Fine. Dandy. We'd do it. I replied, "He'd love to," while we got gas, and by the time we breezed through the McDonald's drive-through for a large vanilla milk shake for Mr. Van Winkle, who'd awakened a tad peckish and in need of sustenance to fuel the pastured turkey pitch he immediately recommenced, I'd forgotten the entire exchange.

Two nights later, the phone rang. Cuy answered upstairs, and I heard him say, "Um, sure, I'll do it for you. Uh-huh. Uh-huh." And then, "*What's* the dog's name?"

The dog? Oh, my God. It's about the dog I said he'd watch. Holy cow. I totally blanked on that text. I raced to the foot of the stairs to catch the rest of the conversation. "Yes, I'll be here. See you Saturday morning. Can't wait to meet him." And then Cuy hung up, walked to the top of the landing, and looked down at me.

"So, Mom, did you plan on telling me I'm dog-sitting *Dick*?"

At the word *dick*, Casey, who'd been busy chatting on

---

191. The number two reason being that, odd as the name Bluetooth is, it moves a lot more product than Looks Like a Water Bug Sucking on Your Ear ever would.

Facebook, let out a howl they could probably hear, well, at Dick's house. "Cuy," he teased, "you're dog-sitting a dog with a dick, or his name is Dick?"

Never one to miss the chance to chime in, Hemingway pulled his nose out of his book long enough to lob his two cents: "Don't be ridiculous, Case. He's not going to watch him with his dick. He's going to use his eyes, right, Cuy?"

Casey snorted and mumbled something about changing his status, and Cuy glared at me. "Mom, what were you thinking?"

"I was thinking you'd want to watch the dog. I didn't know his name was . . . questionable."

"It's not questionable. It's Dick!" He rolled his eyes and took the stairs, two at a time, toward me. "They'll drop him off Saturday morning, and pick him up next Friday."

A week? Dick the dog will be here a week?

More eye rolling, this time accompanied by head shaking and several sighs that spoke volumes, one of which was obviously entitled, Dude, My Mom's a Moron. "Mrs. Wyatt said she sent you a text. But you probably got it in the car, couldn't read it, and forgot about it. Right?"

I nodded. Well, at least now I knew whose dog I'd agreed to watch. And I did get the Friday part right.

"We've got to work on that, Mom."[192]

"Do you think Dick will bring his dick?" Casey bellowed from his bedroom to no one and everyone. He just

---

192. When I'm old and senile and stuck in a wheelchair, I want Cuy taking care of me. Why? Because when the time finally comes to push me off a cliff, I know he'll make sure there's a nice field of lush grass or a body of water to cushion the blow.

couldn't let it go. And why should he? His father's just as bad.

"Yeah, Sue," hollered Hem, "all the other dogs are bringing theirs!"

"Thanks, hon. Thanks, Case. Sam Kinison would be proud." And then I turned to Cuy. "Come on. Let's go talk Dick. I mean, about Dick."

Oh, dear God. This was not going to go well.

In the end, it was really no big deal having a fourth dog in the house. Particularly since I made them stay outside the house until Hemingway threatened to call the Humane Society. I don't get it. A little lightning never hurt anybody.

Anyway, in the end, it all worked out.

But first I had to survive the middle.

Now, just to fill in the blanks a bit, Cuy, who was supposed to be watching Dick, had really been doing, if you'll pardon the expression, dick. Why? Because the day after Dick arrived, Cuy took off with my girlfriend and her two sons for a stay on the Shenandoah River. He had his Xbox controller, half a dozen video games, a fishing pole, bait, a bathing suit, and enough junk food to positively impact Frito-Lay's second-quarter P&L.

And I had Dick duty.

To be fair, Dick, a small, wiry beagle pup with huge pet-me-feed-me-let–me-sleep-and-poop-wherever-I-please eyes, looked nothing like a penis. And yes, I expected him to. I mean, why name a dog Dick if he doesn't actually resemble one? There are other perfectly good names to pick from, like Max and Spot and Duke and Roscoe and even Richard, which, of course, leaves the doggy door wide-open for calling the dog Dick when he behaves like one.

In any case, little Dick got along just fine with our three perpetually dirty farm dogs. Grundy, our easygoing German shepherd/Lab mix; Tug, our purebred and impetuous golden retriever; and Pete, our squat, red-haired hound who can best be described as a cross between a bratwurst and a water buffalo.[193] They spent the majority of their time getting muddy, drinking from the cow manure–filled streams, and attempting to fornicate. With one another. Throw in some togas, a couple of kegs of beer, and a visit from the police, and it could have been pledge week here in the wilds.

Even the routine during Dick's visit was pretty much the same as it is every day. I got up in the pitch-black before dawn darkness and tripped over the dogs strewn like land mines all over the bedroom rug. Then, after doing my best not to break my neck on the stairs with all four "out of my way, I gotta pee!" pups accompanying me, I let them out, made coffee, and let them back in again. It was all working perfectly until the morning of Hem's bone scan.

You remember the further investigation of the "spot" I mentioned earlier? It was scheduled for the Thursday during spring break. Casey would be helping to replace fence

---

193. And about whom Casey's guitar teacher, Mike, once said, "Susan, I've roasted things smaller than that dog."

boards on the farm he worked at last summer. Cuyler would be away with his friends. And our band of merry mutts would be locked in the kitchen.

Or they would've been if they'd returned from relieving themselves.

At five thirty that morning, I let four dogs out. At five forty, I let two dogs in: the easygoing Grundy, and the desperate-to-eat Pete. I figured Tug and Dick would be right behind them.

I figured wrong. Very wrong.

By quarter to eight, there was still no sign of either dog. If they didn't materialize in fifteen minutes, we ran the risk of being late for Hem's ten-o'clock appointment. And that was a risk I wasn't willing to run.

My husband, on the other hand, was only too happy to postpone the entire endeavor.

"If they're not back, I'm not going." He was staring out the kitchen window, scanning the fields for his favorite four-legged, cold-nosed blonde and his petite playmate, and watching a dozen or so "girls" grazing in the pasture behind our house.

"You're kidding, right?" I stopped tossing his anxiety, nausea, and pain pills into my purse, but not before considering helping myself to a handful. "You're going to put off a test because our dogs are out digging up groundhogs or humping one another or whatever?"

"One of them's not our dog."

"But they're together. They'll be back. They always come back. No matter how hard I try to dissuade them." I smiled.

"What if they don't come back? Do you want to call the Wyatts and tell them we lost . . . lost . . . What's the dog's name?"

"Dick. Dick the dog." At the D-word, the two of us cracked up. I know it's juvenile, but I don't care. I'm just happy that in the midst of all the sickness and the stress and the tests and the fear, we still find stuff funny. "And in any case, we didn't lose him. He's just out for an extended stroll."

I decided to give the dogs ten more minutes and behave like it was business as usual. I gathered Hem's X-rays and the scan orders, stuck them in a folder, and put them in the car. I grabbed two bottles of water, his book, and his reading glasses, stuck them in his backpack, and put it in the car. Then, since it was a little chilly, I decided to start the car. I turned the ignition and the engine roared. Loud. Really loud. Way too loud for a Dodge Durango.

But not too loud for a Dodge Ram pickup truck. Specifically our Dodge Ram pickup truck, a glistening silver behemoth with more than a little resemblance to the Coors Light train, which suddenly streaked past me in my rearview mirror, Hemingway at the helm.

God forgive me, I thought, *but when I catch that man, cancer will be the least of his concerns.*

I jumped out of the car and ran after him. Sure, I could have taken the Durango, but I didn't think high-speed pursuit of a man wearing a fifty-microgram Fentanyl patch (which, in English, means Caution: Mega Amounts of Pain Medication. Can Cause Memory Loss, Drowsiness, and Stupid Decisions. DO NOT OPERATE HEAVY

MACHINERY. McCORKINDALE, THIS MEANS YOU!) was the best approach.

Luckily he didn't go far. He stopped right before he came to the cattle guard, which was good, because I was wearing high-heeled boots, and hopping that thing in those things would've meant the end of several big things I had planned. Like a career in the Ice Capades.[194] And kicking my dog-addicted husband's butt.

"What are you thinking?" I shouted, limping to the driver's-side door.

"I'm thinking you look like Big Bird when you run. Or maybe a floppy scarecrow." He glanced at my feet. "It could be the boots. You wouldn't wobble so much if you were wearing sneakers."

"I wouldn't wobble so much if I weren't running after you." My right foot was killing me. I pulled off my boot and shook out two pointy pieces of gravel.

"Guess I owe you a foot massage."

I didn't want a foot massage. And clearly he didn't want a bone scan if it meant leaving the farm before we found the dogs.

"We're not going to the hospital, are we?"

"I can't." He shrugged. "I'm sorry."

Hem and I agree on a million things. But I would never put a pet ahead of my health. In fact, if the situation were reversed and he was taking me for a bone scan, he wouldn't think twice about leaving Tug and Dick to fend for themselves. And if I protested and wanted to skip the

---

194. So don't relax just yet, Ms. Yamaguchi.

test and wait at home until the prodigal pups returned? He'd hogtie and superglue me to the roof of the car. The point is, there'd be no saying no.

"You're making me nuts; you know that?"

"What can they tell me, Suz? That I have more cancer? Different cancer? Cancer they can only treat with . . ."

"Bourbon?"

He laughed. "At least then I'd get to have some."

"I'll tell you what. When we find the dogs, I'll make you a big old Tennessee Snow Cone to celebrate."

"With lots of Jack Daniel's?"

"And lots of crushed ice."

"But more Jack Daniel's, right?" He gave me a wry smile. "It's not like it's going to give me cancer."

You gotta love the McLogic.

So we took the pickup and went looking for Tug and Dick, or as I like to call them, Tick. And no, Hem didn't drive. We found Tug easily enough; he was sitting in the passenger seat of the Durango when I went to turn it off, panting and obviously expecting to take a head-out-the-window, drool-blowing-in-the-breeze ride. I asked him where he'd been and where Dick was, but you know dogs; the only one they ever let speak is Lassie.[195] Instead he barked and offered me a muddy paw, but no leads on his little pal.

"Okay, you're rescheduled for next Tuesday." I flipped my cell phone closed and stepped out onto the porch. Hem

---

195. Must be some sort of union thing.

was sitting in one of our two bird-poop-pocked rocking chairs, bundled up against the breeze in his huge blue Carhartt jacket. It didn't used to be huge. It used to fit. In fact, it used to be snug. Now he and Tug could wear it, and have room for portly Pete, too.

"We should call the Wyatts," he said, rocking back and forth, one foot rubbing Tug's fluffy exposed belly. The damn hound looked like he was in heaven.

"Not a chance, pal. That dog'll be back." I plopped into the other bird-poop-pocked rocker and watched a couple of mama cows and their calves playing in, doing their business in, and drinking from the stream[196] around the springhouse. The springhouse is a beautiful stone structure literally built over a spring. A hundred years ago, people sat inside it to escape the heat. These days, six-foot black snakes use it for the same purpose, which is good because it limits the number we find cooling themselves in our cellar.

"Face it, Suz. We've looked everywhere. The barn, the equipment shed, the workshop, the old cattle sheds, the hog pen, the chicken coop, the woods . . ."

"I know, I know. I was there, remember?" I love my husband, but he's such an Aquarian. Ask him the time, and he'll tell you how to make the watch. "I think we're looking in the wrong places. He's someplace . . . else. Someplace . . . Dickish."

"You took one of my pain pills, didn't you?"

"Very funny."

"An Ativan, then."

---

196. And now you know why Black Angus beef tastes best!

"I have not set foot near the McPharmacy," I replied, walking toward the railing. "But I think the McLiquor cabinet is calling my name. Correction: your name."

"You're jumping the gun. No Dick, no Jack."

"Well, unless that right there," I said, pointing toward the springhouse, "is a very premature calf, a floppy-eared fox, or a really tiny reindeer, I'd say it's happy hour, handsome."

Sure enough, Dick was peering out at us from the snakes' favorite vacation spot. Hem shot me a look. "We were both too chicken to check it."

"That's 'cause we've seen what snakes can do to chickens."

"Dick! Here, Dickie boy!" Hem clapped his hands and shouted, and Tug raced out to meet our missing house-guest. Even from the porch it was evident Dick was caked in mud and manure and God knows what else (and I thank You, God, for keeping that information to Yourself). "Too bad Cuy's not home," Hem added. "We could have him give Dick a bath."

"Oh, yeah. I forgot," I said, hooking our frenetic, foul-smelling charge to a leash as Tug licked him. "Cuy sent me a text before. Guys! Easy! My arm needs to stay in its socket!" Tug was doing his nip-and-run routine, and Dick was trying to take off after him, and he just about took my arm off in the process. "Gentlemen, sit!" Miraculously, they both sat. And then I saw something stuck right above Dick's right eye, like a fake eyelash askew after one too many appletinis and a run-in with a pink feather boa.[197]

---

197. Not that I have firsthand experience with that sort of thing, of course.

"And he said?"

"Who?"

"Cuyler. Our son. He sent you a text?"

"Oh. Yeah. Something about coming home a day earlier. Or maybe staying a day longer." I bent over to inspect the thing on Dick's head and got a whiff of manure and pond scum so piercing I was sure I'd lose the Oreos I sneaked for lunch. "I'm not sure. I—"

"Couldn't see it." He took a deep breath. "Please tell me you didn't respond."

"I think I just said, 'sure.' And I think, believe it or not, that this," I said, plucking what was definitely not a fake eyelash off Dick's forehead and holding it up for Hem's inspection, "is a piece of snakeskin."

"You know what I think?" He looked at the snakeskin, and then at me, and finally at the yipping, yapping, happy-as-a-pup-who-spent-the-day-in-shit Dick.

I shook my head.

"I think you really need to start using your reading glasses."

Chapter Thirty-eight

NEEDY AND NOT PROUD OF IT

I'm sitting at my desk putting the finishing touches on a piece I've killed myself on. It's taken weeks of writing and rewriting, massaging, editing, and walking away in utter frustration to achieve what my dear friend Trish calls "reads like you just let it rip, Sue" status. I review it again, add a comma, delete it, and know in my gut I've nailed it.

At least, I think I know.

The piece is tight. It's funny. It's poignant. It is quite possibly—dare I say it?—perfect. But what if it's not? I mean, why should it be? It's me we're talking about here. Not Nora Ephron.

I need to know, and I need to know now. And for that I need my number one editor, critic, taskmaster, and fan, the guy who gave me the guts to start writing in the first place.[198] I need my sounding board and soul mate, aka Hemingway, to give me his seal of approval. Or at least a round of edits I'll argue but ultimately acquiesce to because, frankly? The man's usually on the money.

I snatch the pages from the printer, grab a red pen I pray he won't need, and head into the den. He's stretched out on the couch. Our cat Coca is on his chest. Tug, our dim-witted, hyper, and perpetually burr-covered but beautiful golden retriever, is quite literally blanketing his feet. And our two laid-back mutts, Grundy the Throw Rug and What Have You Got to Eat? Pete, are sprawled on the floor, snoring.

So, by the way, is Hem.

He's sweating, too, and the sharp, sickly sweet scent stops me cold. His salt-and-pepper curls cling to his forehead. Every few seconds his shoulders twitch, and the fingers of his left hand pop open, wide, like he's going to wave or pet one of his beloved beasts. Then they snap back, fast, into a fist. If I didn't know better, I'd swear he was having a nightmare.

But I do know better, and he isn't having a nightmare. He's living one. The unyielding fatigue, twitching, and sweating are just some of the side effects of the chemotherapy he endures once a week. Today is two days since his last treatment and visit with the oncologist, a superbright guy who walked in carrying Hem's latest labs and

198. A million years ago, Hem encouraged me to enter an essay contest. For some reason, he was positive I'd win. As I had all the self-confidence of table salt, I was positive he was crazy. But, just to shut him up, I entered. I wound up winning, and Hem wound up finding out how much he and Dr. Frankenstein have in common.

announced wryly, "You're doing really well with all this poison we're putting in your body!"

I, on the other hand, am not doing so well.

Before you jump to conclusions, let me clarify. I thank God every day for the fact that the poison is working. Hemingway's tumor marker is down, and his weight is up. His color is good. His pain is gone.

But so, to a degree, is he.

My whip-smart, well-read, screamingly funny, no longer big, but still, God bless him, brave, blue-eyed former marine is simply not the same. And it's more than the twenty-four/seven, beat-to-the-bone exhaustion that leaves him barely able to get from bed to his butter-soft leather sofa. It's the "brain fog" that's come with the chemo. We were warned about nausea and possible hair loss, neither of which he's experienced. But disorientation, confusion, and memory loss?

We'd swap it for bald and barfing in a heartbeat.

Thanks to the poison that's prolonging his life, the man I met and fell madly in love with thirty long years ago is gone. Sure, I love the new guy. But I miss the old one, badly.

I stand there clutching my stupid chapter and my stupid pen and I feel, well, stupid. Even if he were awake he'd say what he's said a dozen times since he got sick. "You know it's good, Sue. You don't need me to tell you."

Fair enough. I don't need him to tell me. But I want him to tell me. If something I've written works or if it needs work. If the paint color I'm considering for the hall is elegant or borderline bordello. If the motion-sensor lights I got for the equipment shed, the repairs I approved on the skid loader, or the permission I gave a friend of a friend to nurse a hundred mistreated polo ponies back to health on our pastures is fine, or just further proof of the fact that I'll never learn how to handle this place.

He stirs for a second and looks at me. "You okay?" he asks.

"Just checking on you," I lie, ashamed of myself. How did I get to be one of those women who's pushing fifty and still needs a pat on the head?

"I'm good." He nods. "Gonna sleep a little more."

I do my best to adjust his blanket without disturbing the cat, and kiss him on the forehead, and it dawns on me: The only thing good about cancer is that it's not a car crash or a coronary or some other instantaneous death deal, like having your parachute not deploy at thirty thousand feet or your bungee cord go kaput over a rock quarry. Cancer, at least, gives you time. Time to say, *I love you*, and, *Goodbye, this sucks*, and *I can so take you in* Seinfeld *Scene It*.

It also gives you time to grow up and get your big-girl pants on. To figure out how you're going to work without a net. And without your best friend wielding a red pen.

Chapter Thirty-nine

PUZZLED BY KUDZU? ME, TOO.

"*M*om!" I was at my computer penning hate mail to our health insurance company[199] when I heard Cuyler and his best friend, Jeff,[200] come racing into the kitchen. "Hey, Mom!" Cuy shouted again as I caught the familiar sounds of the refrigerator door opening, slamming shut, and the *pop! hiss!* of two cans of Coke being readied for rapid consumption. "Did you know we have kudzu on the farm?"

"What do you mean, on the farm?" I shouted back. "It's in the den."

---

199. Why? For once again approving a particularly pricey procedure, then backtracking, playing the "it's experimental" card, and finally refusing to cover it. The bill we got is bullshit. So that's what I'm paying it with. You know, sometimes living here really comes in handy.

200. Jeff, his parents, and his *five* younger siblings moved into our largest tenant house when it became available. And I don't think the ignition was off in their Suburban before he and Cuy were best friends.

In a flash, both boys were standing in my doorway. They were dirty, sweaty, and sucking down their sodas almost as fast as Jon Gosselin replaced Kate, and looking at me like I'd completely lost what was left of my mind.

"We have kudzu in the *den*?" Cuy asked, incredulously.

"Yeah. Dad has a book of them. Kudzu puzzles. He has crossword puzzles, too. You guys want them?" I stood up and started down the hall. "Come on. I'll show you."

"Mom, that's sudoku." He made a circular motion by his temple with his index finger, and mouthed the word *blond* to his buddy. "Kudzu is a vine."

I whirled around. "I saw that, dude." Both boys looked at the floor. Holy cow, they even had dirt on their eyelids.

"They call it 'the Vine That Ate the South,'" Jeff ventured.

"When you say *vine*," I asked, "do you mean the Tarzan-swinging-from-the-trees-type vine, or the vinca-we've-got-in-the-window-boxes-type vine?"

"That depends," my son replied. "Who's Tarzan?"

Wisely, I didn't try to explain Tarzan and they didn't try to show me how to do sudoku, an unfortunate pastime that involves math and, to my way of non-number-loving thinking, looks about as much fun as having one's large intestine removed laparoscopically and being forced to wear it like a feather boa.

Instead we hit the Internet and searched for "kudzu."

The images of the broad-leafed plant, oftentimes resplendent with blue or purple blooms, were both mesmerizing and horrifying, not to mention startlingly reminiscent of the sets in *Edward Scissorhands*. Picture after picture showed it blanketing abandoned barns and cars, fallen trees and untended pastures all over the South, and site after site described its startling and unstoppable summer growth rate of a foot a day.

A foot a day? And I thought nothing could spring up faster than Casey. If it eats as much as he does, we are so screwed.

I logged off and looked at my younger son and his pal, both of whom were busy adding a lovely orange coating of cheese puffs to their filthy fingers. "Where exactly did you two see this stuff?"

"In the woods, on the old wagon."

"No, it's an old chicken coop!"

"Nuh-uh. Wagon!"

"Guys, guys." I put my hands up in the universal signal for "stop, or I'll cut off the snack foods." "Wagon, coop, who cares? Take me there."

And so they did.

Sure enough, there was an ancient wheeled whatever barely visible beneath some kind of freaky foliage. Was it regular old ivy? Was it poison ivy? Or was it kudzu? And if it was kudzu, would it eventually be known as the Vine That Ate Nate's Place? I didn't know, and I definitely didn't want the kids to get any closer. What if the ghastly thing suddenly did its foot-a-day growth dance and devoured both boys right before my eyes?

No, no, better to stand back and plot its destruction, or at least postponement. You can't kill kudzu, but you can maim it.

I figured we'd start by getting the goats to graze on it.

Then we'd bring in the cows. When they'd chowed it down to nothing but nubs, we'd finish by letting the hens have at it. That would bring it to the brink of the grave.

And if it didn't, we'd resort to sudoku. One look at that stuff and the darn thing would wish it were dead.

Chapter Forty

ONE CHOLECYSTECTOMY, THREE ERCPS,
AND SIX DEAD CHICKENS LATER . . .

We're here, we're hanging tough, and we've learned a few things.

Nothing earth-shattering. Mostly stuff like "shit happens," and "a friend with weed is a friend indeed."[201] To celebrate the fact that we've made it this far with our funny bones intact, I thought I'd share some of what I've picked up. And sure, I hope you laugh. But I really hope you and those you love never need to know any of this nonsense.

The instant the C-word is spoken . . .

You're promoted to caregiver. There's no raise, no one absorbs your old responsibilities, and you get to do your

---

201. For medicinal purposes, of course.

spouse's shit, too. To quote Sid in the original *Toy Story*, "Woo-hoo! Double prizes!" In addition, the job comes without so much as a how-to pamphlet or a packet of NoDoz. To survive your new role as Superspouse, remember two things: One, it's not a sprint; it's a marathon. And two, even caregivers need caregivers.[202]

Go home and have sex. I know, you just got the worst news of your life and I'm telling you to go home and get it on. Crazy as that sounds, I wish someone had told us. Things can go from bad to worse fast, and they did in Hem's case. If we'd known on that long-ago Sunday how our lives would be turned upside down on Monday, there'd have been a whole lot more adult fun on the farm. "Think the kids are cool with pizza and M&M's for dinner? Me, too. You get the masks. I'll rustle up some rope. Meet you in the back of the barn in ten!"

You have to learn a whole new language. And I'm not talking farm speak; that I'm still struggling with. I'm talking medical speak, and I don't care how much *ER* or *Grey's Anatomy* you've watched; you'll still wonder what the hell they're saying. For example, while taking Hemingway's medical history for the first of his three ERCPs,[203] the nurse asked me who performed his chole-

---

202. And those bearing wine are particularly welcome.

203. Endoscopic Retrograde Cholangiopancreatography. Go ahead, say *that* three times fast. The procedure uses X-rays and an endoscope to see inside the digestive system and diagnose all sorts of un-fun stuff like gallstones, inflammation, and tumors in the liver, gallbladder, bile ducts, and pancreas.

cystectomy. Who indeed! I thought. That's the last time
I look the other way when he and his buddies hit Hooters! She meant gallbladder surgery, and no, he's still not
going.

Get your ducks, chickens, and goats in a row. And that
means, if you haven't already done so, do your wills,
powers of attorney, and advance directives. It's not
pleasant, but that's why God invented wine.

Check your checking account. If your joint account hasn't
been set up "with survivorship," fix it. Otherwise, if
something happens to the main account holder—and the
main account holder is the patient—the bank will freeze
your funds. And paying for that case of La Crema—not
to mention your health insurance premium—could pose
a problem.

Pack an overnight bag and put it in the car. Having your
own toiletries, cosmetics, and clothes on hand makes
surprise overnight stays at your sister-in-law's easier,
and it'll stop you from stealing her stuff. "About the
sexy blue tee and the Chanel blush. You didn't want
those back, did you? I mean, they're covered in Suzy
cooties now. . . ."

**Your ten-year-old will want a cap that says "Cancer
Sucks."** You'll say, "No, *sucks* is not a nice word." He'll
say, "*My dad has cancer* are four even worse words."
You will buy him the cap. You will like the cap. In fact,

you will like the cap so much, you'll get a second one and announce, "Kids, it's time for your Christmas picture!"

The dogs will get in on the "get well" gift act. Because to dogs, nothing says "cut the cancer crap" like the bottom half of a dead chicken dropped at the front door. Please note: It's best to acknowledge your pups' presents with a belly rub and the occasional Beggin' Strip. Otherwise they feel their gift has gone unappreciated, and before long, you're down six of your best layers.

It no longer matters whether the Giants win or lose. Just that my kids get to watch the game with their dad. Okay, it would be nice if the nitwits would win. . . .

Dinner in the hospital becomes the height of romance. So what if it's mushy mystery chicken for him and a questionable Caesar salad for you. It's nothing short of the happiest, most romantic meal in the world. Particularly when he hasn't eaten one in eight weeks.

The little boy wearing the "Cancer Sucks" cap will want a cell phone. Why? Because the cell phone is the new security blanket. Necessary when Dad's in the hospital. The perfect paperweight when he's home.

You enter the wonderful world of prescription narcotics. Hem's stash of OxyContin has a street value of nine thousand dollars. Hmmm. Pain-free honey, or Manoloheeled mommy? Of course I'm kidding. I can buy twice as many Kate Spades with that kind of cash.

You develop a new appreciation for those annoying feel-good/cope quotes girlfriends forward one another more frequently than Kohl's sale coupons. Not all of them, of course. Just this one: "Yesterday is history, tomorrow a mystery. Today is a gift. That's why it's called the present."

Chapter Forty-one

I'M DREAMING OF A WHITE
CHRISTMAS TREE. NOT.

Cancer or not, Christmas falls on Mom. So this season, I did what I could to save what little is left of my sanity and simplify things.

For starters, I did a lot less decorating. The kids and I plugged in the porch lights[204] and promptly blew a fuse. This meant someone had to go to the basement in the pitch dark, hope nothing long, black, and slithery was hosting a holiday party with its long, black slithery pals 'round the hot-water heater, and fumble with the fuse box until she heard the telltale sounds of a video game being played above her head. But only because her boys were too busy to stop and tell her the power was back.

Continuing with my less-is-more mantra, I left the HO

---

204. Woo-hoo, go, white! Hey, you snooze, you lose, farm boy.

HO HO doormat, and the fake reindeer, metal Santa, and SANTA, PLEASE STOP HERE! sign I usually place near the steps in storage, and slapped a plain pine wreath on the front door. *Last year's* pine wreath, which for some reason didn't make it to the burn pile and instead got put away with the rest of the holiday decorations and is now brown, odorless, and devoid of any additional adornment save the dead stinkbugs nestled among its needles.

At least, I thought they were dead. The aroma coming from the runner in the hall suggests otherwise.

Undaunted by my decorative disasters, and hoping, quite frankly, that Duke and Willie would finish the wreath off (and why not? They eat everything else), I sallied forth with two traditionally foolproof moves.

First I copped out on making Christmas dinner and ordered Chinese.[205] Again. Lest you be appalled, please know my family prefers this to anything I could make myself. It's tasty, fun, and the fortune cookies typically, and accurately, predict no one will wind up in the hospital.

Second, I did a good chunk of my shopping in the *très* lovely and legendary town of Middleburg. Maybe you've heard of it? No? Well, hit Google when you've got a minute, because my farm management skills (not to mention my math and culinary talents) are rivaled only by what I didn't retain in history.

Sure, there are those who can speak to Middleburg's hallowed role in the development of our country. And

---

205. Up until the tomato-sauce/turpentine debacle of 1973, I was a dyed-in-the-wool "Birth of the Lord Means Lasagna!" Jersey girl. After that it was all downhill and to the left, to Chan's Chinese restaurant.

then there are others who, at the mere mention of the place, would see stars—celebrities, socialites, tycoons, and media types—and recount incredible, true tales of the famous personalities who've sought respite, rejuvenation, and damn fine foxhunting there. Indeed, Middleburg is the equestrian mecca of the country, and there are experts who can talk at length about that, too.

But I, alas, am none of those kinds of people.

I confess. I'm a lightweight. But at least I know my limitations: fifteen thousand on Visa, ten thousand on Master-Card. Of course, there are no restrictions on my AmEx, but that's just because Hemingway cut up my card. No, all that history about the heart of horse country is better imparted by those much more knowledgeable than *moi*.

This girl's shtick is shopping.

And good shopping, close to home,[206] really helps keep things simple.

I have friends who swear by Fair Oaks, and still others who are willing to endure all kinds of traffic to get to Tysons. But I already spend too much time on Route 66. I'd rather spend some in Tully Rector trying on coats and cocktail dresses I don't need but can't pass up 'cause they're so darn cute. And unique. And often on sale. Which makes my "Something for you, something for me" gift-buying system almost a hundred percent justifiable. Almost.

I have pals who'll shop only in New York and buddies who won't buy unless they're abroad. I even have a group

---

206. Middleburg is ten tiny minutes from my front door.

of girlfriends who insist that Los Angeles is the height of fashion.[207] And when they all give and get the same snake-skin belts from J.Crew, the same black sweaters from Banana Republic, and the same oversize totes from Ann Taylor, I shake my head and think, Thank God for Lou Lou. And Lou Lou Too. Jewelry, belts, boots, bags, pants, tops, sunglasses—you name it, they've got it, and I'm giving it.

Christmas list done and dinner ordered, I was on a hot streak of simplification and totally ahead of schedule. Now all I needed was a tree to magically alight in the living room. Since I couldn't count on Harry Potter to help, I went with the next-best thing: the Internet.

Even for me, a counterfeit farm girl, it's painful to confess that I broke down and ordered a fake tree. I mean, I live in the country. We could have gone to a tree farm and cut one down ourselves. Or maybe if I'd taken a good look around the property, I'd have found a spruce or Scotch pine out there somewhere. But I didn't have the energy or the time and, to be honest? My heart wasn't in it.

And so I searched the World Wide Web and discovered a world of fake tree options. I had no idea they came in any color but green. But there they were in red and blue and, be still my childish heart, pink.

Bright, pure, baby-girl-bedroom pink.

I clicked, and a sparkling six-footer popped into my shopping cart. A shiver of delight ran down my spine. And I got an idea. A great idea. I'd give the boys a totally pink

---

207. I keep telling them, "Lunch *at* the Ivy, not *on* it."

Christmas! I'd get a complementary-colored tree skirt, gift wrap, paper goods, even pink stockings! I could see them now, stuffed with iTunes gift cards, *Tropic Thunder* and *The Simpsons Movie* DVDs, and the kids' favorite kinds of candy. But what if I couldn't find pink Christmas stockings? What if Wal-Mart or the dollar store didn't have them?

No problem, I heard myself say, *I'll just be like other mothers and make them!*

The sound of my Suzy Soprano honk snapped me back to my senses. What the hell was I thinking? I don't do crafts. And the McMen don't do pink Christmas trees.

A white one, on the other hand, just might work.

Particularly if it was a spectacular, six-foot-tall, prelit-with-zillions-of-twinkling-white-lights wonder that would've made Peter Allen proud. I typed in my credit card number and mailing address, hit "purchase," and said a prayer.

Why God chose that particular moment to go deaf, I don't know. But it's on my agenda for that "come to Jesus" meeting I mentioned earlier.

The tree was barely out of the box, an undertaking that alone took more than thirty minutes, when Casey said, "Mom, that's so not us." He was right, of course, as my older son frequently is, so I repacked the cheesy cheap mess,[208] hauled it to the post office, and forked over an eyetooth in order to have it back to the manufacturer by Christmas Eve.[209]

---

208. In a lot less than thirty minutes, I assure you.

209. Why the rush? Because otherwise they'd think we actually used the ugly thing and could refuse to refund our funds.

Not exactly the simple, low-stress, time-saving solution I was looking for.

I left the post office and went, in the first snowstorm of the season,[210] to buy a real tree from the Boy Scouts. Or, I should say, their parents. The boys were at a party. Their parents were at the tree sale, doing the boys' dirty work and freezing their buns off. Based on this description, both my sons would make great Scouts.

Casey and Cuyler did, however, help me get the tree up and decorated with garland made from the hospital bands Hem's been collecting since he got sick. You may think that's sick, but we think it's funny.

Almost as funny as my trying to simplify things.

---

210. Because even Mother Nature had to piss on my simplification plans.

Suzy's "Things to Be Thankful For" This Christmas

. . . .

The fact that my honey's weight is up, and his tumor marker is down. God willing, he'll soon be fat and cancer-free. You know, like he used to be.

The goats' habit of getting into the garbage. It's disgusting, but it saves me a trip to the dump.

"You have no new messages." Music to my voice-mail-overloaded ears.

Doctors, physician's assistants, and nurses who answer my questions and calm my fears day and night, on weekends and on holidays. And who still hug me when they see me.

Days I have to bathe Tug only twice.

An empty e-mail in-box.

Chardonnay via IV drip. (Okay, I'm kidding. But a girl can dream, can't she?)

Duct tape. Sort of a stunt husband. Just don't try to spoon with it.

My new automatic poultry feeder. Now if I could just get it to gather eggs . . .

Online shopping. When the going gets tough, the tough click "add to shopping cart." (White faux Christmas trees not included.)

Good friends and wonderful family who listen, do, support, and send care packages bursting with goodies for Hem, the boys, even the dogs. And occasionally vino for Suz-o.

My Turbo Power 4400 Titanium hair dryer. I still stink at straightening my hair with it, but dinner defrosts lickety-split no matter how late I get in from the hospital. Plus I can unfreeze pipes, blow the wolf spiders making themselves comfy in my kitchen into the stratosphere, and dry Tug almost all at the same time. And on that note . . .

My GHD (Good Hair Day) flatiron. My weekly trips to the salon are a thing of the past, but thanks to my flatiron, a whole lot of Garnier Fructis Sleek & Shine, and several private lessons from my favorite hairstylist and friend Ashley, I can actually tame the hay bale that results from my attempts to use a round brush and a blow-dryer.

Fentanyl patches, OxyContin, and oxycodone. And no, we're not drug addicts. We're pain abhorrers.

The teachers and counselors who care so much for Case and Cuy.

My state-of-the-art dog deskunking kit. Liquid soap, baking soda, hydrogen peroxide, three personalized pet towels, and a pair of rubber gloves all wrapped up in a Rubbermaid tub roomy enough for a Barcalounger and a big-screen TV. Thanks, Santa! Dog grooming gift certificates are *so* impersonal.

My therapists. (Yeah, plural. Because I'm twice as nuts as you thought I was.)

Casey and Cuyler. Cuyler and Casey. Sure, they've matured lots since their dad got sick. But they still brawl over who gets top billing.

Hem.

Chapter Forty-two

IS THAT A POINSETTIA IN YOUR POCKET,
OR ARE YOU JUST GLAD TO SEE ME?

*Y*ou know the snowstorm that hit the day I bought our Christmas tree from the Boy Scouts or, more accurately, their poor, frostbitten parents? It was just the overture, the prelude, the preamble to what we in the forest primeval shall forever refer to as Snowmageddon or, more accurately, the Time We Forced Short, Fat Pete to Do His Business in the Cat's Litter Box. It was either that or watch him suffocate in the snow, because there was no way Tug and Grundy were letting him use their—I mean *the*—living room rug.

All told, we got forty-five inches of the white stuff, and now that it's melting and becoming mud, and Tug, our harebrained golden, is anything but, I almost miss it.

Of course, neither Hemingway nor I miss having Casey and Cuyler home for thirteen straight school days. That's right; thirteen *school* days. Counting weekends that's nineteen surprise days of drudging, round-the-clock, full-time, crazy-making family time.[211]

At first, both boys were only too happy with the sudden instructional interlude and found lots of fun ways to enjoy themselves. And then they got bored and things really got recreational. Right this second there isn't a Coca-Cola left in the house. (And they put a darn good dent in the Jack Daniel's, too.)

Of course, the back-to-back (-to-back) snowstorms didn't just leave us with more reasons to toss the living room rug (as well as the brittle, brown, stinkbug-ridden pine wreath not even Duke and Willie would eat) on the burn pile. No, no. We were also awarded a very nice dusting of dead chickens, several rodents seeking respite and, quite possibly, squatters' rights in our utensil drawer, and a clutch of cows in the backyard.

Yes, for the first time in all the time we've lived here, the cattle guard behind our house froze solid. For the uninitiated, a cattle guard is a series of parallel metal bars installed in a roadway over a ditch. The bars are wide enough so a cow's hooves and legs will fall through, but cars can drive over safely. Lest you think we're being cruel, please know that most animals are smart enough to recognize the potential hazard and stay away. In this instance, we got so much snow that it filled the ditch, covered the metal bars, and froze. And then, as I watched from the kitchen window, a dozen or so mama cows, baby cows, and at least one bull

---

211. I had a maternity leave that didn't last that long. I'm telling you, self-employment has so many perks.

sort of skated right across it.[212] They strolled all around our backyard, peeked inside our pickup truck, and then came right up to the door of the mud porch. I didn't have range cubes handy, but they ate the dogs' food just fine.

Short of the fact that all four of us spent about forty-five minutes in twelve-degree weather cajoling the cattle back into the pasture and then locking them in by parking the pickup squarely between the fence posts and over the frozen cattle guard, we really got off easy. We never lost power, ran out of pain medication, or had to make a hospital run, which, frankly, we couldn't have, as the Virginia Department of Transportation had our road closed in both directions for two days. In fact, probably the worst thing that happened was that our satellite went down. This was bad because we had no Internet service, no access to e-mail, and we missed the start of the Olympics and all the cool stuff Shaun White was doing. But it was good because, without Internet service and access to my e-mail, I actually got some work done. And it was great because when we finally reconnected with the world and I could watch all the Shaun White I wanted, I did it my way—in thirty-second snippets on YouTube.

In fact, there were a couple of good things that came out of having a dead satellite dish. For one, we escaped the ceaseless, stultifying weather reports:

212. The smallest of the calves did it like such a pro I christened her Kristi Ya-MOO-guchi, and for a split second even thought she and I should team up for the Ice Capades. But that was before my friend Trish told me it folded. I believe her exact words were, "Yo, country mouse, get your head out of the hay!" Oh, well. Maybe Ms. Ya-MOO-guchi and I have a shot at Disney On Ice. Or maybe I should just try to get out more.

"Here in Fairfax, we've got a lot of snow. And I mean *a lot* of snow. What about by you, Bob?"

"Here in Winchester, too, Dan. And it's so white! I've never seen snow so white! And fluffy! Have you ever seen snow this fluffy?"

"No, Bob, I can't say I have. Snow that's white *and* fluffy; it's truly incredible. To address the issue in such tedious, plodding detail as to make viewers want to throw themselves in front of a train, a move they'll have to wait on, as there's currently no service due to, you guessed it, snow, we turn now to meteorologist Dr. Mark Makesumthinofnuthin. Dr. M., so good of you to join us!"

We also managed to miss the inane "What's Topper's Real Name?" guessing game our local news[213] had going.

No offense, folks. I don't know what Topper's real name is, and, while he seems like a very nice man, I don't care. I only know I'm stuck in the house with a sick husband, two squabbling sons, two dogs that haven't relieved themselves outside in almost a week, a third that will go only in the cat's box (a development that's got the cat in shock and shitting on the couch), a dwindling supply of club soda and paper towels (gee, wonder why), one last, lonely bottle of chardonnay, a container of wood alcohol that's starting to look real good, and the growing possibility that my picture will wind up in the post office if you don't put *The Big Bang Theory* back on.

By the time school recommenced, the kids had eaten

---

213. WUSA Channel 9 is our local news station, and Topper Shutt is the chief meteorologist. He's very charming and usually, unfortunately when it comes to snow, accurate. Oh, and his real name is Charles.

through all the junk food, the sugarcoated cereals, the non-sugarcoated cereals that they coated in sugar, the ice cream, the frozen cookie dough, two packages of Swedish Fish they found behind the couch, and two formerly fun-size but now decomposing bags of M&M's they found between the cushions and had to fight fat Pete for. They were slathering Carr's Table Water Crackers and Triscuits in Hershey's Syrup so as not to go into withdrawal when we got the call that both school and our road were finally open.

Whew.

They left for class, and we went for chemotherapy and a tumor count. In September of 2009, when we began the pancreatic cancer odyssey, Hemingway's tumor marker, aka his CA 19-9, was just under eight thousand. Eight thousand. Last Wednesday, it was thirteen. In case you don't know, and I sincerely hope you don't, anything under thirty-five is considered normal.

Double, triple, quadruple *whew.*

Such fabulous news deserved to be celebrated. And since one of us has been sick for a while and we don't really do the whole dining-and-dancing thing these days, Hem and I raced home from the hospital with grand plans to eat a half gallon of ice cream each (please note: He has to eat like this; I'm just stuffing myself in solidarity, as any good wife would), beat the boys in a rousing game of *Simpsons* Scene It, and enjoy an eight-o'clock comedy. With our eyes open.

Tug, unfortunately, didn't get the memo, and we were greeted with a house that looked as if a muddy golden retriever had run through it.

Oh, wait. One had.

Garbage all over the kitchen floor, items set aside for the local consignment shop pulled apart, shredded, and left for dead on the dining room rug, a fresh bag of cat litter (to be put away later, later! What was I thinking not squeezing in one more task before we took off for Georgetown at seven thirty in the morning? Shame on lazy me!) ripped open and mashed into the runner in the hall, and books—oh, so many books Hem had stacked in piles marked "Fiction," "Nonfiction," "Read First!" and "Skim: May Suck"—torn asunder, covers half-consumed, pages soaked in doggy smothered-in-garbage-and-cat-litter-and-destroyed-household-discards saliva.

And then there were the two poinsettias that once flanked the hospital band–bedecked tree but were now safely, or so I thought, displayed on a table in the living room. Sure, it was only a matter of time before they died at the hands of She Who Should Not Garden,[214] but they certainly didn't deserve to be murdered by that mutt. And my living room rug really didn't need plant stems and potting soil smashed into it. Though it does sort of complement the dog barf and poop stains.

To say we didn't celebrate is an understatement. Unless you consider collecting garbage, washing the kitchen floor, and vacuuming a celebration. Which I would if it included hanging that damn hound.

Kidding. Just kidding.

I'm terrible with knots. But I'm a damn good shot.

---

214. My frequently forgotten, and therefore still alive, jade plant notwithstanding.

Anyway, today, as they say, is a new day, and despite the cold it's a good one for reveling in Hem's good news. I'm not sure what we're going to do, but whatever it is, it'll be here, in the house, where we can keep an eye on the dog, who's had his eye on the sleeper sofa. If he eats it, he'll be asleep. Permanently.

Hemingway still has to go for treatment, and we've got to get some meat back on his bones,[215] but for the first time in a long time he's making big plans for this place.

Once the weather warms up, he's going to get back to farming, planting, and driving the tractor all over God's green earth. I'm all for it. Particularly since, when that happens, he'll also resume Tug demuddying duty. It's my least favorite task, but one I must attend to now. Before the sun sets, the temperature drops, and I need my blow-dryer to deice that damn dog.

---

215. So please send Swedish Fish; yeah, they were his.

Chapter Forty-three

COCK-A-DOODLE SUE, PART TWO

It's three o'clock in the morning[216] and I'm at my desk. I'm not writing ad copy, like I should be, or tweeting, like I'd like to be. I'm not putting silly status updates on Facebook[217] or Googling pancreatic cancer and pancreatic cancer treatments, like I usually do when I can't sleep. Believe it or not, I'm not even up this early because Tug and Grundy need to be deskunked[218] or Duke needs to be physically removed from the front porch because he's ramming his head against the storm door in a desperate attempt to get in and say, "Howdy!" and "Where the hell ya been?" to Hem.

---

216. Which, even for me, is too friggin' early.

217. Like, "And now I'm keeping Hem, and Casey, and the *cat* compliant with their medications. I spend all day pushing pills and liquids and getting spit at. Really, Hem, it has to stop."

218. No, that I did yesterday at o'dark thirty.

No, right this second I'm online looking at night-vision goggles and ski masks, and considering a subscription to *Soldier of Fortune* magazine. I've bookmarked several sites that promise to teach me how to crack a safe and override an alarm system, and I've made *Inside Man* number one in my Netflix queue. I've also requested it be sent stat, priority, mucho pronto,[219] because I'm running out of time.

I need to learn how to break in and rob a bank without getting caught, and I'm counting on Clive Owen to show me the ropes.[220] Just to clarify beyond a shadow of a doubt the seriousness of the situation, I am not even going to comment on how hot and sexy I think Clive Owen is, or how I'd happily brick myself up in a bank with him any day. No, I'm not going to say any of that stuff. I'm just going to stay focused and stick to the facts.

And the fact is, I'm planning a crime spree.

I've given it a lot of thought, weighed the options, and looked at several alternatives, and, right this moment, two cups of light, sweet coffee and a tablespoon of strawberry preserves straight from the jar into my day, I've come to the following conclusion: My becoming the Counterfeit Bank Bandit is really the only way we're going to be able to pay for the medication Hem needs.

Sure, I feel bad about it. I'm not a thief,[221] and I'd much

---

219. I'd stream it and watch it right this second, but high-speed Internet isn't an option here at our house. Hell, I'm just lucky I'm not doing this whole thing via dial-up.

220. Of course, I'm unsure there are actual ropes involved, but I'll let you know when Clive arrives.

221. My behavior with Cuy's hundred-dollar bill notwithstanding.

rather our health insurance company and the pharmaceutical firm involved play nice (read: stop screwing us). But on the other hand, I've always fantasized about being one of those Navy SEALs, Special Forces, or Delta Force dudes. I think it would be a blast.

And I'll use any excuse to wear black.

To be clear, my sudden interest in robbing from the rich[222] and giving to the poor[223] is this: The chemotherapy Hem's been taking has stopped working. That's the bad news. The good news is that we're not out of treatment options. It's just that the treatment he's opted for, and the one the doctor thinks is his best bet, involves two new medications. One the hospital will supply as part of Hem's participation in a clinical trial; the second we need to get through our insurance agency.

It's the second that's prompted me to go all black ops–meets–Ma Barker.[224]

The medication in question is called Xeloda.[225] Every morning and every evening, for three weeks straight, Hem will take four five-hundred-milligram pills. Then he'll get one week off before the cycle resumes again.

He'll do this for as long as it's working. Or as long as we can come up with the five hundred and fifty-five dollars and seventy-one cents it's going to cost us per week to fill the prescription.

---

222. Hello, Hoffmann-La Roche!

223. Hello, Hem and Suzy's dwindling savings!

224. But not Bonnie Parker, 'cause we all know what happened to her.

225. Pronounced "Zeloda."

Uh-huh. You read that right. And you're feeling sorry for us because we don't have a prescription plan, right? Wrong. We do. And that's our copay. Our copay!

And if we didn't have health insurance and the aforementioned prescription plan?[226] The Xeloda would cost us—drumroll, please—one thousand, six hundred and ninety-one dollars (say it with me now, people) per week.

Per week! Please forgive me for repeating myself. I seem to have overdone it in the caffeine and sugar departments.

I ask you: Who among regular, hardworking, taxpaying folk has one thousand, six hundred and ninety-one dollars just lying around, waiting to be forked over to some pharmaceutical company every seven days?

And among regular, hardworking, taxpaying, monthly-health-insurance–(with a prescription plan!)–premium-paying folk, how many have an extra five hundred and fifty-five dollars and seventy-one cents just lying around, waiting to be forked over to some pharmaceutical company every seven days?

My guess? Not a whole hell of a lot.

Clearly the system is broken, so I'm back to planning my break-ins. I've changed my mind about robbing the local SunTrust, BB&T, and PNC, though. It sickens me to think I might steal from someone who doesn't have four mansions and a private jet, or worse, some family that's in a position similar to ours. No, I've decided to scrap the whole Special Forces, prance-around-in-the-dark-dressed-

---

226. Which already runs us nine hundred and ninety-one dollars a month.

like-Catwoman[227] plan, and get personal. I'm going super-high-tech and senior-exec targeted. I'm thinking computer hacking and money transfers and offshore accounts in the Caymans, real *Girl with the Dragon Tattoo*–type stuff.

Hem gets what he needs, the pigs at the pharmaceutical company get what they deserve, and I get to sit here and do the whole thing in my pajamas. Black pajamas with a matching ski mask.

And the pair of night-vision goggles Clive gave me.

---

227. I mean, I wasn't going to look anywhere near as good as Michelle Pfeiffer or Halle Berry anyway.

Chapter Forty-four

JAILBIRD IN A SCRUFFY BLUE BATH TOWEL

It's around ten in the morning. The kids are celebrating another hot, sunny day of summer vacation by killing each other via video game, and I'm at my desk.[228] Suddenly there's a knock on the door. What Have You Got to Eat? Pete, who's lying on my sea-grass rug contributing his distinctive stink[229] to the ever-growing list of reasons to toss the damn thing and replace it with something almost as plush, like pavers, flips out and starts barking at a decibel level reminiscent of dearly departed Cluckster. For a split second I wonder what size plant it would take to take him out,[230] and then I stand up to answer the door.

---

228. I'm always at my desk, if I'm not at the hospital, doing laundry, or driving someone somewhere. I don't actually do any work, but the kids don't need to know that, do they?

229. Which can best be described as dry dog food meets wet, dead anything.

230. I'm not sure I have the strength to throw a redwood tree, but I'm willing to try.

And sit back down really fast.

Oh, dear God, I'm not dressed. Am I naked? No, but not by much. I'm wrapped in an old green bath towel, and my hair is sopping wet. Sure, at four a.m. my work attire is either pajamas or yoga pants.[231] But by midmorning I'm in jeans and jewelry, full makeup, hair, and, of course, heels.

And ten a.m. is definitely midmorning. Hell, when you've been up since dawn, it's damn near dinnertime.

In any case, I'm not in my typical work attire, and Pete's still howling like Animal Control's finally accepted my invitation to visit. "Hush, stink bomb," I hiss. The towel, the noise, the knocking. I can't think straight. Where are my clothes? Why am I soaked like I just stepped out of the shower? And who the hell is at the door? Doesn't anybody around here know Northerners hate drop-ins?

Particularly drop-ins that involve a sheriff's deputy.

"Morning, ma'am," said Mr. Deputy when I opened the door, like, a crack, 'cause, well, duh, I'm not exactly dressed. "You the manager here?"

"Yes. Well, sort of." I stumbled. My brain was racing. Why is there a policeman on my porch? Did they catch wind of the whole hacking thing I was planning?[232] Did I not pay a bill? And even if I didn't, since when do cops do collections? "It's kind of a new job, Deputy . . ."

"Gray." He tapped his nameplate, a little strip of silver pinned to a brown button-down shirt that was tucked into

---

231. And a jogging bra, of course. I haven't worked topless since my stint at the Bada Bing.

232. Which, by the way, went nowhere. And that's the last time I ask Clive Owen for anything.

tan pants and topped off (bottomed off?) by black shoes. I'd have gone with brown, but I'm also one of those people who think the fashion police should police the police. You know, when they're not ticketing teenage boys for wearing their pants beneath their butt cheeks. "Sorry to catch you at a bad time," he continued, silently acknowledging the whole shower-fresh and freaked-out thing I had happening.[233] "Why don't I wait while you take a second to get organized?"

Get organized? I felt like Guy Pearce in *Memento*. It was going to take way more than a second to sort this shit out.

"Sure. Okay," I replied. "But can you just, first, tell me what this is about?"

"Honestly, ma'am?"

I nodded.

"It's about the towel."

I glanced down. "You're here to arrest the towel?" On what charges? Fading? Poor absorbency? Softness comparable only to my aforementioned stinky, stained sea-grass rug? The teeny, tiny hole near the hem that lets me hook it to the end of the towel rack? You know, sort of like an oven mitt, only a lot bigger and not nearly as burned?

"No, ma'am. I'd just like to talk with you about wearing it when you're, um"—he paused and looked over at the cattle—"when you're working."

Dude. What I wear at my desk is my business. "Officer, since when do the police care what I write ad copy in?" This was getting more surreal by the moment.

---

233. It's never fun to find cops at your door. Unless you've called them to come cut you out of a dress.

"Ad copy, ma'am? I thought you said you managed the farm."

"I do that, too. You know, now."

"So you're still getting used to the job. I understand, ma'am." And he did look understanding. For a full nano-second, and then it was right back to business. "But it's dangerous to herd cattle in nothing but a bath towel." He paused and looked me straight in the eye.[234] "And more important, in these parts, it's indecent exposure."

What was he talking about, indecent exposure? I don't walk around naked even when I'm home alone for fear the dogs will rat me out to the Humane Society.[235] And herd cattle in a towel? Five-hundred-dollar designer shoes,[236] maybe. But never in a washed-out, slightly singed Spring-maid I got at Costco, like, six years ago. Please. I have a reputation to uphold.

And it's one of improper dress. Not no dress.

"How 'bout I give you a few minutes to get some clothes on," Deputy Gray continued. "Then we'll take a ride to the sheriff's office." He reached out and pulled the screen door open so I could go in.

In?

When had I gone out?

I had absolutely no recollection of stepping out onto the porch. And yet here I was, hair frizzing in the humid-ity like an order of curly fries, barefoot, and facing the

234. Or more accurately, eyes, both of which were bursting from their sockets so fast they made Janet Jackson's fleeting wardrobe malfunction look like a striptease.

235. Again.

236. That actually match my outfit, Officer.

prospect of sitting in a jail cell wearing little more than a scarf. A six-year-old scarf that, while rough and scruffy, was a whole lot better than the jumpsuit they were going to stick me in.[237] None of this made any sense.

"Um, Officer?"

"Yes?"

"I thought indecent exposure was exposing yourself. Like a flasher. Or a streaker. You know, one of those people who run across the stage naked at a college graduation or across the field at a Yankees game." I smiled. He didn't. Dammit, Suz. You couldn't say Nats game? Or Skins? Assimilate already! I was panicking, and not just because Deputy Gray was looking at me like, *Listen, little lady, you wouldn't be the first perp to have a mug shot taken in little more than your birthday suit. Now move!*

But I couldn't move. It was as if my whole body were frozen. Except my gums. And those were flapping Jersey-girl fast.

"I mean, even if I did take care of the cows wearing just a towel, which I didn't, or at least I don't think I did, I mean, I really can't recall doing it, so I definitely don't think it happened and I've no idea why you do, I wouldn't have been exposed. I'd have been covered. By the towel." To make my point, I tugged at it and of course it slipped. I caught the soggy, scruffy thing, but not before Deputy Gray's hand flew to his holster.[238]

---

237. An orange jumpsuit. Against my complexion. Criminal.

238. And here I thought only big breasts were to die for.

"The great state of Virginia doesn't see it that way, ma'am."

"But this is my property. I can do anything I want on my property."[239]

"Exposing yourself's illegal even on your own property, ma'am."

"Deputy Gray, no disrespect, but this is insane. Look around." I made a sweeping motion with one hand (because I'm really not fond of gunfire), and paused while he took the place in. "Do you see any people?"

Deputy Gray looked out at the cows and the goats, and a couple of broken fence boards, and then at two of the hens brooding in their favorite window box, and shook his head no.

"That's because there are almost no people. I could do all my farm chores in a pair of heels and a hat[240] and no one would know, because no one would see me. So even if I did herd cattle wearing nothing but a bath towel, which I didn't, how would you know? And please don't tell me the cows called you."[241]

"We received a report that you were running up and down right here"—he pointed to where his patrol car was idling on our private road, and then referred to his notepad—"chasing a golden retriever that was chasing a bull calf, and you were wearing nothing but a towel. A green

---

239. Including build a mental hospital and move in. Which I intend to do. Right after I figure out what the hell is happening here.

240. Sun on one pair of cheeks is fine. Sun on the other is not.

241. Big mistake, ladies. I pulled the fowl off our family plan. Don't think the same fate can't befall you bovines.

towel, the description of which matches the one you've got on now."

Well, color me happy. He had the wrong cowpoke.

"Deputy Gray, I'm telling you, you've got the wrong girl. This is one of those . . . what do you call it? Cases of mistaken identity. You want to haul me in, hook me up to a polygraph, and pepper me with questions? I'll pass." I raised my right hand[242] as if I were on the witness stand. "I solemnly swear, Your Honor, that I have never, ever chased a golden retriever chasing a baby bull in a green bath towel."

Now if you'd said something about a blue one . . .

But he hadn't, had he? And I was absolutely, positively, beyond-a-shadow-of-a-doubt sure that Cuy's friend Jeff? He didn't see me. Nuh-uh. Nope. No way. He was too far away.

Then again, if he didn't see me, who called in the complaint?

Who cares? It doesn't matter. What matters is that I wasn't indecent, dammit. Not then, and not now.

I put my hand down. Sure, it's safer at my side, but I'd have been even safer if I'd slapped it across my mouth. "You know what?" I continued. "The bottom line, Officer, is that I wasn't exposed. Not in the least. And come on, I had to do something. That damn dog was chasing that sweet baby bull up the road, down the road, around the equipment shed, through the stalls and the barn, and back again. The poor little guy was panting so hard and the

---

242. Carefully, of course.

mama cows were wailing so loud I couldn't help but hear them. So all right already. Yes! Yes, I confess! I'd just stepped out of the shower and wrapped myself in a towel, and I was on my way upstairs to get dressed[243] when I glanced out the window and caught sight of our crazy dog Tug barreling down on what looked like a small black-and-white dog. But the cows wouldn't be wailing over a dog, now, would they? Would they?"

Deputy Gray shook his head. "No, ma'am, I guess not. But there's really no need to get worked up."

"Yeah, well, I can't help it. And I'm sure you're wondering what happened next. Or maybe not, since you already know what happened. I didn't stop to think. I just took off out the door and down the steps in my scruffy blue—*blue*, not green—Springmaid,[244] and did what any farm manager would do. As Tug and the baby bull flew past me, I threw myself between them. Yes, I confess! Tug crashed snout-first into me and my towel slipped a tad and I might have flashed just an itty-bitty, teensy-weensy bit of, er, you know, but the baby bull was saved. And I guess it was while I was tugging Tug up here, onto the porch, by his collar, that I saw my son's friend Jeff. He and his family live here on the farm. And, well, I didn't think anything of it. He was pretty far away, so I just smiled and waved. I might've even yelled, 'Dumb dog!' But I don't even think I did that."

No response. Just lots of scribbling on a pad. I couldn't

---

243. In the whole jeans, hair, heels, and jewelry thing I mentioned earlier.

244. You're right if you're thinking it's time I buy new towels. And maybe even replace my sea-grass rug.

tell if he was writing me a ticket or taking notes for his book about suburbanites who move to the country and completely crack up. It didn't matter. What mattered was that I had to get in the house and get Hem. He'd fix this.

"Really, I was just trying to do the right thing. And I really, truly, cross-my-heart-and-hope-to-die[245] promise never to do farm chores in a bath towel or a robe or anything short of a burka ever again. See? I'm already reformed. So there's no need to arrest me, right? Please, Officer, I don't want to go to jail. Jail's for murderers and corporate scum suckers and anyone who casts Andy Dick in anything. Sure, I steal my kids' Hershey's Kisses and occasionally a ride on a Clydesdale that doesn't belong to me. But I'm not a bad person. I'm stupid and impulsive, but I'm also more than willing to pay for the dozen or so years of psychotherapy Jeff's probably going to need to recover from the shock of seeing my disturbingly white body in broad daylight. Just ask my husband. He'll tell you."

I stepped into the hall and was immediately bowled over by the silence.[246] Had the kids finally made good on their threats to run away? And if so, please tell me they took Tug.

"Hem!" I shouted. "Honey? Can you come down here a sec?" No response. Behind me, Deputy Gray's radio went off. How cops can understand what's being said with all that static, I don't know. But he said something and they said something and he said something back, and

---

245. And spend eternity in an orange jumpsuit.

246. Not to mention Pete's stink. I guess I should have let him out when I went out, but hell, I didn't even realize I'd gone out.

all I could think was, Oh, my God, they're probably telling him to reel me in already.

So of course I started to scream.

"Hem? Hem! Can you please come here and talk to this nice policeman for me? I need you to tell him, hon, please, please tell him that I'm silly, really silly, okay, stupid, and impulsive, let's not forget impulsive!—but I've got a good heart and there's really no reason to arrest me for being outside in a bath towel. I mean, they let Stacy's mom skate and she actually *talked* to the kid. Remember that song? 'Stacy's Mom'? She may have had it going on, but *I* saved a baby bull, for Pete's sake!"

"Susan." Deputy Gray was through waiting. He tugged on my arm.

"Hem!" I screamed. "Hem! Help!"

"Susan, come on now." He was shaking my arm, hard, and pulling me back onto the porch.

"No! Let go!" I tried to twist out of his grasp. "Hem! Hem, where are you?"

"Susan. It's okay."

"You bet it's okay. I didn't do anything!" He pulled; I pulled back. Any harder and he was going to rip my arm right out of its socket. But at least then I'd be able to run. "You'll never take me alive!" I cried.

"Susan! Susan, dammit! You're not supposed to take Tylenol PM with wine!"

Huh?

"Hem?" My eyes popped open and I sat up. Oh, thank God, I thought. I'm in bed! I'm in bed with my honey in my thousand-year-old p.j. pants and the Jonas Brothers'

concert tee I bought and promptly bleached to death.[247]
And there isn't a towel in sight.

"You were having that dream again, the one about Tug,
and the bull calf, and the cop."

I could barely breathe, and worse, I was actually crying. "They wanted to take me to jail. And I couldn't find
you." I sniffled. "It was terrible."

He pulled me to him. "I'd never let anyone take you to
jail, Suz. But you've gotta stop this business of running
outside in just a towel or your bathrobe. What if you'd gotten stepped on that day? Or knocked down and dragged?
Whatever's happening with the animals can wait—"

I cut him off. "Till I'm dressed, I know. It won't happen
again."

"It'd better not," he said, hugging me. "I can't afford
for you to get hurt. And we really can't afford the shrink
fees for all of Cuy's friends."

---

247. Clearly a trip to Target is in order.

Chapter Forty-five

PUTTING MY FAITH IN THE FUNNY STUFF

$\mathcal{I}$'m ashamed to admit this, but it's true: Hemingway and I were once cheaters. Not in the *Scarlet Letter* sense of the word, of course. But in the fact that long ago, when we were wild and childless, we'd go to the movies, see the feature we paid for, and then sneak into one of the other films and watch it (*shhhh*) without buying another ticket.

We were strolling down memory lane and laughing about this and a dozen other things we did preparenthood on our way home from the hospital. It was a wonderful way to pass the ninety-minute ride, way better than wondering what kind of Tug havoc we were coming home to or rehashing every single detail of the doctor visit. We see Hem's oncologist about every three weeks, and every time I show up with my purple pen and my big green Day Runner crammed with Hem's med list, pain log, chemo schedule, latest blood work results, past and pending test dates, and occasionally history homework somebody was supposed to hand in (but I scooped up by mistake—sorry, Case!), and a heart so filled with hope I'm surprised my head doesn't pop off.

And every three weeks I leave a little less hopeful, a little more frightened, and certain only of the uncertainty of my husband's cancer.

It's not the doctor's fault, by any means. He's a brilliant guy. He radiates concern and care and most important, optimism. He never rushes Hem, listens like he's got all the time in the world, and answers all our questions. He always has a plan and, it bears repeating, is always positive and optimistic. It's just that I want what he can't give us: a cure.

Or, barring that, a crystal ball so we can see what's coming and when. Too bad they don't teach fortune-telling in medical school.

"Remember when Spike ran through the white paint and tracked paw prints across the gray couch?" Hemingway's cracking up at the thought of a cat we had way back before the boys were born. "And it was new, too."

"It wasn't just the couch," I respond, glancing quickly at him, then back at the highway. "Remember how hard it was to clean the rug?"

He squeezes my knee. "We didn't spend too much time cleaning it, if I remember correctly."

Ah, the good old days, when we were footloose and cancer-free. Before tumors and Whipples and metastases and ERCPs and a stash of narcotic painkillers that could give the Medellin drug cartel a run for its money. Before jaundice and nausea and weight loss the likes of which *The Biggest Loser*'s never seen. Before mediports and infusion centers and scared kids who keep asking whether Dad will ever get better.

Screw medical school. The crystal ball should pass with the placenta.

I know they say whatever doesn't kill you makes you stronger. But I'm pretty sure that expression means shit. At least when it comes to cancer. Despite the fact that at this point I could probably lift a crystal ball the size of one of those Hampshires I so wanted but didn't get[248] over my head, I sometimes think it would be easier to declare myself the ninety-pound weakling of the caregiver world and lie down and die.

All right, maybe not die. But sleep would be nice. A really, really deep sleep, for a really, really long time. Or at least more than the four hours a night I typically get before Cuyler appears on my side of the bed shaking and mumbling, "Another bad one, Mom," as he scrambles into his favorite spot between me and Hemingway, aka the man of his dreams.

Or, more accurately, the man of his bad dreams.

Almost every night, the poor kid has nightmares about his dad. He dreams his dad never gets better. He dreams his dad dies. And then, as if that's not enough to make him afraid to close his mischievous blue eyes for the rest of his little life, he dreams *I* die and there's no

---

248. And it's a darn good thing, too.

one to take care of him and Casey. Or keep them in cookies.

This, of course, leads me to one of the other things they say. And that's that when someone in your family has cancer, the whole family has cancer.

They got that right.

In addition to the fact that Cuy can't sleep, Casey doesn't have a single mood that seems to last for more than five minutes. He's up, he's down. One moment, he's threatening to run away and join the marines. (Please don't, honey; I'll worry.) The next he's threatening to "stay right here at home with you, Mom" for the rest of his life. (On second thought, I could give you a lift to the recruiter's office!)

Even the four-legged members of the family are feeling the effects of Hem's illness. The dogs sleep all day at his feet, the cattle still loiter in the pasture closest to the house, and the goats would like nothing more than to join the dogs on guard duty. As for Coca, Hem's favorite cat, he refuses to leave Hem's side even to pee. Which means I wash sheets, blankets, pillowcases, and the mattress cover 'round the clock, spend several nights a week in the guest room, and have given serious thought to moving my husband and his menagerie to the living room. The pups already treat it like a Porta Potti; why not let the cat make a contribution? At least it'll keep the stink in one spot.

As for me, I'm losing my hair. No, it's not falling out. I'm pulling it out. All along my temples, around my ears, and at the base of my skull. Hemingway's had several rounds of chemo and he hasn't lost a single strand. I, on the other hand, am beginning to look like Britney Spears during her breakdown. Remember? They took away her kids.

Hmm. Maybe they'll take mine, too.

Just joshing; they can't have my kids. They have to pay me for them.[249]

Of course, the fun doesn't really start until my hair pulling progresses to scalp scratching. This quickly leads to bleeding, which leads, less quickly but much more satisfyingly, to scabbing. And who can resist a scab?

You're right. A mature adult can resist picking a scab. And if one shows up, I'll tell her to keep her hands off my head.

In the interim, Miss Self-inflicted Bald Spot is doing her best to help her stressed kids and sick spouse navigate the nasty world of cancer. I've got the little one taking melatonin before bed, the big one taking driving lessons so, should he decide to flee, he won't have to do it on foot, and the whole family on a strict diet of situation comedies, Dave Barry books, and funny movies, several of which were playing at the Regal Cinema, coming up fast on our right. Fourteen movies: a veritable feast for former film filchers like us.

"Good to see you getting all hot and bothered, farm boy." I laugh. "Want to duck into a movie and make out?"

"Only if we can sneak into a second."

"With our luck we'll get arrested and the boys will have to bail us out."

---

249. Best offer gets a billy goat, or two!

The thought cracks us both up.

Sure, I cook and clean, do laundry, shoo cattle back into the pasture, dole out meds, fix the occasional fence board, make the doctor appointments, and drive everybody everywhere—with one hand, no less; the other's practically superglued to my scalp—in an effort to keep things as "normal" as possible around here. But I firmly believe it's the funny stuff—and the fact that we still find stuff funny—that's going to save us.

Nothing about cancer is easy, and most of it's absolutely exhausting, but on the days it threatens to get the best of us, I just keep repeating the two expressions I totally agree with: *Laughter is the best medicine*, and, *If God brings you to it, He'll bring you through it.*

I can't be sure I'll have any hair left by the time that happens, but I'm certain we'll all be smiling.

You Know You're Overtired When . . .

. . . .

- You give the stock clerk at the home farm co-op your husband's med list and the receptionist in the radiology department your farm shopping list. It's bad enough the kid at the co-op suspects you're trying to score OxyContin (for the cows, no less), but having to explain to the hospital staff that Laymore is not a new erectile dysfunction drug is really embarrassing.

- You discover the dogs disemboweling a chicken and think, Thank God. Now I don't have to lug that damn big bag of dog food.

- You give the last of the Kibbles N Bits to the cats, 'cause it's late, you're out of little Friskies, and you just can't count on your two pacifist kitties to go kill their own grub.

- It's easier to buy more clothes for the kids than face the mountain of laundry that's been wrinkling in the dryer for over a week. (Sure, I keep hitting "fluff." But there isn't enough wine in the world that will get me to "fold" at eleven o'clock at night.)

- You find the goats eating out of the window boxes and your first thought is, Too bad they can't take 'em down and put 'em away for the winter, too. (Except for the one the hens call home, of course. Who needs more complaints from the poultry?)

- It's four o'clock in the morning, you're racing to the hospital with your husband, who's sick with pain from what you'll soon learn are kidney stones the size of raisins, and you're wondering why Route 66 is so dark. Hmm. Might help if you turned on your headlights.

- Both your kids want cake for dinner, and not only do you say yes; you—the fitness freak—go get three forks.

- Your internal alarm clock fails, you awaken at seven rather than four, and think, Screw it; the boys can skip school. Which they'd be happy about if they went on Saturdays.

- You put your Schick Slim Twin in your mouth so you can use both hands to lather your furry legs, and you bite down *on the blade*.

- The message light blinking on the kitchen phone makes you cry.

- The messages themselves, from folks worried you're as overtired as they think you are, make you cry even harder.

- A cop pulls you over for writing this list. While driving. He thinks you're texting and isn't the least relieved to learn you're "Just good ol'-fashioned paper-and-penciling, Officer!" He lets you off with a warning and a stern, "Ma'am, go home and get some sleep." Which you intend to do. Right after you find the cure for cancer.

Part Four

Epilogue
500 Acres and No Place to Hide

$\mathcal{B}$ack when Hemingway and I were engaged, and I mean way back, when he was Stu "Master of the Universe" McCorkindale and I was Sue "Wrinkle-, Pouch-, and Crow's Feet–free" Costantino,[250] and we were both kicking ass and taking names at our big jobs in the Big Apple, we lived in a brand-new condominium in a brand-new condominium complex in an ugly old town right outside New York City.

Why live in a brand-new home in an ugly old town? For its beautiful commute. Thirty-five minutes via express bus from front door to desk, with time to spare to pick up and eat breakfast[251] and enjoy a few more chapters of whatever book on tape I was listening to.

---

250. I would have hyphenated my name, but they don't make business cards the size of billboards.

251. Coffee light and sweet and a buttered bagel; is it any wonder I had hips as broad as the bus lane?

We got to work fast and we got home fast. And home, once we whispered the secret password that opened the huge iron gates to our courtyard, unlocked the two locks on the exterior door and the four on the interior door, turned off the alarm, and stored the Mace and billy clubs we carried just in case things got dicey on the walk back from the bus stop, was lovely.

Small, but lovely.

Now, I'm all for small. In fact, you could say I'm a big small fan. (Which is kind of a funny thing to say, don't you think?) Small means less time vacuuming and dusting and scrubbing and scouring, and more time hanging out with my honey.[252]

But small also means that when I need a good cry there's no place to hide to have one. Hey, I'm a woman. Women cry. At least, this one does. I also suffer from depression, and that makes me a tad more prone to tears. Not all the time, of course. Just in the spring. And when I miss my medication. Or when I can't buy a particularly cute Coach bag because, while it's only the fifth of the month, I've already blown my clothing budget on a pair of boots I just had to have.

In all seriousness, no matter where I went in the condo, Hem could hear me. And, sweetheart that he is, he wanted to console me. But I didn't need to be consoled. I needed Kleenex, my trusty Pond's cold cream ('cause, God, my mascara would be a mess), and ten minutes under the

---

252. After he's finished, that is. "There'll be no Budweiser till that sink sparkles, big guy!" (And if you believe that, I have a barn you might like to buy. Really. Best offer gets the grain silo, too.)

kitchen sink or in a cabinet ('cause really, privacy is crucial to a good cry), and I'd be cured.

Or at least tear-free for the foreseeable future.

And so, despite the fact that I really did like our brand-new condominium, and I certainly loved the beautiful commute, when Casey was born and I couldn't stop blubbering,[253] I knew the time was right to push for a bigger place.

Casey needed a bedroom.

Hem needed space for the HO scale train layout he longed to build.

And I'd have been happy with a dusty attic, dank basement, dirty garage (preferably detached), or dingy crawl space to call my own. And guess what? When we bought our house in Ridgewood I got all four.

I just neglected to specify that they be soundproof.

In the ten years we lived in that pretty, bustling town of yummy restaurants (the signature dishes of which were delivered almost nightly to Chez McCorkindale by the Takeout Taxi—oh, how I miss the Takeout Taxi!), cutting-edge hair salons, chic boutiques, and what had to be two banks and an Edward Jones a block,[254] I built a business, had another baby, and made a dozen dear friends with whom I sat on the sidelines during every junior football

---

253. Because, as you can probably guess, postpartum depression + generalized anxiety + clinical depression = buy stock in Kimberly-Clark/Kleenex, stat!

254. Can somebody tell me why banks are reproducing like bunnies? Even here, in my sweet one-stoplight town, we have a BB&T and a PNC within fifty feet of each other. Why? What we need is a good coffee shop, or a movie theater, or a mental health center that will certainly do a brisk business if one of the aforementioned financial institutions isn't replaced by a Starbucks soon.

game and practice, freezing our buns off rooting for our respective sons ("Go, Casey!") and several of our husbands ("Go, Hem!") who coached. I went back to work in the city,[255] took the top marketing spot at one of the country's top women's magazines, and helped my honey launch his career as a Web site writer. That's also when I started kidding around, calling him Hemingway. Up until then it was Stu or Mac or Buddy or sometimes even Puddin', which he found totally distasteful and I found surprising, considering how much he loves the stuff.

My point is, I accomplished a lot while we lived in what I firmly believe to be New Jersey's best suburb. But I never did find a place to be by myself when I got the blues.

No, that little quest came to a close the first time I set foot on the farm. . . .

"It's too quiet." Hem and I were standing in what would eventually become our front yard, staring at what would eventually become our house. He was smiling. I was sweating and trying not to hyperventilate. Some people panic in crowds. I panic from a lack of crowds.

He put his arm around me. "Don't you hear the cows? Listen," he whispered. "They're saying, 'Soooozy, there's a shooooe sale at Neiman Moooocus.'"

"And I'm missing it 'cause I'm here at what's obviously the end of the earth with you." I laughed nervously, like I do at the dentist when I get great news, like my gum

---

255. Via a commute that was anything but beautiful. An hour and fifteen minutes each way. On a good day. During the holidays, Route 17 in Paramus is nothing short of a parking lot. Commuters are lucky if they get home with enough time to change clothes, finish their letter to Santa, and put their butt back on the bus.

recession's so severe Alan Greenspan couldn't save me, and leaned my sweaty self into him.

"Jeez, you're warm."

"I can't believe you're not hot. I'm sweating like a pig."

"See? You'll fit right in."

I gave him a playful shove. "Of course I hear the cows," I replied. "Bees, too. But some buzzing and a couple of moos does not Manhattan make." Sweat was running down into my bra, pooling in my belly button, and forming a stain the size of an orange on the front of my shirt. Delightful. We weren't here half an hour and not only was I already a *Glamour* "don't," I was now wearing a T-shirt with a design. Charla Krupp[256] would kill me.

"Suz, this place can give you something the city never could. Something you've always wanted."

"Funny, I don't recall wanting no people, a ton of cow poop, and a whole lot of spooky red farm buildings." I nodded in the direction of the ghost town adjacent to our future home: a collection of structures of varying size and in various states of disrepair, all painted the same shade of red.

"Don't think of them as spooky. Think of them as . . . as . . ."

Oh, this was going to be good. Think of them as what? The places where the bodies are buried? Where Hannibal Lecter and Patrick Bateman's new raw-food restaurant is opening? Where the local Al-Qaeda cell plots and plans, and plays its weekly card game?

---

256. Former beauty guru at *Glamour* magazine and author of *How Not to Look Old* and *How to Never Look Fat Again*.

"Think of them as what?" I prompted, arms folded across my chest, foot tapping in mock impatience.

"As sanctuary!" Hem said finally, smiling and clearly pleased with himself at having found what he thought was the perfect word.

Sanctuary? Storage, maybe. But sanctuary?

Oh, my God. Was he suggesting what I thought he was suggesting?

"Please don't tell me you think I'd come out here, lock myself in a corncrib, and cry."

He nodded, and I thought I'd cry at the prospect of living in a place where corncribs, a chicken coop, and a couple of decrepit barns and stalls were my options for a little privacy.

But at least I'd have some.

"This is your pitch? I give up the city, lunchtime trips to Bloomingdale's, not to mention easy access to Starbucks, for a little solitude?"

"Pretty much."

Despite the fact that I don't cry nearly as much as I shop or drink coffee, I bought his pitch and a bunch of other stuff he was selling that day,[257] and was even sort of, in a weird, science-experiment kind of way, looking forward to the first time I got the blues in the backcountry. I mean, not only were there the aforementioned spooky buildings in which to steal away (twenty-eight of them, in fact), there were five hundred acres of pasture and woods and hills and ponds and rocks big enough to sunbathe on.

---

257. Ah, country air; there's nothing quite like it for fucking with your head.

I remember thinking, This could be good for me. Maybe I'll get outdoorsy, read a gardening magazine. I might even plant something! Don't they say gardening's good for depression? Maybe I'll take up hiking, and find a special spot just for me, where I can meditate and center myself. Aren't there studies that link all that yoga stuff to an increase in serotonin? I might even discover a new, deeper, spiritual Suzy. A Suzy who's more than shoe sales and great bags and sparkly baubles. And lunch. (Although a girl's gotta have lunch. You can work up quite an appetite shopping for accessories.) Maybe I'll become a Suzy who helps others, gives back to her community, and gives away her entire designer suit collection to women who just aren't lucky enough to be able to spend all day in sneakers and jeans and T-shirts that say, "What happens in the barn stays in the barn." You know, like that woman at the BP station was wearing. Maybe I'll become a Suzy who cans her own vegetables and cooks from scratch. A Suzy who scrapbooks and knits socks and caps and matching ponchos and maybe even sells them at a roadside stand like the ones we passed! A Suzy who reduces, reuses, and recycles. A Suzy who's concerned about her carbon footprint (and not just the scratches she makes in her stilettos). A Suzy so grounded and healthy she can let her Wellbutrin and Ativan prescriptions lapse! A Suzy who's calm, focused, caring, and committed.

And who just might end up committed if she stops taking either of the aforementioned medications.

Five years later, let me tell you: five *thousand* acres, an ocean, and complete, catastrophic blindness couldn't stop my family from finding me.

There isn't a run-down, forgotten shack or hollowed-out tree trunk on the back forty that Casey and Cuyler don't know about. Not a building they haven't explored or can't break into. Not an inch of pasture or a path they haven't ridden their ATVs all over.

Oh, no. They know this place like they know every line of dialogue to every single season of *The Simpsons*, and every last episode of *SpongeBob SquarePants*.[258] (And now I'm going to stop before my mom reads this and reminds me how I spent seven years in remedial math trying, and failing, to learn the times tables. But every line of *I Love Lucy*? Please. Not a problem.[259])

Suffice it to say, my sons have our spread memorized.

And never has this been more apparent than since Hemingway got sick.

Now, just to be clear, I don't often try to disappear. Not before my husband's diagnosis, and definitely not since. Why? Because, surprise, surprise, I almost no longer need to. I finally find myself in a place where I just might be able to boo-hoo my brains out, and my bimonthly breakdowns dwindle to twice a year, tops.

Some would call that cosmic justice.

Others would say my Wellbutrin's working.

I just think I got gypped.

Of course I'm joking. I don't need a chemical imbal-

---

258. To be honest, I think SpongeBob is sweet. It's those two malcontents, Plankton and Squidward, I could do without. I've actually written to the show's creators asking if once, just once, Sandy could give 'em a nip. After all, she's a rodent. Let's find out if she's rabid.

259. Clearly, the apple doesn't fall far from the TV. I mean tree.

ance to make me cuckoo. I have kids. Kids who don't understand that sometimes Mom needs ten minutes alone. Not to cry, but to collect herself. Shake off a panic attack. Get her shit together.

How do I get those crucial ten minutes? I usually don't. But sometimes, if I resort to a little trickery, the Hardy Boys I gave birth to fall for it. I simply open the kitchen door, pause, and then slam it shut *without having stepped through it*, and then tiptoe into the laundry room. "Frank" and "Joe" think I've departed the premises, and before I can settle myself in behind the hamper, they've snapped off the Xbox, raced down the stairs, and are hopping around the mud porch trying desperately to stick their feet into sneakers they kicked off when they came in, because Lord knows it would take too long to untie them. There're usually a few seconds of, "These dumb things don't fit!" and, "I keep telling her I hate these shoes!" and my personal favorite, "Who the hell tied these?" before they spill out into the backyard, race off to retrieve their four-wheelers, and commence their hot pursuit of a woman who just happens to be in the house.

Oh, come on now. Stop looking at this page like, "That Susan McCorkindale is the world's worst mother!" I didn't leave my kids locked in the car in hundred-degree heat. I'm not at happy hour scarfing down buffalo chicken wings while my kids are home hungry. I don't have as much as a bottle of Poland Spring with me in my teeny-tiny haven of stinky clothes and Clorox.

Now that I think of it, I could hide a nice cabernet and a plastic wineglass behind my hundred-and-fifty-ounce bottle of Tide.[260] Hell, I could leave it right out in the open with a corkscrew. And a package of cashews. And maybe even a box of crackers and one of those cheese spreads that don't require refrigeration. No one would notice, because no one besides me ever sets foot in the laundry room. (Unless it's to dig through the hamper for a pair of jeans or "lucky" sweat socks they just *have* to wear, despite the fact that the item in question is filthy and fragrant as a compost heap.)

But hey, a girl can dream.

And if she does it right, a girl can hide in the (quasi) comfort of her own home.

Why? Because a girl can get tired of having her kid bring her the phone while she's tucked into the tractor, in a dark corner of the equipment shed,[261] catching her breath, reviewing the day's events and deciding how best to tackle tomorrow's.

"Hey, Mom, this computer keeps calling about some appointment for Dad. I thought you might want to hear what it's saying. You okay out here?"

"Yes, sweetheart. Thank you, sweetheart."

Or while she's taking five on a hay bale, enjoying the sweet, crisp scent that she hopes to God will someday replace the burned-coffee-and-peach-air-freshener smell of the waiting room at the chemotherapy infusion center that's forever singed into her sinuses, and listening to the sounds of mice scurrying among the stacks that still, sort

---

260. Frankly, you could hide a toddler riding a Big Wheel behind that thing.

261. Don't worry; I wear a hat.

of, freaks her out. But not so badly that she'll move her butt.

"Sorry to bother you, Mom, but I figured you'd want to talk to the pharmacy. You okay out here?"

"Yes, sweetheart. Thank you, sweetheart."

I'm not really complaining. My kids are incredible. They've always been well behaved and helpful. And since their dad's diagnosis, they've really matured. Right before my eyes, they've become responsible, terrific young men, both of whom are blessed with a good heart, a wonderful sense of humor, and the uncanny, almost psychic ability to find me no matter where I attempt to disappear to.

That or the little bastards stuck a tracking chip in my neck one night.

Of course, they don't always have to look for me. Sometimes they just have to listen. And since listening isn't exactly my sons' strong suit, I did try, just once, to hide in plain sight and have a brief cry.

They were upstairs in the guest room playing Call of Duty.

I was downstairs in the kitchen playing call the doctor.

I could hear them above my head, busting each other about who was winning and who shot whose guy and how one of them didn't mean to kill his own man.[262] They were laughing and cheering and being a little too loud and I thought, Just listen to them carrying on!

And then I heard myself. They're carrying on. Despite

---

262. Clearly we will not be pushing military careers in the McCorkindale house. You're welcome.

everything. They're putting one foot in front of the other and getting on with their lives. They're doing their best to navigate this new normal. To survive it, even thrive in it. They're doing exactly what we asked of them the night Hem told them he had cancer. They're carrying on.

The weight of it caught me right in the throat. I swallowed hard, but it was too late. All the horror, the immeasurable, indescribable sadness, and the sense of utter frustration and powerlessness that I stuff and deny and do anything to distract myself from thinking about, exploded inside me.

My kids were going to lose their dad.

I was going to lose my husband.

And my husband was going to lose his life.

Maybe it's just me, but this carrying-on business is a bunch of crap.

Right this second, though, our kids were doing just that. Being so strong and so brave, I thought my heart might break from pride and pain.

A lot of pain. As if I were being tied into a corset, or worse, getting a bear hug from a really pissed-off bear. I couldn't breathe. And I couldn't see anything but black and blue dots. Fear and nausea rose in my throat and I thought, Oh, dear God, please don't let me vomit. I hate to vomit. But more important, please don't let me pass out. I'd rather throw up than pass out any day. Of course, what I really, really hate is passing out into my vomit,[263] so if we

---

263. Back in college, my friends and I spent a lot of time at a bar called The Beach. No sun, sand, or surf. Just the world's best Bloody Marys. And I haven't had four on an empty stomach since.

can skip that, I'll happily faint right here on the floor. The floor. How did I get on the floor?

If I didn't have years of experience with this stuff, I'd have sworn I was having a heart attack. But alas, depression and anxiety are good for one thing: I know the difference between needing an ambulance and needing an Ativan.

This was a panic attack, plain and simple. And it left me as they always do: sweaty and spent and sobbing.

And making all those ugly, stupid crying sounds, too. Slowly (really slowly, because I was still pretty green around the gills), I crawled into the bathroom and closed the door. I ran the water in both faucets, turned on the shower, and flipped the switch for the fan. Then I wrapped my entire head—including my face, which I managed to cover *twice*—in a towel, flushed the toilet, and let it rip.

For five minutes or so, I sat on the floor hugging my knees, one hand pressing the towel to my mouth, crying.[264] And begging God to save my husband and spare my sons the pain of having their dad die. And getting good and pissed off at the Big Guy for making Hem sick in the first place. And then, of course, apologizing profusely, sobbing some more, and finally, cried out and aching with exhaustion, praying simply for the strength and courage to get all of us through this.

I pulled the towel off my head. Great. Not only had I grabbed a yellow one, I proved yet again that waterproof mascara is a figment of my imagination. And Maybelline's.

---

264. And probably looking a whole lot like a hostage in my terry-cloth hood.

Somewhere in the time it took to stand, rub my butt (which was surprisingly sore, considering the amount of padding I'm blessed with), and turn off everything I turned on in order to camouflage my momentary lapse of self-control, it dawned on me that I had actually managed to have a good cry without an audience. Had I finally found the perfect hiding place? Hit on the right combination of acoustics and sob-muffling accessories? Or could the Hardy Boys be hard of hearing?

Hardly.

I opened the door to find Casey and Cuyler waiting in the hall.

"Dammit!" The word came out of my mouth before I could stop myself.

"We're sorry, Mom. We didn't mean to be so loud." Casey spoke first.

"No, no. I just . . . I thought . . . You could hear me?"

"We thought you were throwing up," Cuy offered, "with the moaning and the toilet flushing and all."

Crap. Now it was back to the Find a Perfect Spot to Cry, Think, and Catch My Breath in Private drawing board.

"Please don't cry," Casey continued. "We'll play more quietly."

"And we'll stop cursing." Cuy looked at his feet.

"Cursing, huh?" Obviously it's the Hardy Boys' mom who's hard of hearing.

"I got mad when he killed me."

I hear you, dude, I thought. Death ticks me off, too. "Okay, here's the plan," I said, trying not to laugh and barely able to see through the clouds of protein covering my contacts.[265] "I'm going to get cleaned up. You guys go back to your game." I bent over and kissed Cuy on the head, then stood on my tiptoes to kiss Case. "But do me a favor," I added. "Don't play quietly. Make noise. Have fun. Laugh." I hugged them both tight to me. "Getting on with living says we win. Now go."

But nobody moved. We just stood there in the hall, arms wrapped around one another, the three dogs looking at us like, What the hell? And then my cell rang.

"That's the doctor," I said, herding them toward the stairs. "Go. Play. Knock each other's blocks off. And, guys?" I paused, and pressed the little green receiver sign on my BlackBerry. "Try to keep the cursing to a minimum."

At least until I get off the phone.

---

265. Due to reality rearing its ugly head, there've been some significant delays in the development of Dr. Suzy's Fantasy Pharmaceuticals' Protein Removal Pill. She has, however, managed to grow a packet of Sea-Monkeys and is happy to report that they do indeed like her hair. Or at least what's left of it.

Acknowledgments

By the time this book comes out, it will be almost two years since my husband was diagnosed with pancreatic cancer. It's tough to see the silver lining in a cloud that black, but it's there. Since those first frightening days, we've been blessed to have many new and wonderful people come into our lives. Compassionate, talented people who, together with our family and friends, have created an incredible network of love and care and support that I can never sufficiently thank them all for.

But that doesn't mean I'm not going to try.

I gave some thought to taking everyone out to dinner or hosting a big shebang, but then I said, "Nah." If it were me, I'd much prefer seeing my name in a book. And so, on that note, my deepest and most heartfelt thanks:

To my agent, Abigail Koons, for having my back, and my editor, Danielle Perez, for her superior instincts and direction.

To my besties, Trisha Clark and Lisa Orban, for being my besties.

To Ellen Dolce, Melissa Duvall, Jennifer Heyns, Joanne and Kevin Jackson, Dr. Martha Mann, Bill Martin, Wendy and Willie Miller, Kimberly Petro, Lisa Tinnesz, Marypat Warter, the Ridgewood Gang, and the Marshall Mafia for listening, running errands, making meals, fixing fence boards, cutting grass, caring for the boys, sending wine, and, even better, bringing wine and staying to drink it with me.

To Andy, Janet, Kevin, and Wayne at the Marshall Pharmacy, for all their help, guidance, and willingness to keep a fire extinguisher near the register for the day my MasterCard finally bursts into flames.

To the doctors and staff at Georgetown University Hospital and the Lombardi Comprehensive Cancer Center, specifically Dr. Firas H. Al-Kawas; Dr. John E. Carroll; Julie Feurtado, RN, BSN; Dr. Thomas Fishbein; Amy Hankin, MMSc, PA-C; Jane Hanna, RN, OCN; Dr. Farhan S. Imran; Dr. John J. Pahira; Dr. Andrew T. Putnam; and the nurses, techs, and staff in the BLES building and the fifth floor infusion center, for being, in no uncertain terms, exceptional. Extra special thanks to Dr. John L. Marshall for always having a plan.

To the four funniest men I've ever met: my dad, Gene Costantino, and my brothers, David, Nick, and Dan, for their encouragement and letting me steal their best lines.

To my mom, Joan Costantino, for everything.

To my brother-in-law, Doug McCorkindale, for his unyielding concern and generosity, and to my sweet sister-in-law, Nancy McCorkindale, for her immeasurable love and friendship, for listening, and for bringing La Crema and J. Lohr chardonnay into my life.

To my sons, Casey and Cuyler, for being my rocks, having my heart, and looking so damn handsome in their CANCER SUCKS caps.

To Stu, for loving and inspiring me. Miss you madly, farm boy.